Simple Prosperity

Simple Prosperity

Finding Real Wealth
in a Sustainable
Lifestyle

David Wann

 St. Martin's Griffin New York

www.stmartins.com

Library of Congress Cataloging-in-Publication Data

Wann, David.
    Simple prosperity : finding real wealth in a sustainable lifestyle / David Wann. —1st ed.
        p.   cm.
    ISBN-13: 978-0-312-36141-9
    ISBN-10: 0-312-36141-6
    1. Social values—United States. 2. Quality of life—United States. 3. Sustainable living—United States. 4. Wealth—Social aspects—United States. 2. Lifestyles—United States. I. Title

HN90.M6W36 2008
306.0973—dc22

                                                                    2007038543

First Edition: January 2008

10 9 8 7 6 5 4 3 2 1

This book is dedicated to all who are ready and able

to open their hearts and minds to a new era.

Contents

Public and Cultural Assets

Acknowledgments

I want to express my deepest gratitude and admiration to all the mentors and exceptional humans whose words and actions inspired me over the years. I learned from them that hope is a self-fulfilling prophecy. It's true that the challenges that lie ahead are vast, but so are our talents, empathies, and collective imagination. We will do what needs to be done, because anything else is unthinkable.

Special thanks to the people directly involved in the completion of this book: my industry-savvy agent, Jane Dystel; the book's intuitive editor, Michael Flamini, his very capable assistant, Vicki Lame, and others at St. Martin's Press; and all the friends and family who supported me on my two-year journey. Thanks for believing in the project and giving me a chance to knead these thoughts and suggestions together.

It was such a pleasure to interview the many experts and everyday acquaintances that ground this book in direct experience. What a relief to discover how many of us are asking the same questions about new priorities and how to bring them—quickly—into our lives. My very significant other, Susan, was the manuscript's constant reality check before submission, and I credit her frank, literate instincts and advice—to throw out the first few, unsteady chapters and start over. The book was also greatly enriched by the librarians at the Golden Public Library, who miraculously met my online requests for more than 250 books and all but read them to me. What a phenomenal network of knowledge we share.

I took the work very seriously, telling a few close friends that if I were struck by lightning, I would want to have written this book first. (They gave me space to do it, maybe wary that I was having a premonition!) Anyway, I hope the book is useful and empowering. If so, I'm delighted we made the climb together.

Preface:
A Generation's Journey
Back to Health

This is a book about how to recover from the debilitating disease of overconsumption. Although the origins of "affluenza" go back at least to the birth of free-market capitalism several centuries ago, the disease has only become a full-fledged pandemic in the last fifty years. But like other pandemics, it will inevitably run its course, and we'll create a more sustainable, healthier culture—either by design or by default. The suggestions in this book, including 17 essential assets to beat affluenza, can help bring the fever down, get our strength back, and build up our immune systems.

Back when I was a teenager in the 1960s, I felt queasiness lurking in the euphoria of the American lifestyle. Gandhi once said, speed is irrelevant if you're traveling in the wrong direction, and it was obvious to me that the accelerating pace of life in the United States didn't *have* a real direction. Everything was becoming automatic, comfortable, and "convenient," yet other than going to the moon, banishing germs from our kitchens, and scrapping with the communists, we seemed to be floating up and away from reality like soap bubbles. We each wanted to expend as little effort as possible but still get paid handsomely for it so we could live the good life, before we . . . popped.

But somehow the cost and dimensions of the good life kept morphing, first into a "new, improved life," then a "better" life. (There was always a better life.) Americans began to send all household hands into the workplace, and soon we were working longer hours than employees of any other country in the world. In fact, we worked longer hours per year than medieval peasants did! A few politicians in the 1950s and '60s proposed federally mandated, shorter workweeks, because technology had doubled our productivity and we could have the same standard of living for less work. But instead of choosing the door marked life/time, we chose the one marked money/stuff.

I began to notice that people whose lifestyle didn't center on money were often healthier and more interesting. They seemed more caring and unselfish, and they were passionate about doing active, celebratory things like playing music, dancing, playing chess or bridge, embroidering, fly fishing, cooking delicious meals, studying history, gardening, and staying current with political issues. TV wasn't a central part of their lives; they were less distracted by commercial hype and less detoured by all the products. What they earned seemed less important than what they learned. I watched how they focused directly on the tasks at hand and accomplished them with finesse and artistry. I was fascinated that in many cases, the ordinary, American Dream-life was much more expensive than the *extraordinary* lives of these unique, self-creating people who lived their lives rather than trying to buy them. They had real wealth, or you might say, the right stuff.

Still, it was confusing to see most individuals stretching and contorting to climb beyond the good life to the more coveted better life. Was the better life any better, really, or was it just a variation on a theme: creativity as a commodity purchased from various technicians and persuaders who brought us Twinkies, air conditioners, and a Technicolor way of thinking? It seemed like all that was new or improved were the colors and shapes of the products, the increasing number of cars on our streets, and okay, the introduction of breakthrough technologies, some of which were *brilliant*. (As a guy who first experimented with writing on an Underwood typewriter and compiled research data on index cards with rubber bands around them, I thank the gods for computers and the Internet!)

But despite the technological miracles, it felt strange and threatening that our world was being shaped by corporate returns on investment rather than by passionate political leaders who listened carefully to *us*, the people who live here. I wondered how companies and industries could possibly provide a humane, integrated vision of the future and a strategy for getting there, since their focus was both narrow and vested. Yet federal government, increasingly on the leash of big business, seemed to be forbidden to do it.

And I wondered if this economy that kept accelerating was equipped with brakes . . . ?

It boggled my mind to think of the seventy-five million people who hurried to work at roughly the same time each morning, clogging highways, trains, and buses—somewhat like the cholesterol in our arteries. Very few of

us had any real sense of what we were building—and more ominously, what we were tearing apart. It felt like we were converting the planet's richest and finest resources into products of dubious quality, busily drilling holes in the environment and living systems to do it. What was the *point* of all the commuting and consuming? What was the economy *for*? We were burning up our time and our lives pursuing happiness but it seemed like we were happier before the pursuit began. For example, the more successful my father was in his work, the less time he had for Boy Scout weekend activities with me or even walks in the nearby forest with the dog, like before—and the same story unfolded in millions of other households. Once we were proud and hardy producers, living by our instincts and skills, but in my generation we'd become passive consumers, living in 115 million overstuffed households that some federal agencies now refer to as "consumer units."

I saw so many people pour their energy into making and spending money while other important aspects of life were neglected! Because the better life required so much of their attention, they stopped learning about the way other cultures and other species live; they stopped eating fresh food and cooking traditional family recipes; stopped going to national parks and even neighborhood parks; stopped learning about political candidates; stopped voting. They stopped saving, and they stopped learning how to fix things. They just threw everything away that needed repair and got replacements at discount chain stores.

➤ Tickling the Bear

Beginning when I was about four and continuing for several decades beyond that, a lumbering grizzly bear invaded my dreams whenever my life felt out of control—at least a few times a year. The bear was a thousand pounds of snarling, razor-clawed mammal, blundering up the dark stairway toward my bedroom. I told my parents about the bear but they assured me he wasn't real. (Why then, I wondered, did he have so much power?)

Thankfully, somewhere in my late twenties, I began to get a grip. One very significant night, I leaped onto the stage of my own nightmare—a lucid dream they call it—and decided to try *tickling* the bear, of all things. Miraculously, it worked; the bear chuckled like a huge, shy, department store teddy bear! My unconscious mind had staged a coup, asserting my right and power to come out of the shadows and live fearlessly in the light—never mind the horror of rejection slips or credit card interest rates that jump fivefold if you miss a payment by two and a half hours. The confused and defused bear plodded, mumbling, out of my life forever.

Tickling the bear became a life strategy (and I believe it can be a cultural strategy, too, for taking back our power). It seemed like the bear's ghostly mission was to terrorize we humans who inhabit a harried, self-destructive Dream of too many choices, too many competitors, and too much to know. I wondered, even then, why didn't we just *start out* content and let that be more than enough? Why didn't we unplug from the fear, the shame, and the fantasy-based expectations, rather than chasing a Dream all our lives? Many remember how the Bomb hung over our lives in those days, but I suspect it really was the *chasing* that was making the country so nervous.

How had we become so preoccupied with the *quantity* of life and so little concerned about preserving our towns, traditions, rivers and forests? How could we be so distracted that we didn't notice the menace that was creeping into our lives? We let the free market make our decisions, unaware or unconcerned that this abstract mechanism has no compassion and very little foresight. I remember reading a thick, academic book called *Man's Role in Changing the Face of the Earth* in the early 1970s, a collection of essays about the effects of human activity throughout history. It made me realize that cutting down all the trees on a mountainside left fish in the streams below choking on sediment; that building a house *here* required a cumulative house-size hole *there* and *there*; that the materials that went into a TV came from twenty or thirty different countries, and that the workers in some of those countries were essentially slaves.

I began to write earnest letters to the editor and guest editorials about our brakeless economy, to which editors sometimes gave titles like "We're Being Swallowed by the Growth Machine," or even—true story—"Chicken Little Says Sky Is Falling." An equation I came across, I = PAT, made our dilemma alarmingly simple. The Impact of human activities on the environment and people equals Population times the level of Affluence (consumption) times the scale and power of Technology. It was ominously clear that P, A, and T were all expanding like hot-air balloons, with support and subsidy from governments, corporations, churches, and consumers. What had been a stream-size flow of economic activity had become a flood; Impact would inevitably keep growing, too, but few people seemed interested. After all, our "friends" on TV didn't seem concerned—in fact, their purpose was to help us *escape* from being concerned. The myths—that "good" would always prevail, God would always protect us, and technology would always provide—seemed to be stronger than the reality. We had learned to hear only what we *wanted* to hear.

(The Affluence or consumption variable in the above equation is the focus of this book. It's quite possible and quite necessary to shrink that vari-

able as if it were a tumor—and lead *more* satisfying lives! My aim here is to give shape to that proposition.)

➤ Waking Up from the American Dream

Just to be clear, I'm not talking about a "conspiracy theory" (let others discuss that), just a command and control mentality that has prevailed because of largely uncontested assumptions such as "all growth is good." My question as a teenager was growth of what? Good for whom, for how long? Everyone was chasing a vision of success, but I kept wondering, mostly to myself in those early days, "Successfully *what*?" It felt to me like we were only successful enough to bring down the civilization, if we stayed on the same path. When I sensed what an unrestricted free market would ultimately do to our health, the economically disadvantaged, and the environment, I began to swim against the current, confident there would be many others swimming with me, and there are! (Now, we'll see what we're made of. We'll see what we've learned as a species.)

With a keen sense of hope and purpose, I watched public concern for the environment slowly build. We started with the "Keep America Beautiful" days of litter busting and moved on to citizen crusades that would result in cleaner air and water. We recovered from the Love Canal days of industrial wastes and came to the realization that only by changing production and consumption systems could we really *prevent* pollution. As each new environmental problem had its media moment, the public gained an increasingly wider understanding of the implications of our way of life. "Oh, I see . . . the toxic pesticides that are sprayed from airplanes wash off the fields into the rivers, into the bodies of fish, then get into *our* bodies . . ."

At EPA where I worked, I studied America's response to the alarming issues that reverberated one after another, like undead zombies in some grade C movie. Now, as the American mind continues to piece the concepts of ecology together, the stakes have gotten so much higher. The "I" variable in the $I = PAT$ equation has become a hulking, feverish monster in a sequel movie, and the public is beginning to comprehend very complex, disturbing concepts at high school Earth Science levels. Our children learn how major planetary cycles are being disrupted by human activities. They begin to understand (we hope) that life-essential nutrients like nitrogen, sulfur, carbon, and phosphorus have all gone hyperactive, far surpassing the natural cycle-rates familiar to life on Earth for eons. And of course, we've all learned the lessons of global warming: too many carbon emissions from burning fossil fuels too fast and the world's glaciers begin to melt.

The point is, in a single booming generation, environmental challenges have grown from the nuisance of McDonald's wrappers on the street to the potential loss of real estate like Florida, Bangladesh, and Holland due to rising sea levels. Now, we begin to see all too clearly how overconsumption of resources has resulted in strip mines the size of counties, played-out oil wells too depleted to pump economically; aquifers that are reduced to dry, echoing caverns; and amber fields of grain whose nutrients were "refined," reassembled into Hot Pockets and Doritos, and exported to all shores on the planet.

To my own amusement and horror, I became a salesperson for sustainability—a product not exactly in high demand in the 1980s. It was the perfect get-rich-quick scheme, in slow motion. But really, money wasn't the game I was playing, or I suppose I could have struck a more convincing pose. I constantly thought, talked, and wrote about how we can deliberately slow down and focus our attention on qualities like fairness in the market and durability in our products; on health and wellness rather than just wealth and "hellness." I wanted to help create a world where people pay attention to how things are really going, and where we have time to take care of living things like children and Bristlecone pine trees that sprouted even before superheroes like Jesus, Buddha, and Muhammad walked their dusty paths. If we changed the *direction* of our economy, from extraction/disposal to preservation/restoration, we'd have the same number of jobs (or more, because many of the new jobs will require more direct human involvement) and they'd be better jobs because they'd be part of a new, purposeful national mission to meet needs without endless detours and side effects.

I realized that the fatal flaw in our culture (as in so many before ours) was to assume that everything was going fine on the farms, grasslands, and construction sites; that everything was fine in the fisheries, factories, and mines. We assumed everything was growing back; that mine tailings were tucked neatly back into the ground and reseeded; that synthetic fertilizers somehow replaced all the nutrients extracted when crops are harvested; that pop cans and milk jugs were all migrating like salmon back to the factories as raw material. Pollution and resource depletion were okay within certain limits because we were making so much money. We could see the GDP rising and the smiles on each other's faces; and we just assumed that what was good for the economy was good for life on Earth. Whenever scientists or economists cautioned that we were drawing down the principle (nature's abundance and stability) rather than wisely spending just the interest, they were either ignored or lampooned as "party poopers." We left it to the experts, unaware of how little they actually knew about biology, systems thinking, or human needs.

➤ Swimming Against a Virtual Current

I got stung, professionally, by America's naive optimism. I'd chosen to write books and make films about environmental and social solutions, mostly for the general public. For eight books, twenty videos and TV programs, and hundreds of articles, I traveled to America's best farms, factories, and sustainable communities, examining intelligent ways of living, growing, eating, and buying. But if the public took refuge in optimism, they wouldn't be receptive to solutions that in their opinion "rocked the boat." What they wanted was quick and easy "tips" that would let them continue the pursuit of happiness-by-consumption with just a few little twists. I was frustrated that many people didn't seem to realize that many environmental and economic problems originate *in our minds, designs, economic assumptions, and value systems*—the way we view and interact with the world. These huge challenges can't just be tweaked with tips, because the paradigm of overproduction and overconsumption just keeps pumping.

We're living a *Catch-22* lifestyle: we aren't sure we can make fundamental changes in our personal lives because the mainstream American lifestyle eats up our time, focus, and human energy. Yet, we can't create more time until we make adjustments in our lifestyle. And we won't do that until we collectively grasp the *benefits* of changing; until we see that we have far more to gain than lose by adopting a more moderate way of life.

In a career focused on change, I've tiptoed through many a book or video, trying to present information in a way that doesn't overwhelm or estrange readers and viewers: "Excuse me, I'm not trying to alarm you or make you feel bad, I just want to tell you about many great ideas and innovations that are out there. Choices we can make based on what people really value and what nature actually needs." It felt like I was sitting in the reader's living room asking—as if casually—if they'd noticed that *bear* hibernating behind the sofa, which *could* kill the baby.

Being a risk-taker, I decided to parachute from the mainstream a decade ago and focus on what really matters—what life is really about at its core—to see if my observations might be satisfying to me and useful to others. In 1996, at the age of forty-seven, I left the forty-hour workweek, the world of people-with-paychecks, to try my luck as a freelancer. By surviving, even thriving, on about half the income I'd made before, and giving myself more discretionary time, I found some of the treasure I was looking for—in the kindness, art, and energy of remarkable people; the richness of organic garden soil; and the realization that life, after all, is not for sale. That's what brought me to this book.

I hope you enjoy reading about all the tools and talents we have—as individuals and as a culture—to help us alter the course of history. We are a very clever species, and right about *now* is when we'll begin to come back into blossom. May it be so.

Be well!

You can never get enough of what you don't need to make you happy.

    —Eric Hoffer

If you have a garden and a library, you have everything you need.

    —Cicero

For fast-acting relief, try slowing down.

    —Lily Tomlin

Humankind has so much become one family that we cannot ensure our own security unless we ensure the security of all others.

    —Bertrand Russell

Since the Earth is finite, and we will have to stop expanding sometime, should we do it before or after nature's diversity is gone?

    —Donella Meadows

To climb these coming crests, one word to you and your children: Stay together. Learn the flowers. Go light.

    —Gary Snyder

We are the leaders that we have been waiting for. We are the social innovators and entrepreneurs that we have been seeking.

    —Duane Elgin

Creating the world we want is a much more subtle but more powerful mode of operation than destroying the one we don't want.

    —Marianne Williamson

When the wind is strong, the seed-feather will be ready.

    —David Wann

Hope is the thing with feathers—that perches in the soul.

    —Emily Dickinson

Simple Prosperity

Introduction

The central premise of this book is that significant changes are now occurring in the way we live our lives, with many more changes on the way. As in a huge game of gin rummy, we are deciding which cards are not worth keeping and which ones would make a great hand. We're reevaluating many aspects of daily life, including what we eat, where we live, how well we take care of each other, how much and how far we travel, what kind of work we do, and how much free time we have. We're starting to imagine what a more moderate, efficient, compassionate lifestyle will look like, and feel like.

Frankly, the main impetus for these changes is not enlightenment but discomfort; it's become more painful to stay here than it is to move, en masse, to a new era. Our current way of life is not meeting our needs, and *is* destroying the place we call home. Although mainstream America has resisted change (as mainstreams usually do), it's become apparent to many people that a decrease in the flow of fossil fuel energy and consumer products is not only inevitable but actually desirable, if other aspects of our lives become richer. That's what this book is about—the deliberate substitution of "real wealth" for overconsumption. The fact that our excessive lifestyle can't and won't continue is not just a moralistic guilt trip or the opinion of a pack of nature nuts; it's the scientific conclusion of some of the world's most brilliant minds. The global economy is moving too fast for natural systems (including us) to keep up. Current rates of consumption are impossible with so many people consuming so much energy and so many products, so fast.

It's time for a new way of valuing the world and our place in it. The good news is that curing the pandemic of overconsumption at both the personal and cultural scale is not about *giving up* the good life but getting it back. If the United States and other wayward nations are wise enough to substitute moderation for excess, our world can come back into balance, maybe just in time. What will we give up? Mostly unwanted side effects like rising sea levels, debt, depression, waste, war, and inflation. Which would *you* rather have—a moderate, joyful lifestyle with fewer of these side effects, or the same old blowout with an even more miserable hangover?

Despite a quadrupling of average income since 1960, surveys show that Americans are no happier now than we were back then. We live on a huge life-support system, passively dependent on the economy for our survival needs; sometimes this feels more like insanity than convenience (mental patients, too, are incapable of meeting their own needs). Furthermore, if we examine the way our needs are actually being met, we see that profits are the typical priority, while needs are really only secondary. In fact, sometimes needs are deliberately *un*met to ensure future sales. For example, American carmakers have rarely given priority to vital qualities like durability, safety, and efficiency, instead going with features that move cars off the lot, such as size, speed, and sexiness. Meanwhile, Swedish and Japanese manufacturers are meeting and surpassing one socially valuable benchmark after another. For example, a 1989 Saab 900 recently crossed the million-mile marker before being retired to a museum. The superefficient Toyota Prius is steadily rolling toward its millionth sale, and Toyota's prototype plug-in hybrids already get more than 100 miles per gallon.

➤ Supply and Demand: Double Trouble

It's easy enough to point the finger at companies whose CEOs make more in a hour than we make in a year, yet we consumers are far from innocent, since we've been more than willing to let consumption be the centerpiece of our lives. Shell-shocked by the shrapnel of advertising and bloated from way too much sitting, we can still regain our sense of pride and dignity if we look at value in a different way, and begin to meet our needs more directly. For example, is it really huge houses that we need, or a sense that we've accomplished something in our lives; that we've expressed who we are, and that our lives are large enough to include the people we love? There are more direct ways of meeting these needs. Is it a string of exotic vacations we need, or the realization that life is an adventure no matter where we are? We don't all have to be millionaires, but we do need creative challenges and a sense of purpose.

Inconceivable amounts of money and effort are spent to fill every consumer moment with a product, leaving little time for healthy food, great relationships, or learning new skills. Because the real wealth makes us feel content, the marketers have learned how to ridicule it and portray it as "boring." You don't see a lot of ads for small, well-designed houses, backpacking adventures, potluck dinners, or other experiences and products that reduce the GDP yet elevate our gladness to be alive.

Humans need a sense of autonomy, but the scale and power of big industry often strips that away. The health-care industry, for example, has become the arbiter of life and death; the final court of appeals. It feels like the only choice we have is to fork over the money to institutions that often pay more attention to graphs of profits than electronic graphs of vital signs. Yet, how many Americans are negligent about diet, exercise, strong relationships, and stress control—all factors that can *prevent* illness? A potential tidal wave of interest in preventive approaches is just over the horizon. Whole foods, yoga, herbal remedies, meditation, acupuncture, and exercise are coming into the mainstream, along with an empowering realization that we can meet many of our own health needs, for far less money. (See chapter 7 for sage advice from the centenarians.)

Nutrition is another fundamental need that the U.S. food industry doesn't even begin to meet, as discussed in chapters 7 and 14. But again, the responsibility lies on both the supply and demand sides of the plate. For example, consumers can just say no to soft drinks that are now the nation's most widely consumed "food" in a society where obesity and diabetes are epidemic. The average American slurps 53 gallons of soda a year—equivalent in more ways than one to a drum of hazardous waste. Trans fat, for many years a standard ingredient in baked goods and fried foods, has recently been outlawed from all New York City restaurants because of its potentially lethal effects. (One out of every eight of that city's residents now has diabetes.) Even wild monkeys have healthier diets than most Americans, according to anthropologist Katharine Milton. Again, in our money-mad world, the focus is on snackability, convenience, and shelf life rather than *human* life. Fossil-fueled food, it seems, is good for everyone except the eater; and though the word "companion" literally means "with bread," today's processed foods are perhaps better eaten alone.

➤ You Just Might Find You Get What You Need

Humans need connections with other people, as the data in chapter 5 demonstrate. For example, cancer patients with social support have a much higher rate of survival than those without. Yet, a recent study by the National Science Foundation concluded that one-fourth of all Americans have *no one* to confide in. So, why have we just spent sixty years and trillions of dollars constructing a car-dependent, suburban universe that physically and socially isolates us from each other? Mostly because it was extremely profitable. Two-thirds of Americans would choose a small town over a large suburb, but there aren't enough small towns left to go around. (We need to restructure the suburbs, as sustainable, interconnected small towns, as discussed in chapter 10.) We also need to be refreshed and renewed by daily contact with nature. In research studies discussed in chapter 8, when people view slides of nature, their blood pressure falls. Hospital patients go home much sooner if they have a view of trees and sky. But there are fewer and fewer places to access nature in a landscape so littered with instant, would-be castles made of dry wall, and chain stores made of money.

Environmental protection is also crippled by affluenza. We look the other way when it comes to environmental impacts—toward the money. As in health care (and crime control) prevention receives much less emphasis than after-the-fact containment and treatment. For example, prevention of pollution is less appealing to the marketers of such products as pesticides. Organic growers may buy a single truckload of beneficial insects, but once the insects begin to reproduce, no further purchases are necessary—a great example of how nature and knowledge can replace the use of resources. Ingenious though it may be, some economists don't like organic farming because it doesn't boost the GDP the way conventional, soil-mining agribusiness does.

At this turning point in history, U.S. policy continues to heavily subsidize oil and gas extraction, and every year, the average U.S. taxpayer contributes about $2,000 in support of automobile use (even if he doesn't drive), according to the nonprofit group Redefining Progress. An average-salaried American also shoulders about $700 annually in advertising expenditures, payable at the cash register, and is subject to land use, wage, worker benefit and other policies that are often in synch with big business: more focused on economic growth than human welfare. Once again, consumers are partly to blame for the fact that the United States is 5 percent of the world's population yet consumes a fourth of its energy. Until we take advantage of efficient lighting, appliances, and windows, and live in well-insulated homes with at least some natural lighting and passive solar heating, we can't really chastise the power companies. Chapter 12 offers ideas on how to meet some of your own energy needs and finesse your utility bill.

Many human needs are hard to see—they are in our psyches and our social interactions. Corporations don't and can't do a very good job meeting our need for freedom of expression, creativity, beauty, autonomy, acceptance, respect, and a sense of meaning and purpose; so we, the people, have to take charge of these needs ourselves. In fact, if we don't meet these needs fully, we become victims of affluenza, hoping that, somehow, what we buy can heal our wounds.

➤ Renewable Resources of Real Wealth

When Dr. Dean Ornish encouraged one of his patients to adopt a healthier lifestyle, the patient's response was, "I have twenty friends in this pack of cigarettes that I can always depend on—what can you offer me that's any better?" Similarly, if we make a heroic effort to break our widespread addiction to overconsumption, what will take its place? This book proposes that when we change a few key priorities, many of our material wants will cease to be obsessions. It's not just that we won't *need* the next generation of gadgets and clothes; we truly won't even *want* them. Instead of perpetuating fidgety, addictive consumption, our lives will be filled with the real wealth of sanity, health, hope, caring, connection, participation, and purpose. All we have to do is unplug, and change our priorities.

We try to buy real wealth with money, often unsuccessfully. There's no price tag for some of life's most essential values; for example, an abundance of memorable moments completely free of stress. Real wealth is the calmness and contentedness that comes with feeling good, physically; the sense of well being that makes *anything* seem like an event. Real wealth is finding the rhythm of natural cycles, and jumping in. It's understanding how the world works and substituting information and brilliant design for resources.

Consider the bonds between people—what some call "social capital." This kind of wealth never runs out; in fact, the more we spend, the more we have! Similarly, the stocks of natural capital are the best investment we can make because they are based on the most reliable source of income—the sun. If nature is rich on a continuing basis, we don't have to be. Many other assets are also self-perpetuating, like curiosity, which stimulates more curiosity. When we're surfing the Web or completing a master's degree in a field we love, curiosity pulls us along like a large puppy on a leash. Similarly, the more creativity and inspiration we spend, the more we seem to generate; one developing skill often leads to another; cultural traditions constantly build on and perfect themselves. Sexual desire keeps coming back, delivering "interest" that has nothing to do with corporate profits. And democracy is an empowering, self-fulfilling prophecy, a source of real wealth, if we just join in.

When we choose real wealth, we can have things like healthy, great-tasting food; exciting hobbies and adventures; work that challenges and stimulates us; and spiritual connection with a universe that's so much larger than we are. Instead of more stuff in our already-stuffed lives, we can have fewer things of higher quality; fewer visits to the doctor and more visits to museums and to see neighbors. More joyful intimacy, more restful sleep, and more brilliantly sunny mornings in campsites on the beach—bacon and eggs sizzling in the skillet and coffee brewing in the pot. Greater use of our hands and minds in creative activities like playing a flute, knitting a sweater, building a table, or harvesting the season's first juicy, heirloom tomato. These are the things that matter, and we can *choose* them, if we spend less time, money, and energy being such conscientious consumers.

How many people do you know who convey the message, "I am enough. I have enough. I'm content." When people reach this stage of self-acceptance, they often make very poor consumers, because if they *are* enough they may not need or want more. I believe this is where America's collective psyche gets scrambled; too few of us feel that we're good enough; that life is intrinsically abundant. However, in this group therapy session called America, many do move beyond personal doubts and insecurities by being less absorbed in their own fortunes and more involved with the real wealth of the world.

Imagine how much lighter we'll feel if we work together to meet the huge challenges that lie ahead. Why carry mountains of stuff when our needs can be met more precisely with great design, ingenious efficiency, and a few basic changes in our priorities? Why settle for confusion when we're well equipped with human strengths like community, creativity, and compassion? Why permit our minds to be filled with useless static when clarity and purpose feel so much better?

The new, emerging lifestyle described here is not about guilt, shame, judgment, or sacrifice—it's about a strategic, enlightened reduction in our use of resources, and a corresponding, deliberate increase in efficiency, quality, care giving, trust, and teamwork. Using tools like these, it's quite possible for each American to gracefully reduce her or his resource consumption by half, along with all the stress, anger, and dysfunction that often go with it. This book offers many ideas for how to do that, showing that by reducing our reliance on energy hogs like aluminum cans, airplane travel, feedlot meat, and suburbs-without-stores, we can each reduce our "ecological footprints." By meeting basic physical and psychological needs *better* we can and will make the transition to a lifestyle that feels more comfortable in the present and does not clear-cut the future. As a special bonus, we can also ensure that the planet we call home does not ultimately resemble a fried egg, sunny-side up.

While the material in this book is mostly very good news—how we can make a few fundamental changes to *live* life rather than trying to buy it—

· How to Prepare a More Delicious Lifestyle ·

Ingredients:

Flexibility, foresight, instinct for happiness, self-knowledge, pride, quality, equality, connection, health, vitality, sensuality, natural abundance, useful skills, durability, purposeful work, passionate play, exploration, adventure, experience, delight, efficiency, precision, sufficiency, appropriate scale, information, knowledge, ingenuity, curiosity, design, compassion, respect, grace, gratitude, hindsight, cooperation, community, generosity, aesthetic brilliance, democracy, courage, vision, tradition, moderation, trust, loyalty, wisdom, spirituality, grace, humility, mutuality, contentment.

Instructions:

Mix ingredients together in the workplace, political arena, home, neighborhood, media, marketplace, and natural world to create cultural prosperity. Don't overcook!

---

we can't just ignore the not-so-good news if we want to permanently rid the world of the affluenza virus. As I organized the book, it didn't make sense to put that not-so-good news at the end, so it's up front with the findings, forecasts, and suggestions of dozens of biologists, psychologists, economists, geologists (and unicyclists). Together, we conclude that continuing to consume excessively as a way of life is neither desirable nor *possible.* The epidemic has nearly depleted our resources as well as stripped away our resolve and passion. It's time to create a more moderate, more enjoyable, less frantic American lifestyle.

1

Taking Stock

How Foresight Can Cut Our Losses

*Currently, more money is being spent on breast implants and Viagra
than on Alzheimer's research. So in the very near future there should
be a large elderly population with impressive breasts and magnificent
erections, but no recollection of what to do with them.*
   —Sally Feldman

*We've been born into a cult that has made a god of numbers. We
worship rankings, quantities, statistics, profit margins, and polls . . .
We want to know first, last, biggest, best, most, least, latest, and how
much the baby weighs. We've mapped the genome. We've captured
the quark. By God or by Newton we will know.*
   —Marilyn Ferguson

*It would be possible to describe everything scientifically, but it would
make no sense, as if you described a Beethoven symphony as a
variation of wave pressure.*
   —Albert Einstein

*We must make the rescue of the environment the central organizing
principle for civilization.*
   —Al Gore

have an embarrassing confession to make, right up front: I'm not
a "confident consumer." This morning's *New York Times* may report that consumer confidence has risen to its highest level in
more than three years, but as I begin writing this first chapter, I'm not any
more confident than I was back then that our mainstream lifestyle can
take us where we need to go. I'm confident enough in general, I guess, but
I'm very *un*comfortable being labeled a "consumer." We're far more than

consumers, aren't we? We're a brilliant species that creates human-scaled tools and art, works cooperatively, takes care of natural assets, and uses its awesome brainpower to solve both small and large challenges. But we aren't giving ourselves the time, permission, or focus to do these things *well*.

What's up? We aren't eating like humans who need energy and vitality to feel great. We're not taking care of the children the way humans have always done. We're not designing products that last. And we're overriding many of our most tried and tested instincts, taking direction mostly from the relatively "new," rational side of the human brain that creates assembly lines, profit-and-loss statements, and missiles. We're suppressing the more playful, empathetic, and intuitive side, missing great opportunities for fun and fulfillment.

I have a proposal. Rather than settle for a passive/aggressive, dysfunctional American Dream, let's just recycle it. The people who track "consumer confidence" have their metrics on backward, in my humble opinion. Overconsumption is clearly a fundamental *problem*, not solution, in the maintenance of a healthy economy and planet. I believe it's not just oil production that's about to peak, but also human satisfaction. If we picture our position on a graph called "The Benefits of Consumption," it appears we're on a slope of diminishing returns. We're consuming more now but enjoying it less, to paraphrase an old cigarette commercial.

Here are what I consider to be the two most critical economic screwups: First, our economy is out of alignment with the values that make us feel grateful to be alive. Values such as health, relationships with people, connection with nature, satisfying work, a sense of purpose, abundance of personal time, and freedom of expression are the real wealth, far more valuable than money and mountains of manufactured stuff. If we obtain these values directly, without money as a constant, meddling middleman, we don't *need* as much money, and we don't need to tear things apart to get it. The whole industrial metabolism of civilization—what some call "throughput"—can slow down to match the rhythms of nature.

Second, although we're trained to think of the environment as a subset of the economy, when we think about it, we see it's just the opposite. *Everything* is inside the environment. The economy is really just an opportunistic system of ideas and rules we made up, but the environment is reality itself—a wonderful place for our homes, farms, schools, and businesses to locate—as long as we're trustworthy tenants. But without a more grounded, respectful ethic, we'll never get back our damage deposit. In this era of overconsumption, production is allowed to be careless, and, as a result, the faster we produce and consume, the faster natural and cultural assets get trashed. For example, of the roughly five thousand languages now spoken in the world, fewer than 20 percent will still be spoken by the year 2100. The disappearing languages, though rich in tradition, ties to the land, and loyalties to people, simply don't translate in the global economy.[1]

It's important to remember that the economy was invented when world population was ten times smaller but the planet seemed infinitely large and filled to the brim with resources. It seemed foolish not to produce and consume all we wanted, especially since this seemed to liberate the downtrodden individual. But in the guardian economy now being born—that acknowledges how small the world really is and how fragile its web of life—only the *interest* provided by nature will be consumed, never the principle. In the new "mindful money" lifestyle, there will be more sensible boundaries and constraints, just as there is when an architect begins to design a house on a new site. The lot is only so big, with a certain type of soil, certain solar exposure, and so on. We can be as creative as we want within sustainable parameters, but the limits of the Earth are as tangible and finite as the characteristics of a building lot.

Changing just one idea can change the whole world: the accumulation of money and consumption of manufactured stuff is not why we're here. There are other ways to meet human needs, many of which are not currently being met. *When we change the way we think about value, the world will begin to regenerate, almost overnight*. We're ready! One piece of evidence is that, according to the World Values Survey, a near majority of Americans (61 percent) believe that protecting the environment should be a higher priority than economic growth; that we should prevent the natural world from coming unraveled even if that were to mean some loss of jobs and a slower-growing economy. The good news is, saving our civilization from collapse will *create* jobs and *help* the economy, which can't flourish in a battered, depleted environment.

➤ Cutting Our Losses and Reinventing the Economy

In the book *Affluenza: The All-Consuming Epidemic,* my coauthors and I observe that people in the money-obsessed societies of the world—especially the United Sates—are victims of a disease with crippling impacts on individuals, families, communities, cultural traditions, and the environment. It leaves people feeling disoriented and disconnected—ideal consumer traits from a business perspective! We point out that affluenza is far from being a disease of the rich; the compulsion to purchase and possess happiness has now infected all economic sectors in most countries of the world. Consumer researcher Van Kempen saw farmers in Mali wearing digital watches without batteries, and Tibetan nomads who proudly display their cell phones even though there's no reception. And it's the same in American low-income neighborhoods, where iPods, high-end running shoes, and leased or illicit Porsches are frequently on display. In a full 98 percent of American homes, at least one color TV beams thousands of behavior-defining commercial messages into occupants' jingle-filled brains every week.

Isn't this barrage of media a primary reason why so many people can readily identify one hundred commercial logos but fewer than ten plants? In a recent poll, average Americans were asked to name three Supreme Court Justices, and while only 17 percent could do that, 59 percent knew the names of the Three Stooges. This is America, where we spend more on garbage bags than ninety of the world's countries spend on everything. Where, in 2005, more than two million filed for bankruptcy yet 13 percent of all homes purchased were second or even third homes. As Homer Simpson observed in an episode of *The Simpsons*, animals at the zoo are "bored, obese, and have lost their sense of meaning. The American Dream."

Many of the symptoms we reported in *Affluenza* have gotten worse since the revised edition came out in 2005. The world is in effect spinning even faster; the global economy is heating up the new millennium with activities that are often inefficient, unjust, and unnecessary. Americans now fly 750 *billion* miles every year (an average of 2,200 miles per person, up from 650 in 1970). Even more astonishing, we collectively drive the equivalent of a billion times around the planet's 25,000-mile circumference every year. No wonder we, and the Earth, are tired! We annually throw away more than 2.5 million tons of obsolete computers, TVs, cell phones, and other electronic products. We each burn the equivalent of 2,500 gallons of gasoline annually, when all energy uses are considered. It takes a lot of time and human energy to accomplish all this. The question is, do we deserve an award or a subpoena?

This year's annual "directory of billionaires," compiled by *Forbes* magazine, lists 15 percent more ultra-rich Americans than last year. The rich get richer, that's nothing new. But what is new is the *scope* of the problem: the top 1 percent of American households now own 58 percent of all corporate wealth, according to the Congressional Budget Office. Yet, about 50 percent of Americans do not own any stock at all. In 2004, the top one percent of earners, including CEOs, received 11.2 percent of all wage income—up from 8.7 percent a decade earlier and almost twice the 6 percent from three decades ago.[2]

Admittedly, most Americans are fascinated that software magnate Larry Ellison's private yacht, the *Rising Sun*—453 feet in length—is as imposing as a luxury cruise liner (or battleship); and that Paul Allen's slightly smaller yacht sports its own, portable submarine. But if we really examine the spectrum of wealth in America, it's easy to see that many can't even afford to float a Wal-Mart rubber ducky in their bathtub, since the price of tap water is rising as steadily as the price of petroleum. (Since 2001, its price has risen an average of 27 percent in the United States, according to the Earth Policy Institute). In fact, many at the very bottom of the economy don't even have a bathtub. (Nearly one in three hundred are homeless and twice as many are in prison.) But while street people manage to fit all worldly belongings into a shopping cart or packing crate, we middle- and upper-class Americans, almost universally infected with affluenza, can't seem to cram our stuff into houses twice the size of a typical 1950s American home.

In recent years American household budgets have skyrocketed for day care, elder care, health care, lawn care, pet care, house care, and hair care—in direct proportion to our often-frustrated quest to be "carefree." Much of U.S. spending is for purchases far beyond subsistence, but there's a growing segment of American society whose boats haven't risen at all in the economic high tide of recent years, as the prices for such essentials as housing, food, health care, education, and transportation continue to creep up. Close to fifty million Americans are without health insurance; hundreds of thousands have had their retirement benefits cut; and tens of thousands have recently waved good-bye to jobs that were shipped overseas. From 1998 to 2005, U.S. consumer debt almost doubled, from about $1.3 trillion to $2.16 trillion, according to Federal Reserve analysts, and in 2006, Americans spent one percent more than they earned, the worst "savings" rate since the Depression. Many homeowners regard home equity as a "savings" account, and collectively they borrowed almost a *trillion* dollars from their equity in 2006. But experts say that financial well is going dry.

Where will the capital come from to keep consumer spending pumped up? Says Robert J. Samuelson, a columnist for *The Washington Post* for the last thirty years, "The great workhorse of the U.S. economy—consumer spending—will slow. For six decades, consumer debt and spending have risen faster than income, but we're approaching a turning point."[3] Since consumers are responsible for more than two-thirds of U.S. Gross Domestic Product, what will happen when household debt, lack of savings, an increase in the cost of living and other variables combine to reduce consumer spending?

Answer: The economy will continue to reinvent itself. The average

American, and the three hundred million people he represents, will become less wasteful and more conscious of durability, quality, and efficiency. He'll rediscover real wealth—what really matters—as people always do when the game changes. He'll become more conscious of what other people need and less obsessed with his own, often-trivial gratifications. He'll become more active in local politics, and his TV time will shrink from an average of five or six hours a day (!) to thirty-five minutes. The U.S. GDP might possibly be smaller in the future, but it could represent greater *real* wealth overall if negative values like waste, pollution, climate change, stress, and environmentally related disease *decrease* while positive values like social relationships, renewable energy, bike trails, preventive health care, and compact communities with town centers *increase*.

Here's the bear trap we've caught ourselves in: Our economy is geared up to produce far more than we *need* to be content, and we've obediently bent ourselves out of shape to accommodate over-production. We do things that are unintelligent and inhumane to keep up with production. And the more goods we buy, consume, and throw away, the more energy we use up, since products and the materials they're made of are filled with energy—for their extraction, transport, manufacture, and use. Since 1900, the U.S. population tripled, but the use of materials went up seventeenfold; annual emissions of carbon dioxide grew by a factor of fifteen. Life in America became

According to the McDonald's Corporation Web site, in 2007 McDonald's has more than thirty thousand local restaurants serving nearly fifty million people in more than 119 countries each day. How many billion burgers (and cows) have been consumed now? Credit: Susan Benton

an all-you-can-eat cafeteria in which the atmosphere quickly turned from circus-like to sinister. It's now all but illegal to stop eating, since corporate economists and politicians count on tireless consumer spending. One of the greatest, most nagging stresses we feel is, "How can we find the time to consume all this stuff?" But whenever that thought begins to cross our minds, a game show buzzer sounds, instructing us to "just keep eating."

The truth is, maybe we just can't eat anymore. The research firm Yankelovich Partners concluded in a 2004 survey that consumer resistance to marketing is peaking: 65 percent of American consumers feel they are constantly being bombarded, and 61 percent feel that marketers do not treat consumers with respect. Even more telling are the first tinges of green in a grassroots movement to throw advertising in the dumpster. While 65 percent think there should be more limits and regulations imposed on marketers; 69 percent are interested in products and services that would block marketing; and in keeping with the theme of this book, a full 33 percent (and growing) would be willing to have a slightly lower standard of living in order to live in a society with less marketing and advertising![4]

I think of these various symptoms of affluenza as messages assuring us that our way of life is changing. They are evidence that shoddiness, manic advertising, and excess have just about run their course, and that we are waking up from the Dream—or is it the Nightmare—to invent a new way of thinking; a new way of appreciating life. If health, happiness, and humility become new American benchmarks of success, we'll no longer need hypergrowth or overconsumption. As a result, we'll generate less stress, environmental destruction, depression, and debt! There doesn't seem to be a downside.

➤ Looking Behind the Screen

In my ongoing encounters with affluenza, I sometimes compare the Western economy to a huge movie screen positioned right in front of life itself. We want and need to experience life directly and celebrate it with the plants and animals that also live here, but the big screen keeps getting in the way, numbing us down, booming commercials and redundant stories about rags-to-riches entrepreneurs, or heroes who "never said die" but died anyway. Meanwhile, behind that movie screen, the drilling rigs, cranes, draglines, semi trucks, chainsaws, and conveyor belts are hungrily converting materials and energy into products and profits.

It's true that when we are extremely careful in the mining, forestry, farming, fishing, manufacturing and transporting processes that create the products, *less* harm is done. And in some cases, as in well-orchestrated organic farming and local purchasing of food, *no* harm is done. The soil continues to be built even as crops are harvested; side effects from transportation, packaging and processing of the food are minimized. A system like this is an overall plus. However, with so many people demanding so many products, we find ourselves at a major tipping point. Like a man dying from several diseases at one time, the era of overconsumption is on its last legs because limits have been reached in several fundamental areas at once. These tangible, indisputable limits, all directly linked to excessive production and consumption, include economic limits like low savings rates and rampant debt throughout all levels of the economy; geophysical limits related to coming shortages of our essential resources, oil, water, soil, minerals, and climatic stability; biological limits like the loss of species, the shortfall of grain and the diminishing resilience of ecosystems; and psychological limits such as depression, hopelessness, and aggression.

While we banter on our cell phones and noodle around in our SUVs, battles-to-the-death are being fought for control of such resources as diamonds, copper, and exotic hardwoods. Says Worldwatch Institute researcher Michael Renner, "If you purchase a cell phone, for example, you may very well be paying to keep the war going in the Democratic Republic of the Congo, where rival armies fight for control over deposits of coltan, a commodity that just over a decade ago had little commercial value, but is now vital for the one billion plus cell phones in use today." Guerrilla wars in Africa, Asia, and South America (mostly Columbia) have killed or displaced more than twenty million people and have raised at least $12 billion a year for rebels, warlords, and repressive governments around the world, according to Renner, author of *The Anatomy of Resource Wars*.[5]

In Nigeria, oil thieves known as "bunkerers" drill into pipelines, often blowing themselves up along with many others. About a quarter of Nigeria's 2.3 million-barrel-a-day production-flow is regularly choked off by warlords who demand a better quality of life for Nigerian citizens—especially themselves. When insurgents send e-mails announcing they plan to attack an oil platform, they also send tremors of financial insecurity into oil futures markets from Tokyo to New York.[6]

The good news? By reducing consumption, we also reduce war, fear, and despair.

➤ Last Rites for a Used-Up American Dream

Certainly, we need to have a sense of hope and joy about the world and our place in it. We need to be confident we can create a better world. But we also need to base our actions and behavior on the truth. The discomfort we feel when we hear the "bad news" is something we should acknowledge, not shrink away from. We're strong enough to deal with the challenges—we've been training for them for thousands of years. The clarity of purpose, camaraderie, and lightness we'll gain by attacking these challenges together as a species that used its strong cards (our brains and social instincts) will give us the momentum we need. Truthfully, discomfort has always been a powerful catalyst for change. This important evolutionary warning prompts us, "Hey, wake up, we need to move on, now!" When we perceive the way things actually are, we also see that it's far more desirable to change than to have hell come looking for us ("We deliver").

As we listen to reports about climate change or the rising prices of food, oil, and water, my friends and I often ask one another, "*When* will we make the fundamental changes that will make our lives less destructive and less fearful?" Some suggest that our addiction is so strong that we won't change until we absolutely have to, when global catastrophe strikes and resource prices spiral out of most people's reach. My own comments usually go in two directions: First, if we perceive that life can be better without the detours and dysfunction, we may decide to change our priorities *in this decade*, and become historical superheroes! (This is the good news). Second (the bad news), we are in fact *already* experiencing catastrophe, most easily perceived region-ally. For example, some eastern cities ran out of landfill space years ago and are now begging neighboring states to take their waste. (New York City alone ships six hundred tractor-trailers out of state every single day.) Cities from Sacramento, California, to Sydney, Australia, are running out of potable water

Polar bears have become a graphic symbol of global warming. Because the small islands of sea ice where they hunt are melting so rapidly, even these world-class swimmers are drowning in alarming numbers. Credit: Dan Crosbie Canadian Ice Service

supplies and a new industry is emerging: the tug-boating of huge plastic bags containing up to *five million gallons* of "bottled" water from water-rich countries like Turkey to arid ones like Cyprus. Already, insurance companies refuse to provide coverage to residents of coastal, hurricane-prone areas; meanwhile, many inland areas are experiencing such record-setting, regional catastrophes as flashfloods, forest fires, drought, and plummeting water tables—all related to our lifestyle and its side effects.

In the United States, Venezuela, the United Kingdom, Norway, and about eight other major oil-producing countries, oil production has already reached maximum output and begun to decline, forever. Even in nations where production is still on the upswing, major *fields* are declining. Back in the 1940s, the United States was the Saudi Arabia of the world, producing about two-thirds of the world's oil; brashly, we built our economy around the idea of limitless supplies. Today, U.S. output contributes less than one-tenth of global production from roughly 3 percent of the world's reserves. Our fields are played out.[7]

We already see what regional catastrophe looks like in places like New Orleans, with its one million environmental refugees; in famine-stricken Africa, where millions have died from civil war and lack of clean water; and the great plains of China, where chronic dust storms turn day into night and farmland into desert. But it's also true that we can *prevent* the holocaust of planetary catastrophe if we read the persistent warning signs, stay calm, and take strategic steps to create a more efficient, less consumptive world. Consider this book to be last rites for an era dying of affluenza, as well as a birth announcement for a brilliant new economy that historians may refer to as a just-in-time renaissance. Long live our emerging, moderate lifestyle, rich in green technologies, relevant information, human relationships, great health, and magnificent art!

In her work on the process of dying, Elisabeth Kübler-Ross identified denial, anger, bargaining, depression, and acceptance as the five stages that precede death. Regarding the passing of our excessive way of life, I'd guess that we Americans are collectively in the bargaining phase, though of course some individuals are in denial and others are quite angry about the price of gasoline, for example. Many others are moving through depression about the scope of the problem. Fortunately, many have come to accept that changes are not only necessary but can be quite positive. Why carry the heavy baggage of overconsumption? These front-runners have already rolled up their sleeves and are ready to do whatever it takes to change the world for the better. Indeed, our future may rest on their good energies and sense of hope.

What's being born is far more important and exciting than what's dying.

We're moving toward a sustainable, zero-waste economy that wasn't possible without some of the lessons we've learned along the way. But first—let's face it—we each need to acknowledge that we have a common ailment. ("I'm a citizen of the industrial world and I have . . . affluenza.") Confident there's something better waiting for us on the other side of change, we need to accept the diagnosis with finality: It's impossible for overconsumption as a way of life to continue. This is no fire drill, ladies and gentlemen! Let's look, together, at the sobering but very real evidence, remembering to forgive ourselves, drop the anger, and prepare to move on. Hearts and minds are like parachutes: They work best when they are open.

Throughout history, we've lost an Easter Island here, a Roman Empire there, but now we face major ecological and economic disruptions at the planetary scale—the whole ball of wax, so to speak. These challenges can't just fix themselves if our current, high-impact lifestyle continues. They aren't about interest rates or stock indexes but something much more fundamental: empty shelves, resource exhaustion, and human despair. Just since 1950, the U.S. economy expanded fivefold as demand for such materials as timber, steel, copper, meat, energy, aluminum, cement, and plastic climbed higher and higher. (The global economy expanded sevenfold in the same time frame, as world population *tripled*.) Many economists regard this awesome trajectory as the world's greatest success story, but it can also be seen as history's darkest hour.

Neglecting to monitor the busy activities behind the movie screen that separates us from industry, we didn't see how quickly the Earth was being stripped and how quickly habitats were being destroyed. We didn't realize that *every day*, about four hundred pounds *per capita* of earth are moved to construct highways and buildings, mine for copper, drill for oil, and harvest timber. It didn't really occur to us that each product we use leaves a pile of rubble back at the source; for example, that a one-tenth-of-an-ounce gold ring requires the mining of three tons of ore that typically smother another critical piece of biological habitat.

At the time my life began, marketing analysts such as Victor Lebow were formulating a game plan for America—one they believed would make each of us extremely happy, and some (of them) extremely wealthy. In 1955, Lebow wrote, "Our enormously productive economy demands that we make consumption a way of life, that we convert the buying and use of goods into rituals, that we seek our spiritual satisfaction, our ego satisfaction, in consumption . . . We need things consumed, burned up, worn out, replaced, and discarded at an ever-increasing rate."[8] In the giddy years of what seemed like an economic miracle, most of us shrugged our shoulders, smiled naively, and hit the accelerator, saying, "That works for me."

➤ It Happened So Quickly

Every day, most Americans sacrifice four pounds of unrecyclable stuff to the garbage truck gods—trash bags bulging mostly with packaging, food waste, and paper advertisements. We don't question this familiar scene; it's just the way we do it. But behind the huge movie screen that obstructs our view, the story is far bloodier. This is where things got so quickly out of control, while we floated in a pleasant American Dream-world. ("Row, row, row your boat . . .") Do you ever wonder why the seashore has fewer pretty shells than it used to? For roughly the same reason that the Earth has fewer pretty species . . . billions of people demand a constant supply of resources to furnish oversize houses with exotic hardwoods and delicate ivory sculptures for the mantel. The problem is, what looks cute on the mantle can be a holocaust back at the source, or at the end of a product's useful life. For example, many of the millions of recycled computers that have died of viruses, dust, or obsolescence end up creating health and ecological havoc on the other side of the globe.

In Guiyu, China, and villages throughout Asia and Africa, thousands of laborers work for $1.50 a day, scavenging precious metals from electronic waste. This is where our mountains of recycled computers, cell phones, and TVs end up—in scavenge heaps far from the eyes of the media. In Guiyu, laborers burn plastics and smash hard drives, wearing no protective equipment. They breathe in bits of a thousand different chemicals and compounds, many of them toxic. (One of the computers is probably my old IBM—I can imagine bits and bytes of articles and book chapters, smashed unceremoniously as circuit boards are drenched with acid to extract tinctures of gold and silver.) The lead in cathode-ray tubes is scavenged from monitors, and leftovers are thrown in a pile or into the nearby river where water samples contain up to 190 times the acceptable level of pollutants allowed by the World Health Organization.[9]

I witnessed a similar story in a village near Hanoi, Vietnam, where furniture makers apply very volatile coatings to shoddy plywood furniture, right in their own homes. When our team of environmental consultants toured the factories, the air was hazy with fumes that settled onto open woodstove pits in the worker's kitchens. The workers held cigarettes in fingers caked with toxic toluene, potentially contracting cancer from several sources at once. Some wore steady-release aspirin patches on their temples because of chronic pain caused by their work. The truth is, we saw broader smiles on the faces of the less "fortunate" Vietnamese, whose yearly incomes averaged $400 a year compared with the furniture makers' $6,000. Every morning at six, we'd walk past thousands of low-income Hanoi residents doing tai chi by West Lake; or playing badminton before going to work. Each small house or apartment in Hanoi had colorful potted flowers in front, and most people seemed content just to be alive.

➤ The Stories Behind the Stuff: Burgers and T-shirts

We know, of course, that a fast-food burger comes from somewhere, though we'd rather not know *all* the details (we've heard just enough rumors of the livestock factories and slaughterhouses where billions of animals meet their fate). We can easily grasp the fact that each hamburger patty has used enough energy to drive 20 miles (growing of the grain that feeds the cow; the transportation, the processing, the packaging, and so on). But most people are surprised to learn that the water expended to produce a single burger could supply half a year's worth of showers for the burger eater. (This water is used to irrigate the feed grain; the wheat for the bun; to wash down factory floors; and so on). Food scholars tell us that if we ate just 10 percent less meat in America, sixty million people could eat the grain, directly, that livestock would have consumed at the feedlots. The hang-up seems to be one of recipes and cultural tastes. We eat what we've learned how to cook. "Hmmm, what can Hamburger Helper help besides hamburgers?" But a trip to the bookstore or library yields the perfect cookbook, with fifteen-minute, meatless recipes like we enjoy in five-star restaurants these days.

In the classic little book *Stuff: The Secret Lives of Everyday Things*, by Alan Durning and John Ryan, the life stories of such things as coffee, shoes, and computers are narrated in great detail, taking us behind the scenes to how things are made. For example, the typical T-shirt may say Cancun or Disneyland on its chest, but it's been many more places than that. (I'm paraphrasing their great research and colorful writing in this discussion.)[10]

Look down. That 4-ounce shirt you're wearing—half cotton and half polyester—began its life as a few tablespoons of petroleum from Venezuela, as well as the cotton harvested from 14 square feet of Mississippi cropland. Its life will be over when the collar starts to fray—or when you stop exercising and it "shrinks"—but in between the shirt's birth and death are a universe of people, technologies, and places, including migrant farm workers who make a living spraying pesticides that damage their central nervous systems, kill the life in the soil, and only minimally hit the target crops; irrigation systems that water exceptionally thirsty cotton crops; huge air-conditioned harvesters whose parts come from twenty different countries;

diesel fuel that comes from Mexico; cotton gin operators who separate fibers from seeds; and truck drivers who deliver the fibers to a textile mill in North Carolina, where the yarn is coated with polystyrene for easier handling. At each step, energy is expended and wastes are generated—many of them toxic. And that's just for the shirt's cotton!

To provide petroleum for the polyester, workers spin a diamond drill bit into a Venezuelan oilfield. After spilling a mixture of diesel fuel, heavy metals and water in the process of lubricating and cooling the drill bit, the operators pump oil and gas to the surface, as crude oil leaks from derricks, pipelines and storage tanks. The crude oil is refined in the Caribbean city of Curaçao, where the factory emits dark clouds of air pollution. Then 3 percent of the crude oil is shipped to Wilmington, Delaware, to be used for petrochemicals, and it's there that the T-shirt begins to emerge, as long chains of PET plastic are drawn apart to form polyester fibers. Then the T-shirt's fabric is dyed and sewn in a Taiwanese-owned apparel factory in Honduras, where the workers make about thirty cents an hour. Your shirt is mounted on a cardboard sheet made of pinewood pulp from Georgia, wrapped in a polyethylene wrapper from Mexico, and stacked in a corrugated box from Maine.

The box is shipped by freighter to Baltimore, by train to San Francisco, and by truck to Seattle. It's displayed on a department store shelf brightly lit by a 150-watt flood lamp, and that's where you find it, calling out to you. A lot of work has gone into it, but you've never once thought about that. (It's not like in the old world, when the village tailor asked, "How do you like the shirt I made for you?") Still, it's a bargain at $12, and you take it home in a low-density polyethylene bag from Louisiana, feeling like one shrewd consumer. Pulling the shirt out of the dryer (where, if it was mine, it shrank), you wonder, come to think of it, why retailers shouldn't be *paying you* to display the shirt's very profitable commercial logo. The energy that will go into washing and drying your shirt over its useful lifetime will dwarf the energy that went into its manufacture. Of course, it would help if you got out your clothespins and clothesline rather than using fossil fuels to bake and shrink it dry . . .

The story of your T-shirt is only one small episode among many billion stories of products that occur *every day*. Yet many continue to believe that all economic growth is unquestionably *good* for the environment and people—that the products we use leave squeaky-clean footprints in the environment as well as pumping up the Dow Jones and NASDAQ indices. In a recent poll about the health of species, 44 percent agreed with the statement, "What I do does *not* impact the health of natural habitats."[11]

In the absence of a resurgent grassroots voice, most politicians and media-meisters continue to report what their sponsors and the general public want to hear: The Earth has limitless resources and a limitless capacity to clean up after us. This story may be a soothing one but it's not factually correct. We're on a collision course with dwindling resources and disrupted systems, including the inconvenient truths of climatic instability and short-falls of grain, oil, and water that support the economy. Impacts like these have already occurred on a regional scale many times in human history, with civilization-crunching results, and now they are beginning to happen at a planetary scale. As the number and appetite of global consumers continues to expand, in effect the Earth shrinks.

The average American's "ecological footprint" (the land needed to provide the materials supporting his or her lifestyle) is 30 acres, or roughly *thirty football fields* of prime land and sea, year after year—which is roughly twice what the average Italian or German thrives on. As engineer Mathis Wackernagel explains, there is of course a finite amount of land on the planet—28 billion acres of biologically productive land and sea. Dividing that finite acreage by 6.5 billion humans, each of us has a theoretical right to about 4.3 acres. (However, that acreage also includes the rest of the world's species, which are steadily and alarmingly being crowded out.)[12] Using up in just a few generations resources that nature concentrated over the eons is a bit like going temporarily insane and gambling away your life savings in a single casino spree. But that's exactly what we're doing.

Let's face it, the working, spending, and consuming life can really drain a person's energy. And for what? As Lily Tomlin points out, "Even if you win the rat race, you're still a rat." The thought of being just one more rat-like species is not very exciting, is it? We buy a plastic wastebasket at a

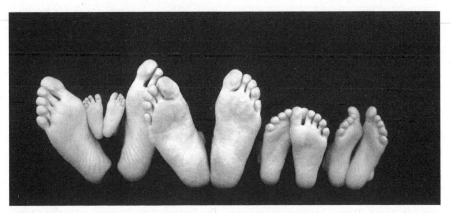

The average American baby will be taught to expect a lifestyle that requires 30 acres of productive land and sea on a continuing basis. A wealthy American's lifestyle might require more than fifty acres—ten times a fairly distributed amount available for each human. Credit: Marjolane, *See Through Me*

discount store and take it home in a plastic bag. Then we take the waste-basket out of the plastic bag and put the bag in the plastic wastebasket—over and over again. That's why I believe we need to create a new, better-fitting lifestyle as quickly as possible. All the baggage we carry (phys-ical, emotional, and psychological) is getting very heavy; it's time for us to reinvent a more moderate economy based on how nature actually works and what humans actually need. I have to admit, however, that there are still many, many people who aren't willing to listen to mounting evidence about environmental dysfunction. Their mantra is, "If it ain't broke, don't fix it," but mine is, "If it ain't fixable, don't break it."

➤ How I Became a Terrorist Without Even Trying

The week before Christmas in the year of 9/11, many Americans were still reeling in a state of post-traumatic shock—baking cookies for neighbors, lighting candles, and waving little flags-on-sticks. A friend called, advising me to get a copy of that week's *Denver Business Journal*, where, he warned me, I'd been slandered in an article called "On the Lookout for Radicals." The journal's editor referred to me as a terrorist, suggesting that I should be tried before a *secret military tribunal*. My first and strongest reaction was a bewildered, "Hunh?"

"Being alert for threats to America," he wrote, "I read Mr. Wann's arti-cle and immediately detected signs of thinking that—if played out to logi-cal conclusions—could lead to the destruction of the United States as we know it. Wann is a weekly columnist at a big metropolitan newspaper. He has influence. He can sway minds. He must be stopped." The thing is, I agreed with him about the "destruction of the United States *as we know it*." I'm an advocate of a much better, much more sensible United States!

It turns out I was stopped—at least temporarily—not too long after that editorial. After an intense yet exciting stint as a columnist with the *Denver Post*, I was dismissed via a short, perfunctory e-mail that also went to the paper's owner. It appeared that others had also found my wise-consumption commentary unpatriotic—or at least unprofitable; some were CEOs whose companies advertised in the newspaper.

Hanging my head on that wintry day, rereading the article that con-demned me, I wondered how I'd fallen so far, so fast. Change-agent, maybe even sustainability superhero (in my dreams) one week, and terrorist the next! I'd been getting phone calls and e-mails from dozens of readers telling me to keep up the good work—someone needed to be saying what I was saying—when all of a sudden I was being pilloried by free marketeers for "shaking the foundations of our society." The *Business Journal* editor continued, "Wann believes our society is built on ever-expanding consumption and personal dissatisfaction with a perceived lack of material goods. He calls it 'affluenza,' like it's some kind of disease. I don't know about you, but I could use a touch *more* affluenza, if you know what I mean."

I did indeed know what he meant. I was well familiar with this kind of attitude after twenty-some years on the environmental front. Tell them about rising temperatures or falling water tables and somehow they'll turn it into "progress." At the age of thirty-five, I'd gone back for a master's degree in environmental science, then spent ten years as an EPA analyst and communicator and twelve years (and counting) as a freelance writer and filmmaker. I'd been bumping into people like this editor every step of the way. It was easy to imagine him elbowing a colleague and whispering, with a wink, "I don't know about you, but we could use a bit more environmental degradation, if you know what I mean."

All right, so maybe that's an exaggeration (or maybe not), but I have, without a doubt, witnessed selective and calculated blindness throughout my career. I've researched and written in depth about the large percentage of our economy that's conveniently ignored—waste, pollution, fraud, negligence, planned obsolescence, and other profitable spin-offs. While the Gross Domestic Product continues to climb, the Genuine Progress Indicator (a more accurate tracking system that subtracts the "bads" from the total) continues to fall. Our official national yardstick doesn't allow us to subtract the oil spills, car accidents, energy waste, and lawsuits from the GDP, to come up with a more sensible assessment on how we are really doing. In terms of GDP, the economic hero is a terminal cancer patient going through a messy, expensive divorce, whose sports car is totaled in an accident that was his fault. The data from his misfortunes make the GDP go up. But the reasonably happy guy with a solid marriage who cooks at home, walks to work and doesn't smoke or gamble is an economic nobody, in the eyes of economists.

The editor quoted directly from my column: "While we frantically climb the peak toward economic milestones that are always still further up the trail, less time and care are given to things that really matter, like family and friends, personal health, environmental vitality, community and cultural traditions. Rather than exhilaration, we often experience vertigo, from uncertainty as to whether we're living well. Are we spending our time, human energy and money in ways that really make sense? We may be the no-contest world champions in economic prestige, but at what real cost?" He responded to this earnest, out-of-context paragraph, writing, "Yeah well, and your point is, Dave? What could be more American than spending money?"

He had me. Spending has become the quintessential American trait. Maybe I *was* being un-American. Maybe I shouldn't question the direction America is headed, and just go along with it. Maybe I should just download the latest lifestyle software and go deeply in debt to buy a Hummer that gets eight miles per gallon, because it's good for the economy, and darn it, God Bless America!

Or maybe not.

I wrote a tactfully worded e-mail inviting the editor to join me for lunch so I could explain how patriotic I really am. How I'm trying to base my lifestyle on biological and social realities rather than oblivious optimism and returns on investment. How I've actively promoted sustainable, economically viable technology and design for thirty years; have written eight books, and produced many TV programs and videos on these topics. I wanted to tell him how I helped design the neighborhood I now live in, where people know and support each other; and how I personally use less than half the resources the average American does. Predictably, he wriggled out of the invitation, assuring me that he had "only been kidding" in the editorial.

I'd been infected by a carrier of affluenza (it made me feel better to think of him as a germ), the very disease I was trying to fight. *The Denver Post* soon replaced my print "inches" with those of a consumer advocate who was also a TV commentator, whose columns seemed to be mostly about new gadgets and how they could make our lives more convenient. For the next half-year or so, people asked me when my columns would reappear. Like me, many believed that dissent is what fine-tunes and maintains a healthy democracy. Like me, they refused to perceive overconsumption—a highly destructive and often *morally* questionable pursuit—as a national religion and patriotic duty.

Ironically, the staggering increases in income, mobility, and information don't appear to be increasing our happiness, as the next chapter demonstrates. The things we value the most—meaning, purpose, relationships, and time to enjoy life—are being swept away. The burning question is, Can we wake up in time to make personal and social changes that can still prevent cultural death-by-overconsumption? Only if we agree to seek help to break our various addictions: to drugs, naive optimism, hyperactivity, media, and stuffed lifestyles. Good riddance to all of it—there's something much better now being born.

2

Evolutionary Income

An Instinct for Happiness

Happiness is like a cat. If you try to coax it or call it, it will avoid you. But if you pay no attention to it and go about your business, you'll find it rubbing against your legs and jumping into your lap.
   —William Bennett

Happiness is a way station between too much and too little.
   —Channing Pollack

The optimist proclaims that we live in the best of all possible worlds; the pessimist fears this is true.
   —James Branch Cabell

Happiness makes up in height what it lacks in length.
   —Robert Frost

I f I were to ask you what you want out of life, I can guess what you'd say. You want less stress than you have now, and more laughter. You want a greater sense of control over how you spend your time, including fewer everyday details like security codes, telephone calls to be made, and endless consumer choices (which health insurance? which sunscreen? which mutual fund?). You want more energy and vitality, and fewer "worn out" days. You want the people in your life to really understand and care about you—people who you love and respect. You want activities and passions that foster creativity and self-expression; a sense that your life has meaning and purpose; a feeling of being safe in your neighborhood—and in our expansive, mysterious, starry "neighborhood," too—these are the kinds of things that make us happy.

When we're lucky enough to have the important things in our lives, we are less likely to beg doctors for antidepressants and more likely to sleep soundly on a cushion of well-being. We're less likely to be dependent on the approval of others, and more likely to know in our own hearts that we're on the right track. We spend less time at the mall hunting/gathering what we hope are the latest fashions and hippest products, and more time completely absorbed in activities that make the time fly past. When we understand who we are and what we want, we have a greater sense of clarity and direction. Rather than feeling that something is wrong or insufficient, we feel content. We know instinctively that we have "enough," and those nagging, insecure voices go silent at last.

➤ For the Greatest Good

Humans have an instinct to seek happiness partly because the things that make us truly happy also help us survive—as individuals and as a species. Charles Darwin acknowledged the value of pleasurable sensations such as eating healthy food, socializing, and the joyful intimacy of sex, which promote the perpetuation of our species. He also believed that humans have a strong, innate sense of altruism—that beyond self-gratification we are hard-wired to cooperate for the good of all. "When a man endeavors to save a fellow creature without a moment's hesitation, he can hardly feel pleasure," wrote Darwin. "There lies within him an impulsive power widely different from a search after pleasure or happiness; and this seems to be the deeply planted social instinct".[1] Recent examples of this social impulse are the heroism of passengers on Flight 93, who lost their lives preventing a 9/11 hijacker from smashing into the White House. Other heroes were, at the same moment, rescuing survivors from the smoldering, collapsing World Trade Center, later suffering lung damage for their efforts. And in today's paper, the story of fifty-year-old construction worker Wesley Autrey, who jumped onto New York City subway tracks even though a train was coming, to save a young man who'd fallen after having a seizure. Two passenger cars thundered inches over their heads before the train screeched to a stop. Navy veteran Autrey called up, "We're O.K. down here, but I've got two daughters up there. Please let them know their father's O.K."[2]

We're fond of believing, "When the chips are down, we'll roll up our sleeves and get busy!" Well, the chips *are* down, and now we'll see what we humans are really capable of. Yet the urgency of our situation doesn't mean we can't live satisfying, enjoyable lives; in fact, taking better care of things and people will bring stimulation and purpose to our lives—which many psychologists say delivers the greatest happiness of all. Sometimes it takes

New York City resident Wesley Autrey, who jumped onto the subway tracks to save a stranger. He may have lost a knit cap, smudged from the grease of the train tracks, but he gained a lot of respect. © Tina Fineberg/New York Times

a crisis to jolt us back to the reality of who we really are as humans. When the chips are down, it doesn't matter how much money we have. More important to our happiness are such qualities as flexibility, generosity, calmness, and a resilient sense of humor.

Elaine Oneto, a sixteen-year resident of Diamondhead, Mississippi, who lost her home to Hurricane Katrina, would agree. Everything she valued most highly was in her car when she fled the city before the hurricane. But the loss of her house seemed very insignificant a few days later, when her youngest son Robert was killed on a foot patrol west of Baghdad, Iraq. She says, "Possessions, things—material things—they are just so transitory, so temporary. They really are not that important."[3]

Similarly, Czech supermodel Petra Nemkova was used to living the high life—jet-setting everywhere, the finest clothes, money galore. But she happened to be in Phuket, Thailand, when the 2004 tsunami struck. Her boyfriend was swept away forever by the powerful waves, but she survived by clinging to a palm tree for eight hours until she was rescued. Afterward she told reporters the tragedy had transformed her. She cut back on her modeling because her old life of fame, fashion, and fortune felt empty. She funded a school in Thailand to help children affected by the tsunami. What's important in hard times is also important in good times, but we tend to lose sight of the real wealth when the culture, and our own lives, are in autopilot.

To reduce consumption to moderate, much less catastrophic levels, we'll have to rely on our instincts now, to guide us back to the real wealth—that's what our religious mentors have always counseled, and in recent years, many thorough psychological studies concur: An excessively materialistic outlook on life actually gets in the way of true happiness. Psychologist Richard Ryan points out a few reasons why: "Desires to have more and more material goods drive us into an ever more frantic pace of life. Not only must we work harder, but once possessing the goods, we have to maintain, upgrade, replace, insure, and constantly manage them. Thus, materialists end up carrying an ever-heavier load that expends the energy necessary for living, loving, and learning."[4]

It's not that money itself is a bad thing. A person's skills, talents, and good energies often result in monetary as well as other types of rewards. That's great. But the real value lies *beneath* the money—in those things we crave instinctually. What money is worth ultimately depends on how it is earned and how it is spent. When it becomes the central focus in a person's life, the resulting imbalance may well create poverty in other areas, reducing his or her odds of being truly happy. For example, a person may be poor in available time, or else have lots of time but not know what to do with it. He or she may lack meaningful connections with people, be culturally clueless, or lack vitality and playfulness. Natural systems may be less abundant as a result of that individual's business decisions and excessive purchases; or the community the person lives in may lose the benefit of his or her creative, civic energy—all because the individual is off-balance—like most of us.

Ryan and psychologist Tim Kasser have compiled convincing evidence that insecurity and materialism can become a vicious cycle. Not only does insecurity often initiate a quest for material wealth, but when even second homes and sports cars fail to satisfy at a deep level, we doggedly try to "fill ourselves up" with *more* wealth, status, and fame. It's not easy being a human, is it?

Kasser points out that reaching for objects when we feel insecure has always been a human trait. "We were smaller than many of our predators in our early days as a species," he says. "When we felt insecure, we reached for a stone or a stick." Now, we routinely reach for an iPod or a fantasy vacation, but we might do better to reach out to each other. Concludes Kasser, author of *The High Price of Materialism*, "Our research shows that people who focus on materialistic values tend to report more distress, have poorer relationships, contribute less to the community, and engage in more ecologically damaging behaviors." In a society that plays up the value of financial success, fame, and image, Kasser has consistently seen a correlation between outward-looking (what he calls "extrinsic") goals and such negative traits as possessiveness, nongenerosity, and envy.[5]

One executive who owns a global company with three hundred thousand employees confided that people "at the top" are often extremely lonely because they are suspicious of others. They think anyone who approaches them in friendship does so because of their power and only wants to take advantage of them.[6] Another businessman reported that right after closing a big deal, it felt like his life might improve, forever. But, alas, the next deal hovered over his desk, and he calculated that he had "about seven minutes" of elation.

On the other hand, intrinsic goals like personal growth/self-acceptance, community involvement, and a sense of vitality deliver *continuing* satisfaction. Psychologists such as Kasser and Ryan aren't suggesting that we live like monks. Kasser, for example, lives on a small, lush farm in central Illinois and has a great quality of life (without a TV!). He told me that what makes him happy are things like teaching his son how to swim and spending quality time with his wife after the kids are in bed. Tim Kasser reminds us that it's not stuff, stocks and bonds, or the horsepower of one's vehicle that provides true satisfaction, but how well we meet our psychological and physical needs.

➤ Measuring Happiness

Since the 1970s, despite an economy that keeps expanding and personal incomes that have more than doubled, the number of people who report being "very happy" has actually gone down, according to the General Social Survey (an annual survey funded largely by the National Science Foundation). After reaching a certain level—often estimated to be about $50,000—additional income is not proportional to additional happiness. What matters most about money, according to many psychologists, is not how much of it we have, but whether we have more (or less) than *other* people.

I admit that I tend to be skeptical about subjective reports of happiness. After all, what does the word "happy" really mean? Isn't it partly a reflection of the culture and times we live in? If Americans are convinced their country is a happy, optimistic one, won't that affect the results? Yet remarkably similar results were shown in Europe, Japan, and other countries over roughly the same period. Economist Richard Layard, author of the book *Happiness: Lessons from a New Science,* was also skeptical about happiness surveys, until he began looking more deeply into the research. "To overcome the problem of subjective definitions," says Layard, "psychologists asked people's friends whether they thought the person was happy." There was a strong correlation between what friends said and the person's self-assessment. Then they tried asking independent observers to evaluate the person's smile and manner. Again, there were strong correlations between the observer and the observed.[7]

"But the big breakthrough for me came about six years ago," says Layard, "when I learned that neuroscientists have identified the areas in the brain that are active when people feel good and when they feel bad. And this is measurable with MRI technology—you expose the person to some lovely pictures of happy, smiling children and they say they're feeling cheerful. Lo and behold, the MRI shows that they're more active in certain sections of the brain. You expose them to some awful pictures of deformed children and other sections of the brain show activity." It appears, then, that happiness is an objective state, linked up with the endocrine system, the senses, and the brain. We can measure whether or not a person who says he's happy really *is* happy.[8]

➤ *More* Than Happy

One day back in my college years, I noticed I'd been working for a few hours on a poem and thought it was only a few minutes. As opposed to the schoolwork I was *required* to do, the writing was something I did because I loved it. It was a fascinating puzzle, and the more I focused, the faster the time flew by. I suspected back then that writing could be something I might do for a "living." I think my instincts were guiding me toward something that *might* be of use. (I'll leave that up to you.)

I've had many similar experiences before and since then, and a few years ago, I found an explanation for what I often experience in writing, gardening, playing music, or hiking. Psychologist Mihaly Csikszentmihalyi (try saying that name three times backward) calls it "flow." He describes this phenomenon as "being completely involved in an activity for its own sake. The ego falls away. Time flies. Every action, movement, and thought follows inevitably from the previous one, like playing jazz. Your whole being is involved, and you're using your skills to the utmost."[9]

Csikszentmihalyi's research indicates that the process of an activity can be more important than the end product. When we are fully *in* the process, fully focused on a task, we feel alive. The activity becomes its own reward. After a flow experience, we are not only refreshed, but we've increased our skills, sensitivity, and self-confidence. We are more "complex," to use Csikszentmihalyi's term. (It seems we are hard wired to improve ourselves!) He's been researching "optimal experience" at the University of Chicago since the 1970s, and has compiled a large data set involving people from all walks of life. Basically his technique, the "experience sampling method" (ESM), catches people in the middle of their daily activities and asks them to record what they are doing and how much they enjoy it. When they are signaled at random a certain number of times during the day, participants record in a workbook if they are in a condition of flow, or something far less.

To be genuinely happy, observes Csikszentmihalyi, we need to *actively* create our experiences and our lives, rather than passively letting media and marketers create it for us. The pathway to greatest happiness goes beyond mindless consuming to the heightened, enlightened realm of mindful challenge, where we are engaged, connected, and *alive*. Csikszentmihalyi's distinction between pleasure and enjoyment suggests that many of us are settling for grade B happiness—a package of mind-dulling pleasures— rather than reaching for more intrinsic flow experiences. His ESM research indicates that when we challenge ourselves to experience or produce something new, to see things in a different light, and in general, to become actively engaged in what we're doing, true enjoyment transforms moments of our lives from the routine to the extraordinary. The great news is that anyone can do it, with activities that are self-determined.

Conditions that Encourage and Define Flow

1. *Clear goals* (Expectations and rules are discernable.)

2. *Concentrating and focusing*, a high degree of concentration on a limited field of attention (A person engaged in the activity will have the opportunity to focus and to delve deeply into it.)

3. A *loss of the feeling of self-consciousness*, the merging of action and awareness

4. *Distorted sense of time* (our subjective experience of time is altered.)

5. *Direct and immediate feedback* (Successes and failures in the course of the activity are apparent, so that behavior can be adjusted as needed.)

6. *Balance between ability level and challenge* (The activity is not too easy or too difficult.)

7. A sense of control and *mastery* over the situation or activity (as when a golfer's concentration results in a great shot).

8. The activity is *intrinsically rewarding*, so there is an effortlessness of action.

Adapted from Flow: The Psychology of Optimal Experience

University of Pennsylvania psychologist Martin Seligman also prefers a deeper, more resonant definition of the word "happy." The author of *Authentic Happiness* divides the happiness continuum into pleasure (gratification, social compliance), engagement (depth of involvement with people, work, and hobbies) and meaning (such as using personal strengths for the good of society). Says Seligman, "Many Americans build their lives around pursuing pleasure, but it turns out that engagement and meaning are much more important." While most psychological theories focus on an "end product," such as the alleviation of anxiety, Csikszentmihalyi and Seligman come from a more positive perspective, asking, "What makes us feel glad to be alive?"[10]

Many of these psychological insights relate directly to the underlying theme of this book—*how to create a more productive, less consumptive lifestyle*. When we learn how to routinely experience flow, we can sidestep a lot of consumption and never miss it! In a very real sense, consumption is often just a detour that doesn't deliver the real wealth.

Optimal experiences make our doubts and hesitations disappear. We aren't absorbed in ourselves and directed by our egos, but rather by spontaneity, a sense of challenge, and connection with others. Despite the greatest cumulative ad campaign in the history of the universe, many of us still have original thoughts, and memories of peak experiences in which consumption played no role: skating on a late afternoon in January, learning to skate backward on a large pond at the edge of the neighborhood, hardly noticing that it's almost pitch dark. Standing at an overlook of a trail in total silence except the occasional chirp of a wren; gazing out over a valley covered with vineyards. Standing small and amazed beneath a starry sky lit up with shooting stars. Slurping a sweet, blushing organic peach seconds after it was picked. Making love in a huge, cozy hammock in the heart of a rain forest. Many have realized that humans cherish moments when we are active participants in life. We're becoming saturated by images that offer fantasies for sale, and we are realizing, at last, that we are such obedient consumers partly because we're afraid to follow our instincts.

If only life could remain as uncomplicated as it was in the crib! As Adam Phillips writes in *Going Sane*, "The infantile pleasures of being loved, adored, stroked . . . of only sleeping, eating, and playing, these are the truly satisfying pleasures . . . The idea that material objects or money could be any kind of alternative to these fundamental things is unrealistic." Phillips believes, with Sigmund Freud, that it's a form of madness to not know, or to forget, that it's the essential things that make us happy. Having lost our way, we become frightened that there's nothing in life that we really have an appetite for—nothing that really turns us on. At that point, we consume. At the heart of affluenza, and all addictions, is a burning desire to want *something*.[11]

Yet Freud's view of infantile happiness seems incomplete, too. When babies leave the crib, they exist in a wider world—it's not just about "me!" What about the joys of participating in something bigger than one's self? Greek and Roman philosophers of a few thousand years ago—and modern thinkers like Csikszentmihalyi, Seligman, and Abraham Maslow—regard happiness as a goal that requires effort—which begins when we unclutter our heads and ask ourselves if our lives really make sense. For the ancients, happiness was a function of rational development; a reward for leading a virtuous, balanced life. Aristotle, for example, believed that happiness must be evaluated over a lifetime (not just in the lick of an ice-cream cone, as in our world of instant gratification). Happiness, he wrote, consists of a blend of moderation, gentleness, modesty, friendliness, and self-expression. Happiness is harmony and balance in which desire is tempered through rational restraint. His words sound very much like something an enlightened Zen master might say; and like directions to the sunnier shores that may lie ahead, if we choose moderation and balance.[12]

Writes Richard Layard, "Our fundamental problem today is a lack of common feeling between people—instead, we have the notion that life is essentially a competitive struggle." He considers the Scandinavian countries to be among the happiest because they have the clearest concept of the common good. If only a third of our society is "very happy," what's preventing the rest of us from getting there? One of the obstacles may be a lack of that wider sense of the common good. Another very large obstacle is that many of our economic and social systems aren't really designed to make us happy. Really, the world of business would really rather see us *dissatisfied* and *incomplete* so we'll be more faithful customers.

➤ Changing Our Mind

As Daniel Pink explains in the book *A Whole New Mind*, when we first became preoccupied with logic, sequences, and precise measurements, about the time the industrial revolution began, we constructed a logical, left-brained world that can now only be *maintained* with the left brain. He explains what sort of thinking takes place where: the right hemisphere deals with nonlinear concepts (like surfing with great curiosity from one Web site to another); with instinctive, holistic, patterned, nonverbal, and emotional thoughts. The left brain is Spock Central: sequential, literal, functional, textual, and analytic. The left brain is text, the right brain is context; the left side is the single, precise answer, the right is the pattern; the left is abstract and logical, the right is empathetic; the left is the picture, the right is the thousand words. "Use the two together and you have a powerful thinking machine; use either on its own and the result can be bizarre," writes Pink.

The left side of the body controls the right side of the brain, so in a world that's 90 percent right handed, movements such as handwriting, eating, and maneuvering a computer mouse are mostly done on the left side. Moving our head from left to right is controlled by the left side of the brain, so the Western alphabet also reinforces left-brain dominance. "It's no surprise that the left hemisphere has dominated the game," says Pink, "It's the only side that knows how to write the rules."[13]

The two hemispheres are brilliantly counterbalanced, offering different approaches to solving problems; different ways of understanding the world and reacting to events. To me, the exciting piece is that we are increasingly using the right side of the brain in our day-to-day lives. "Left-brain style thinking used to be the driver and right-brain thinking the passenger," writes Pink. "Now R-directed thinking is suddenly grabbing the wheel, stepping on the gas, and determining where we're going and how we'll get there." (It feels like Pink is writing directly to me, a right-brained, pattern-perceiving futurist!) He continues, "L-directed aptitudes, the sorts of things measured by the SAT and deployed by CPAs—are still necessary. But they're no longer sufficient. Instead, the R-directed aptitudes so often disdained and dismissed—artistry, empathy, taking the long view, pursuing the transcendent—will increasingly determine who soars and who stumbles. It's dizzying—but ultimately inspiring—change."[14]

Now there's news that Darwin would readily toast! Not only are we coming up from our primordial brain into our underutilized cortex (where aggression, jealousy, and survivalist hoarding may be less of an issue) but we're also becoming adept at using both *sides* of the cortex. The stage is set: maybe just in time, we're changing our collective mind! To balance the precise, quantitative, and sequential mind-set orchestrated for a millennium by the left brain, here comes a troupe of story-telling, aesthetic, empathetic caregivers, visionaries, and creators. Though still ridiculed by policy makers and engineers, and sorely neglected by test-crazy school administrators, it appears the right brain is rising. YES!

As hard evidence of a surge in empathy in our society, Pink documents changes in the medical profession, long an enclave of analytical, data-heavy thinking. For example, "Students at Columbia University Medical School and elsewhere are being trained in 'narrative medicine,' because research has revealed that despite the power of computer diagnostics, an important part of a diagnosis is contained in a patient's story." Medical students at the Yale School of Medicine are studying famous paintings to hone their abilities to notice details, and at UCLA Medical School, students are admitted to the hospital overnight with fictitious illnesses, to learn bedside manner from a different perspective. Pink reports that the number of jobs in the "caring professions"—counseling, nursing, and hands-on health assistance, is soaring, along with the jobs' salaries. The narrative story—a right-brained stronghold is once again becoming a vital tool in the physician's "black bag." Empathy, not just data, is becoming standard practice.[15]

➤ This Way Out

In the opening scene of the TV documentary *Escape from Affluenza*, the Jones family stands on their front porch, waving a white flag and begging the audience not to try to keep up with them anymore. "We're just going to try to live simply and be happy," says Mom, hopefully. Imagine the benefits of arranging a truce with the Joneses, and all others who are victims of affluenza (that's most of us) that we aren't going to try for absolute perfection in our lawns; for the perfect mix of possessions, or victory in a battle for the highest salary! If the lifestyle we've been leading is making a mess of the environment, using up many of the world's resources and leaving us feeling queasy as a culture, why not just move on to something else?

By redefining our individual and cultural priorities, we can create a more satisfying sustainable American Dream. When our priorities shift, we'll *all* benefit from a greater focus on taking care of things. By meeting our needs directly, less monetary effort (and side effects) will be necessary. With more time, better health, and the substitution of information and art for resources, the American culture will quickly mature. If our insistence on being wealthy is really about being wealth*ier*, we'll get over it when the economy slows down to the speed of the EU economy, for example. Instead of striving to be the wealthiest individual in the firm, maybe we can each strive to be the kindest. Our personal health, families, communities, and environment will all be richer when we change just a few basic assumptions.

It appears that the three-hundred-plus million citizens of the United States have some things to learn from the tiny kingdom of Bhutan, with a population of less than a million. Located high in the mountains and valleys between India and China, this Buddhist culture has adopted an idea well worth looking at: In 1972, its king implemented Gross National Happiness (GNH) as the country's benchmark for success, instead of the same old Gross Domestic Product. Each year, the prime minister issues a progress report on the four pillars of GNH: promotion of equitable and sustainable socioeconomic development, preservation and promotion of cultural values, conservation of the natural environment, and establishment of good governance. Since the GNH was established, public schools began rotating teachers between rural and urban regions to improve the quality of education; both Western and traditional forms of medicine have been widely provided; and at least 60 percent of Bhutan's land has been preserved as forest. Would the United States ever replace GDP with GNH? Not likely in this millennium, but aspects of GNH would greatly enhance our acquired *quantity* of life mentality, to the great benefit of everyone.[16]

A few years ago, the prime minister of a considerably more populous nation than Bhutan, the Netherlands, acknowledged that his country's GDP was not growing, but that he wasn't concerned, because quality of life *was* growing, in the form of bike paths, industries that take responsibility for their wastes, and policies that ensure a fair distribution of wealth. For example, in that country, there are many part-time jobs available—with benefits—enabling the free market to work as it's supposed to: if a person values time off more than the extra money, he or she is free to choose that value, without penalty, making work available to others who want more income.

Why should we all have to work full-time, leaving our children stranded? Why does healthcare have to be so tightly linked with employment? Why does money have to be the only form of wealth we pay attention to? Why do we assume that monetary success is the best measure of a person? Doesn't it make more sense to base our respect on what she knows, how trustworthy she is, how funny, or how healthy and full of energy, rather than just how much money she makes or how many people she supervises? Our basic need to have the respect of our peers is not really met with a "trophy" home if we don't have the time to know our neighbors. (Besides, their houses are just as big as ours, damn!) A more direct way to win the respect of the neighbors might be to help them through an emergency, coach the local basketball team, or organize a community block party.

Personal
Assets

3

Personal Growth

Creating a Rich Life Story

My only regret in life is that I'm not someone else.
  —Woody Allen

Fear less, hope more, eat less, chew more, whine less, breathe more, talk less, say more, hate less, love more, and good things will be yours.
  —Swedish proverb

There is nothing noble about being superior to some other man. The true nobility is in being superior to your previous self.
  —Hindu proverb

No one can make you feel inferior without your permission.
  —Eleanor Roosevelt

One can never consent to creep when one feels an impulse to soar.
  —Helen Keller

Whether deliberately or by default, we each create a personal identity and life story. If we're lucky, we figure out what we're good at, what we believe in, and what we want to accomplish, joyfully, while we're here. However, in this world of media and mirage, there are significant obstacles to "knowing thyself," as the Greek sages counseled, because there are so many stories out there! (It's like a room filled with hundreds of telephones—which one is ringing?) From the moment we understand even a few words, we begin to absorb TV stories complete with laugh tracks, parental parables, religious scriptures, mythological epics, and cultural directives—and we try to figure out which story is most like the life we want to create.

Judging from the many gentle, passionate characters I've had the pleasure of knowing, sometimes our aspirations and instincts *do* guide us in the right direction! These remarkable people create an ethic to guide them; a vehicle of self-identity to carry them securely through life. They meet many of their needs just by knowing who they are. If the script is strong enough, material possessions and monetary wealth often become lower priorities than do other forms of wealth. This is not to say that people with creative, original scripts prefer to be poor, just that money isn't their *primary* goal—it comes as a by-product of other passionate pursuits.

A friend of mine, writer and artist Patricia Lynn Reilly, is definitely a self-scripted individual! She has also become a coach and mentor for other life-minded people who also want to create authentic, rich life stories. Patricia's earliest years were spent as a "lost and tossed" child with alcoholic and drug-addicted parents. Her father would be home for a few days, then take off again. "I made up stories, as any four- or five-year-old would, to make sense of his comings and goings," she says. "*He comes when I'm good. He leaves when I'm bad* . . . One day he left for good."

Within a few years, Patricia's mother also disappeared. "I was taken to an orphanage in a station wagon driven by strangers," she recalls vividly in the book *Words Made Flesh*. An ordinary girl might have let the fire inside go out, but Patricia dug deep and found her core values. During her five years at the Sisters of St. Joseph orphanage, she also found mentors among Catholic nuns who had taken vows of poverty. "Their basic needs were met to support the work which gave great purpose and meaning to their lives," she says. "Their love, focus, and dedication had a strong influence on me; I learned that a purposeful life can be creative and abundant."

I ask if she felt a lack of "stuff" in her life at the orphanage, and she shakes her head emphatically. "Material possessions were not even a blip on the screen for me," she says, "and they still aren't." Clearly, she celebrates her immunity to stuff and the stress that usually goes with it. "I've noticed that some of my friends who grew up in more comfortable surroundings didn't have to reach inward as I did," she tells me, "and they are less likely to question the script they are living and create their own story. But I had to move away from the violence and danger I'd seen. I had to rely on myself." Because she felt drawn to dancing, she sought out a nun who was a dancer to teach her the basics. After weeks of looking in the window of a dance studio near the orphanage, she was invited to take more dance lessons, free; and by hanging around a horse stable and looking cute she also got free horse-riding lessons. "I knew what I wanted, and I went out and got it," she says.

She recently went back to the orphanage for a reunion, and saw the well-preserved videotape of a play in which she starred. "My classmates at the orphanage said they remembered me as "focused, creative, and thriving," she says, with pride. "A few of the nuns commented on how 'resilient' I was." That inner resilience served her well when she began to question the religious script she'd been taught. "In my graduate studies at Princeton Theological Seminary, I began to see that I was studying scriptures that were written solely by men, and that portrayed women as subservient. I was preparing myself for a profession that still didn't accept women as equals. I decided to write a book on that subject. I titled it *A God Who Looks Like Me*, and I traced the problem back to its roots—all the way back to the story's passages about Eve being created from Adam's rib." Adapting her personal script-in-progress, she became a Child of Life rather than a Child of God because she feels a greater sense of abundance and immediacy in the way "life calls out to life."

➤ Measuring Real Wealth

Patricia went "under the story" of another dominant script when she turned her back on the "fear-based, accumulative story about the American Dream that's told on television." In her twenties, when she was living with her partner and his children, she observed, "The creative impulses of the kids were neutralized by television and it was a very sorrowful thing for me. I insisted, 'The TV has to go!' Then I set up an art center in the apartment and watched the kids come back to life." Like so many clear-headed people I know who have permanently turned off the tube, she continued to create a script free of commercials.

She's also arranged a simple life to have more creative freedom, challenging the idea that a successful person must own a house and spend twelve hours a week at the mall. "The lifestyle I've designed is not dependent on whether a company's stock is high or low; not dependent on whether the company is hiring or laying off workers." Patricia finds creative ways to make her freelance career work financially. As one of America's forty-seven million citizens without health insurance, she nevertheless sees the very best specialists—the ones the doctors themselves go to—and persuades them to let her make installment payments for their medical care.

"I measure the wealth in my life by the creativity that flows through me; by the depth of connection I have with interesting people; by the time I spend laughing, exploring, and learning," she summarizes. Where would the world be without people like Patricia, who have the courage of their convictions and who are able to question the weaknesses of prevailing scripts?

. . .

We don't have to wonder if Abraham Lincoln challenged the existing paradigm, giving slaves their freedom and doggedly sticking with a life script that he wrote long before he penned the Gettysburg Address. Honest Abe was persistent! He failed in business in 1831 and again in 1833, and also lost a race for state legislator. He then suffered a nervous breakdown after his loved one died, yet remained rock-certain he could be a contributor in American politics. He ran unsuccessfully for U.S. Congress in 1843, 1848, and 1855; remained unsuccessful as a vice presidential candidate in 1856 and a senatorial candidate in 1858; and then ran, in 1860, for president.

Unless Lincoln had won his place in history, people like environmentalist Lester Brown, who I interviewed for chapter 17, might not have created *their* own scripts. Says Brown, "As a young boy I read the biographies of Lincoln, Washington, Benjamin Franklin, and Daniel Boone, and I realized that these men were addressing the great issues of their time. So I asked myself, 'What are the great issues of *our* time?' And the environment was one of them." Without Lester Brown's dedication and focus, people like me may not have edited our own script. Some people have even told me my work has affected *their* life, and no doubt theirs will affect others, too . . .

➤ How This Skunk Got His Stripes

I've always been a writer. In second grade, when I was recovering at home from a long hospital stay, I dictated a little story to my mother about how skunks got their stripes (a whipped cream accident, of course). She took the story to my classmates and I've been writing ever since.

A formative moment came in my college years on a walk through the Indiana countryside a few miles out of town. My love life wasn't going anywhere, my grades were lousy, and I was up before sunrise to do some backroads soul searching. With a faithful little campus dog by my side, I passed a lush, green pasture where dozens of dairy cattle grazed, just as the sun was coming up. With the Indiana sky's pink, gold, and purple-gray hues as a backdrop, I saw in a storybook-flash-of-insight that life was like an interwoven quilt! The cows ate the grass and made milk, fertilizing more grass with their wastes. The skies contributed rain; farmers were nourished by the milk and had the good health to properly take care of the cattle. I realized that billions of similar relationships were woven productively together, all over the planet. "I see it!" I shouted to my furry friend Pooh, who of course had always seen it.

It wasn't that I knew much about ecology back then—that would come later. Really, my epiphany was more profound than science—I didn't just *know about* the interconnections of life; but in that instant of insight, I was right in the *middle* of them. I suddenly realized that life on Earth had a strategy and a purpose, and that our throwaway style of living was naively oblivious to it. In the years after college, my emerging draft script focused more and more on the evolution of a strong environmental ethic, and it became clear to me that I should combine my two passions. My work at EPA years later did that, but there was something missing. The job paid good money, I had great health and retirement benefits, and I was doing work that the world considered respectable. I knew that if I just kept my head down and went with the bureaucratic flow, my basic needs would be met. But something in me craved sunlight, freedom, and fresh air. I wanted more than a standard career.

In my last days at EPA, I would sometimes sneak out an hour early, shutting my computer off and making a casual-looking (but inwardly desperate) beeline for the fire-escape stairs in the center of the building, as if I was just heading off for still another meeting. I'd leave my daypack in my cubicle as cover, and dance down four flights of stairs into the wide world outside, where the afternoon sun was still shining. I needed to find a different path—one that I chose myself. The bottom line is, I didn't retire from that job, I just got tired. (And if it hadn't been that job, it would have been another.) I remember feeling at first like I was playing hooky from the real world, and that I would get punished for it (bankruptcy? terminal illness?). I'd ride my bike to the grocery store by way of the park, or plant a row of lettuce in the garden, and feel as if everyone else was following the script but I'd forgotten my lines.

Then I began to trust my instincts, relying less on what the world wanted and more on what I needed. I learned that being less conscious of what other people think could save me lots of money, because it required less than the average person spends on new cars, electronic gadgets, and clothes. Gradually, what I was moving away from became less important than what I was moving toward. I was far less dazed and confused than before, and since confusion often results in consumption, I rarely showed my face at the mall. I liked the work I was doing and I didn't feel a huge need to get away for more than a good vacation a year—I was already "away," after all. At an extended family reunion in the beautiful Napa wine country, my mother and I debated the meaning of success and whether I still had a shot at it. I wrote this note afterward, but am only now "sending" it in excerpted form. I think of it as "Successfully What?"

Dear Mom,

The radically honest conversation (okay, shouting match) you and I had in our cottage during the family reunion prompted me to write. You truly care about my well-being, and I really appreciate that! You want me to be successful, the same way I hope your life and my own kids' lives are successful.

The question is, successfully what? When I confided that last year was a financial challenge, you were worried. "A person needs to have enough to live a good life, and to provide for later years," you said. You also seemed to be saying, "Work harder. Make more money. Go back and get a real job again—quick."

When I told you that despite the meager income I had one of the best years of my life, you seemed skeptical. I guess you didn't realize how much meaning the work has for me, and how inspired I was by the insights of the people I interviewed for the film I was working on. In combination with good friends, family, and continuing play in building the community garden, it was enough. I didn't need much money.

When I recently served two very large bowls of organically grown salad from the garden to a group of forty appreciative friends, that also felt like success—good work that we could taste and crunch, and feel proud of. When I went into a music store the other day that stages jam sessions and somebody remembered a song I'd sung six years earlier, I considered that a success, even though it had nothing to do with money.

Last week I got an e-mail thanking me for a talk I gave, telling me that one woman had tears in her eyes because I was speaking from my heart. Wasn't that success, in a real sense? And when I went in for a physical the other day and the doctor told me I had the heart of someone half my age, that felt like success, too, because of all the exercising and healthy food I've chosen to eat.

At breakfast that morning in California, you told me I shouldn't be so demonstrative about my convictions, because I'll turn people off, and I won't be successful. But the way I look at it, unless I express my hopes and suggestions for a more livable future, I can't be successful in the full sense of the word. There's too much evidence now that our young, boisterous economy has designed and mined itself into a very dangerous corner.

That's why I'm writing, Mom. I feel an urgent need to communicate my concern that our country has lost its way, whether or not that brings in money. I want to help find and present better trails. I'm OK,

Mom. I think you already know that I need to "do my own thing."
And you also know how much I love and appreciate you, right?
   Love,
   Dave

That particular year, I'd made less money than some households spend on facelifts for their suburban backyards: state-of-the-art barbecue "stations," tractor-style lawn mowers, and upscale professional stonework for the perennial beds. (I'd also made less money than society spends annually on the average prisoner—about $35,000; but, in contrast, I was *out* of jail.) For the most part, I was happy, partly because the decisions were mine. Money wasn't the game I was playing. My sister Susan confided recently that she, too, had debated with my mother about whether or not I was successful. She'd used rhetoric like this: "Why do people need money? They need it to bring up their kids, and Dave's kids are doing fine—both are college graduates and both are happy. People need shelter, and he owns a great house in a neighborhood he helped design. They need health—he has that; they need something stimulating to do, and his work seems to turn him on. They need occasional breaks from everyday life, and in recent years, he's been to New Zealand, Vietnam, Costa Rica, the Outer Banks of North Carolina, Alaska, Guatemala . . . People need someone to love and his girlfriend, Susan, is wonderful." She concluded that however much money I was making, it was apparently *enough.* After thinking about it in those terms, our mom had agreed—what a relief!

My partner, Susan, made strategic scripting decisions, too, and doesn't regret them for a minute. In her children's formative years, she took twelve years off from a stimulating career as a computer software expert because the kids were her priority. Toward the end of a career distinguished by many awards and achievements, she did the math and opted for an early retirement even though senior managers offered her a small fortune to move up the ladder and direct a whole department.

I'm not suggesting that to create a good script a person has to leave her or his 9-to-5 job! What I am suggesting is that it's a relief to know our own minds, and know what we stand for, and what we are willing to stick our neck out for. I read a great newspaper story last week about a guy, Jim Reddick, who works in a supermarket in the state of Washington. He's become a local hero for going the extra mile with customers. When he does deliveries to seniors, he brings not only groceries but books they might want to read, medicine from the drugstore, or much-needed sweatpants he's found for them, on sale. He checks the mail for them, takes out the garbage, even gives them a lift to town. At the supermarket, old-timers wait in line to have

Jim check out their groceries, even when other checkers are available. You might say that Reddick's script has a wealth of character development.[1]

What will our life stories look like in our last years? Here's hoping that all the people involved with this book—readers, editors, writer, reviewers, binders, printers, and all those I've quoted or interviewed—are happy in our final years because we've all made good decisions and had good experiences! (And if not, maybe we'll get another shot as zebras, orchids, or at least slime molds). I was curious what stories people tell at the end of their lives, and asked my friend Jonathan to tell me what he hears as a hospice chaplain.

➤ Living and Dying Like a Racehorse

For a man who's just thirty years old, Jonathan Daniel has acquired a lot of wisdom. Some of it comes from rigorous meditation and Buddhist practice; some from his challenging work as a chaplain, where he's gotten to know more than a thousand people before they died; and some from the fact that his father, an attorney, was murdered when Jonathan was twelve. Death has always been part of his adult life, and he seems to live more mindfully and intensely as a result.

His daily work begins when he goes into the homes of people who've been told they have less than six months to live. His mission is to help them die with strength, comfort, and dignity. If they're Christians, Jonathan recites scriptures; and if they are Muslims, he finds wisdom in the Koran. "I want to use the truths they've been studying throughout their lives to have a conversation about what's meaningful to them," he says. Every workday, he deals with two very profound questions: How should we live in the time we have left, and how should we regard death? As we sit in a booth at a busy restaurant, I ask him, "What do people tell you in their last days? What do they value in their lives above all else? What are they most proud of?"[2]

"Many of them tell me they've always thought they'd take a trip around the world before they die, or buy impressive trophies, like a stylish new car," he answers. "Instead, what they value in their last days are things like feeling the sun on their face, hearing the intricate beauty of a classical symphony, or smelling the fragrance of a lilac in bloom, out in the backyard. These are the ordinary, everyday surprises that really matter to them, in the end."

He takes a sip of beer and continues, "People who live with purpose and dignity seem to die that way. A woman I worked with recently was a successful writer whose husband was also successful at starting a small company. Every week, about fifteen close friends would come to visit her, and it made her feel great to know that she was loved. That's what people are proudest of—that other people love and respect them. When I came to her house I asked her how she was doing. She shrugged her shoulders and said, 'Well, you know, I'm *dying* . . .' I asked what she thought was going to happen when she died. She smiled, saying, 'Wow, that's unusual for you to ask that! All my friends who come to see me—I can tell they're uncomfortable about death. They sit down stiffly and to reassure me, they tell me exactly what's going to happen when I die; what I need to believe; who I should pray to; and what it will be like, after I die. You're the first person who's asked me what *I* think.'

I interrupt Jonathan's story to comment that the friends had as much anxiety as the woman who was dying.

"We *learn* to be afraid," he says, nodding. "So, then I asked her what she would *want* to have happen, if she could have her way, and she said with a smile, 'I'd want to come back as a racehorse! I know it sounds kind of crazy—I can't tell that to my friends—but as I sit here dying I keep thinking how grand it would be to be a racehorse, because they're so beautiful and majestic, so powerful . . .'

"'I'm wondering if what you're seeing in the racehorse is what you want right now, as you go through your transition,'" I asked, and she answered, 'Yeah, actually that's true—when I see all the grace, all the lack of hesitation, that *is* what I want as I die . . .' Even though she was a Christian, all our conversations became centered on the attributes of racehorses. And it seemed like she did have that sense of strength as she died."

I ask Jonathan, "Are most of the people you see afraid of dying?"

"There's usually some discomfort, because death represents the unknown, the loss of control, unpredictability—and these are the central issues that people fear. They're used to things that feel safe and predictable—things they can control. When we're dying, we lose control of our life. The project is over; there's no longer anything to maintain. Everything we've identified with— our careers, our friends, our ways of thinking, the way we look—is suddenly stripped bare and we're left with the true face of who we really are. We come face to face with ourselves, and that can be uncomfortable."

As Jonathan talks, I'm reminded that the acquisition of material things is often about trying to control life rather than just live it. We surround ourselves with possessions to fortify our lives against uncertainties that lie ahead. It seems apparent that to reduce consumption, we'll need to be less obsessed with controlling life. After all, we each have a solid seat in the universe, and we're not likely to fall out, so why waste our lives worrying about death and possessions? Why not focus on what we have rather than what we don't have? Billions of living creatures die every day—there must be a pattern behind it.

Jonathan continues, "When people have displayed a tremendous amount of generosity in their lives, and been very giving and thoughtful of others, that seems to diminish their suffering. When I ask them what they want to pray for, they don't say themselves. They want to pray for their families, for other people in the care center, for the people on the news they recently saw . . . I find it very poignant, the number of people who are concerned about the survival of the human race. I tell them, 'Here you are with terminal cancer, talking about your death, and yet you're concerned about how this world is going to continue after you're gone . . .' Sometimes it's expressed in a big way, as the entire world of humans as a species, and sometimes at a smaller scale, like how America is going to fare. So there's this real sense of interconnectedness that hits them. Sometimes they don't even realize how strong it is until everything else is stripped away."

I ask Jonathan what people say about their material goals and possessions at the end of their lives. "They often say that financial wealth gets in the way of family relationships, especially at the end. A few days ago, a man I talked with wanted to have deep, meaningful conversations with the family, but couldn't because they were so focused on the money, asking for advances on the inheritance, and pressuring him to sell the house. The poor guy wanted to talk about more important things, but they kept coming back to, 'Mom always said I could have this.' He told me, 'I wish they could wait until I die to have these squabbles.'

"So I think you're saying that the best way to prepare for death—and also live a quality life—is to become more comfortable with the unknown and the unpredictable?"

"To live happily and die comfortably, I think we have to give up trying to be in control," he says. "But at the same time, we can be mindful, and prepared. A man I'm working with right now has taught me a lot about this. I worked with his wife as she died, too; all this stuff came up, all this baggage, all the shadows she'd repressed. But eventually she was able to work through it and die peacefully. The family asked me to perform the funeral service; then, two years later, I get this phone call from their daughter who says, 'My father wants to be ready for death. He wants the same level of care my mother got, but he wants it now—while he's healthy and able to do the work. When his death comes, he wants to die consciously and aware.'

It struck me that the pursuit of real wealth such as mindfulness is a sure way of being ready when death comes.

Jonathan explains, "So I meet with him once a week and we talk about what he wants to do with his remaining time. He wants to learn how to meditate, to calm his mind and release some of the trivialities he's been caught up with. The more he lets go of his worries and doubts, the more he tells me, 'You'll never believe what happened to me today!' He's making friends and having real conversations with them, and feels a great sense of delight. The smallest words of kindness from his daughters completely make his day. Every day is a blessing. He smiles and laughs a lot more than he did just a few weeks ago. Sometimes we'll sit together in complete silence for ten or fifteen minutes, just looking into each other's eyes and smiling. 'When I die,' he tells me, 'I don't want to be overwhelmed by the pain of all my past habits. I want to be present for my death. And I want to learn how to do that now, by *becoming present for my life.*'"[3]

➤ The Value of a Story

"It is not enough to add years to one's life; one must also add life to those years," said John F. Kennedy. One of the most fruitful ways of adding life is to get in the habit of following a script you believe in—based on values that resonate for you. By keeping promises to yourself, you stand a pretty good chance of treating other people—and yourself—well. You become something much bigger than an ego or an appendage of commercial logos. You find activities and passions that match your abilities with the tasks at hand and make the world safer and more sensible. Sometimes, though, the world seems to trap you in your own script. For example, Olympic skier Bode Miller has always skied primarily for the love of it, trusting that the money would follow. And did it ever. With thirteen corporate sponsors, Miller has become a multimillionaire, and isn't sure what to make of it. "As soon as you have millions of dollars, you literally don't have money as a motivating force anymore, unless you just simply try to continue to acquire more and more of it," says Miller. "That process is about as unhealthy as anything else I can think of—so the acquisition of money *alone* is a terrible, terrible goal."[4]

4

Mindful Money

More Value from Better Stuff

I base my fashion taste on what doesn't itch.
   —Gilda Radner

If it works, it's obsolete.
   —Marshall McLuhan

I have enough money to last me the rest of my life, unless I buy something.
   —Jackie Mason

Too many people spend money they haven't earned to buy things they don't want, to impress people they don't like.
   —Will Rogers

No one wants to spend money for products or experiences that don't deliver value, even if one has money to burn. Whether it's kitchenware, a car, or a musician for your daughter's wedding, good quality satisfies but poor quality usually does not. One of the most pleasant changes we are making is learning the difference. We're moving toward a renewed appreciation of durable, crafted, nontoxic, repairable, fair trade objects and services that communicate a sense of trust and pride. For example, classic clothes never go out of style, tile floors have longer life expectancies than humans do, and timeless cast-iron pans don't add ingredients not called for in the recipe—such as potentially toxic aluminum or Teflon (except for iron, which our bodies need). The new lifestyle will contain fewer things but better things, and the typical household will be less cluttered with junk.

We all have bedside lamps, but how many of them are expertly designed to swivel right over your book or look back toward the nightstand with a simple adjustment? A great lamp like this can increase the reading you do, and decrease the mindless, sometimes-troubling TV watching before going to sleep. The things we really value are objects that tie into our lives. Someone gave me their used Venetian blinds last month and even helped me install them. Rather than cuss at the sun for glaring on my computer screen, I just close the blinds for twenty minutes while the world turns a bit. My point is, it's not just a lot of objects we want, but great objects that enrich our lives.

My favorite possession is a 1967 Gibson J-200 guitar I bought used, thirty years ago. Made from Sitka spruce, maple, and rosewood, the instrument just seems to get better in tone quality all the time. Once owned by country musician Buck Owens, it's always been my rainy day or after-work standby. When I want to unfocus I let my fingers do the thinking for a while. How much value has it given me? At least fifty times the $500 I paid for it on layaway.

I love great Belgian, Swiss, or Italian dark chocolate that energizes me in a very smooth way because its ingredients are so pure. I can't say the same for most American chocolate, because it has so much sugar and so many additives that it makes me feel jumpy—and fat. I also love organic produce that has a story connected with it: Maybe it comes from Buffalo Canyon Farm, where growers use heirloom seeds and "green manure" (cover crops) to make the soil rich and full of nutrients. There's a connection between the growers' intentions to grow healthy food and my desire to feel good—it becomes a relationship centered on health.

I value my old car, a 1986 Volvo station wagon with 274,000 miles on it, for atypical yet logical reasons. It enables me to do things like carry potted fruit trees from the nursery without stressing about the carpeting; recycle the neighborhood's cardboard; and take boxes of books to sell at presentations. It helps me feel secure because who would want to steal a twenty-year-old car when there are brand-new Toyotas parked next to it? Even if it suffers a parking lot dent or scrape, I still love it. If my overall goal is to live a life free of stress, my car is a good vehicle to get me there, because I avoid the stress of monthly payments, I carry liability insurance only, and I go easy on borderline repairs. So rather than spending the typical $7,500 a year for a car, I spend less than $2,000. Money not spent on the car can be spent elsewhere. Rather than just miles per gallon, I'm currently opting for miles per vehicle, avoiding for society-at-large (you're welcome) the energy costs of manufacturing a new one—which comprise at least a fourth of the car's lifetime energy use.

In general, I love things that last. Six years after my dad's death, I'm still wearing a pair of his classic Clarks shoes in the garden. (It feels good to be walking in his shoes.) My mother has a Singer Featherweight sewing machine she bought fifty-five years ago that still works great, and a GE clock radio that's also earned "vintage" status. My friend Mary Romano cherished a well-designed German coffee grinder that she maintained for twenty-five years, changing the parts whenever necessary to keep it in great operating condition. When it finally gave out, she replaced it with a grinder from the same company, but it was a sealed-up unit that couldn't be maintained or repaired, and it was fed to the landfill within a year.

➤ The Stuff of Life

Before going on a vacation a few years ago, I told friends my main stimulus was to take a break from work projects. But I have to admit I also craved time away from my stuff. At least ten times a day, things that are not alive intervene in my life, competing for maintenance, payment, and acquisition. The computer printer gets paper-jammed. The packaging on a new CD takes ten minutes of my life to remove. The house needs a paint job. The car needs a lube job. The microwave shorts out. All day long, like a nest full of wide-mouthed baby birds, my stuff cries out for attention.

I decided to escape my stuff by going Down Under. I carefully selected and packed what I hoped was the right stuff, and my son, Colin, and I boarded a jam-packed airliner for New Zealand, courtesy of frequent-flyer miles. The small amount of gear we'd brought was perfectly adequate for making contact with this unique place, but the real stuff-challenge came when we had to consolidate it into backpacks for several treks in New Zealand's spectacular Fjordland. What we'd already boiled down for the vacation needed to be boiled down again, into seven cubic feet or less of backpack space. My favorite objects on those three-day hikes were a two-cup thermos for swallows of green tea throughout the day's hike; my notebook, pencil, and sharpener; the food we'd brought to cook—much of it fresh rather than packaged—and my well-designed clothes that saved me during a chilly, windy, and rainy day on the beautiful Routeburn Track. In an area that gets up to three hundred inches of rain a year, you need to have gear that sheds water and dries quickly. We didn't need a lot of clothes, just good quality clothes.

I like the analogy of a backpacker when I think about the emerging American lifestyle. The backpacker doesn't want a lot of junk in a backpack. She or he wants only items that are ingeniously designed, like a Whisper Lite cookstove, a warm fleece sweater, a good pair of boots that can go the extra miles, and food that's full of slow-release energy. The backpacker brings along acquired skills, stories to tell and an open mind to learn new ones, a well-designed tent, maybe a flute or a great book. During the journey, the world is a splash of light and shadow, with mountain peaks in the distance and bighorn sheep standing guard. If we're smart, the awakening American lifestyle will deliver clarity, a sense of wonder, and great health, as if life itself was an energizing, mind-opening backpacking trip.

➤ Rethinking Priorities in an Average-Income Household

I love it when economists call our hard-earned money "disposable" income, because in many cases, that's exactly what it ends up being! An overlooked but sizable chunk of the household income typically goes straight down the drain for wasted food; poorly designed, wily widgets with their own agenda; appliances that crunch kilowatts like Cracker Jack; and prescription drugs that mask one set of symptoms with another.[1]

Surely, the most perplexing TV commercials in recent memory are the prescription drug announcements that once we've secured a doctor's signature for antidepressants, allergy inhibitors, hair-growth stimulants, and sleep inducers, our troubles will be over. That is, if we learn to accept extreme nausea, erections that won't go away, or elevated risk of stroke as part of the miracle. But we can eliminate many side effects from various consumer choices by directly providing more of our own health, entertainment, food, and transportation. If we make our household more productive and less consumptive, we can also write much lighter checks to Visa.

"Yeah, right," you say. "How? Where will the extra time and human energy come from?" Quite a bit of it comes from letting the Joneses go their own way, as fast as they want. By redefining what we personally value as "wealth," we can reclaim much of the disposable time we've lost in recent years. What if an average household's annual expenditures of roughly $43,000 went to different priorities? What if a family's purchases (and decisions not to purchase) brought more durability, greater vitality, more satisfying entertainment, greater intellectual growth and more laughter into their house? Their choices might result in major attitude adjustments—psychological makeovers—that would make discretionary time seem far more valuable and a huge income seem less necessary. For example, they might begin to enjoy more of their food at home. As recently as the 1970s, the average U.S. family allocated almost three-fourths of food expenditures for food eaten at home and one-fourth for food eaten away from home. In the twenty-first century, however, the average U.S. household allocates almost half of its food budget for food eaten away from home. We're not sure what exactly is in restaurant food, or how it will make us feel, but it has those four basic food groups: crunchy, greasy, salty, and sweet!

According to the federal Bureau of Labor Statistics, roughly 63 percent is spent for housing, transportation, and food. Each of these categories represents huge opportunities for reducing waste, stress, and the dark threat of bankruptcy. About 32 percent is spent for housing (that's the house, utilities, furniture, and supplies). The family could win back time, money, and vitality by living in a smaller, better-designed house with efficient appliances and good natural daylight, buying well-built furniture that doesn't need constant replacing, and having a different attitude about what a house is for. If they consider it a trophy or "display unit," they'll spend hours a week decorating and redecorating it, and cleaning it or paying someone else to clean it. But if their house becomes more of a healthy verb than a passive noun, there may be a vegetable garden out back, a workshop in the garage, and an accessible place to store well-used bicycles and a scooter. The house will be comfortable, and so will its residents.[2]

About 18 percent is spent for transportation. If the house is located near the things the family needs—work, friends, groceries, bank—the average family can reduce transportation costs by at least a tenth, or about $750. Getting rid of the second car and all its insurance and maintenance expenses will yield even greater benefits.

If the food they eat delivers energy rather than lethargy, they'll exercise more, walking to the library or bank, and playing sports rather than buying them. Health-care costs will be lower and weight-loss programs won't be necessary. With better food in their lives, they'll go to the doctor less and require less insurance coverage. They'll spend more social time eating, reducing their entertainment costs. Almost certainly, they'll feel a greater sense of contentment and wellness. By slowing down to the speed of life, the average American family can become more than just an "average" family— they can be an exceptional family. Instead of disposing of their income, they can save it, eat it, and live it.

➤ Lifestyles of the Unashamedly Poor and Not-So-Famous

The Social Security statements that come every year remind me, with the inhuman harshness of data, that I've had a few lean years since jumping ship to become a freelancer. In fact, there have been years when I lived *below the poverty line*, a phrase that seems to require dramatic intonation. It's not that I'm trying to find my way to the bottom of the economy, it's just that I haven't had a lot of time to make money in recent years; I've been contentedly busy pursuing things that aren't about money. Do I sometimes wish I had more cash? Sure, we all do, but I feel like I have many other forms of wealth, so in general, no major complaints. (But tell your friends about this book . . .)

My kids, too, are exploring alternative lifestyles that shed light on the excesses of the American lifestyle. On a recent volunteer mission to Nepal to work in an orphanage near Kathmandu, my daughter, Libby, lived with a Nepalese family for four months. Their lifestyle (no car, no refrigerator, a squat toilet) requires less than a fifteenth as many resources as the average American's, yet she says the host family members usually have smiles on their faces. Each e-mail she sent from the Internet café was a glimpse of a colorfully grounded reality. In her first note, after hellish travels that included misplaced luggage, she reported cheerfully, "My host mother, Songita, is boisterous, pushy, and good natured. Her English is pretty rudimentary, and she frequently gets objects and emotions mixed up. She'll tell me she's very mad at me when I've done something good, and tell me to drink my hot tea very slowly because it is very, very cold. I nod and smile, and at the end of a conversation I get up from the table wondering if I've just agreed to marry someone, or buy each villager a new goat."

She learned to love the rice, lentils, and curried vegetables the family eats twice a day, but opted to pose as mostly vegetarian when she found out that, after being cooked, the meat sits on a shelf for days at a time. On a ten-day trek to the base camp of Mount Everest, she experienced a way of life most Americans will never have the opportunity to see. (Less than a fifth of all Americans even have a passport.) "At night," she wrote, "we stayed in guesthouses run by Sherpa people—keeping ourselves warm by a lone fire stove, burning yak dung in the middle of the dining room."

"The trip was surreal: through valleys where water-powered prayer wheels propelled blessings to the sky, to mountain passes where monks chanted in monasteries, and past ancient Tibetan women wearing Nike tennis shoes and fake Northface down jackets over traditional dresses . . . The Himalayas themselves are almost beautiful enough to make you cry, but the Sherpa peoples' history and their current struggle between tourism dollars and traditional ways are especially fascinating to me. I could sit and watch these beautiful people all day long—I would *pay* to talk to these old-timer porters, these human beasts of burden who so gracefully and humbly haul crates of chocolate bars, boxes of beer, and other tourist luxuries up the mountains each day—hundreds of pounds carted at a time in baskets . . .

When she got home, she explained the challenge she'd stepped into: The director of the orphanage had skipped out with the money and left thirty-five kids without sufficient food or health care, sleeping four to a bed,

Libby Wann helped meet the basic needs of many children when she volunteered in an orphanage near Kathmandu, Nepal. Credit: Libby Wann

and spending much of their time sitting on mats, doing nothing at all. Libby and her volunteer cohorts found emergency funding for food and new bunk beds, got the kids to a health clinic, and enrolled them in school. Although the orphans didn't speak English, she discovered that her abilities to dance, jump rope, and play soccer came in handy. Just showing interest in them brought smiles back to their faces.

I wish I'd been able to visit her in Nepal, but I'd given her most of my frequent-flyer miles for the flight, and besides, I was working on a certain book . . . But I was glad that she, an anthropology major, was learning that many of the world's people are not as obsessed with stuff, spotlessness, and convenience as we are.

I did, however, make a point of visiting a more accessible adventurer in the family this past Christmas, my son, Colin. I saw firsthand how even a person with a third-world level of income can "cut back" on resource consumption. It was my first solo road trip in a few years—the kind where you get behind the wheel and just go, for hundreds, thousands of miles, floating on a magic carpet made of two tons of steel, four fragile tires, and a cumulative 55-gallon drum of credit-card gas.

Colin, the Big Guy, is six foot three and currently living in a bright blue van parked in a friend's driveway, in Prescott, Arizona. Two days a week, he coteaches a course on outdoor education at Prescott College, where he got his undergraduate degree. The other five days, he hikes, bikes, climbs, runs, hangs out with friends, and cooks food from the health food store, on a two-burner propane stove in his van. Life's uncomplicated. I can often hear Thoreau's words when Colin opens his mouth: "The cost of a thing is the amount of life exchanged for it . . ." Like me, he has a relationship with resources—probably more intimate than my own. For example, when I offered to give him some beginning Spanish CDs and a battery-operated player, he didn't accept the player because he didn't want to consume batteries.

Although he owns and highly values a pickup truck with a camper shell, recently its battery has lost its charge because he doesn't want to buy and consume the gas. His friends, who also live in and around the house, likewise refuse to associate with their vehicles. After all, the shops, parks, and institutions of downtown Prescott are at most a ten-minute walk from where Colin lives, and his sturdy, custom-built bicycle can take him anywhere else: to the mountains, to outlying components of Prescott College campus, even to the Grand Canyon and back (about a 200-mile ride). So the truck's primary use, at least for the winter, is storage—a Tuff Shed on wheels.

One of the trip's highlights occurred after we'd set up camp in an isolated spot in the Coronado National Forest—just north of Sonora, Mexico. "Have you ever made fire without matches?" he asked me. I seemed to remember *trying* to, back at scout camp . . . He stood beside the ten-foot-tall flower stalk of a sotol cactus—a relative of the agave and yucca species—and cut a four-foot section of the lightweight wood, about the diameter of a cucumber.

He dissected another section of the stalk into a short, flat platform. He cut a notch into one edge of the platform as an exit ramp for coals, just as he'd done at many outdoor workshops on backpacking expeditions. After assembling a tinder ball out of dried grass roughly in the shape of a bird's nest, he went to work: holding the platform in place with his foot, he created friction by boring a hole into it with the sharpened stalk. His intensity and focus were awesome. I wanted this effort to be successful, just as so many before me did—so many humans, hungrier and colder than me, hoping for fire.

After ten minutes or more of intense effort, a tiny coal slid down the notch into the pile of sawdust. He grabbed the ball of dried grass, carefully dropped the coals into it, and softly breathed fire into the tinder. When the tinder nest began to crackle, he placed it on a large, flat rock, adding a few little sticks to the newborn fire. In that moment, I felt a little less like a father and a little more like the son of many fathers. As we walked back to our campsite, I pondered the idea of forefathers; we consider two thousand

years ago to be ancient history, yet it's really just fifty (forty-year) generations distant. Fifty fathers and mothers who taught their children about
fire, food, and fairness—or else failed to. Ponder this, if you dare: What will
our world be like in another fifty (quick) generations?

➤ Unconsuming—A New Olympic Sport?

I don't mean to imply that our descendants will need to make fire by
friction or hunt javelinas with spears, but with any luck, they will be far
more skillful at minimizing their impact on planetary resources and the living systems that contain them.

In *Radical Simplicity,* author and peace advocate Jim Merkel describes
the Global Living Project, in which seventy-five teachers, students, and activists spent six weeks tracking what a three-acre-footprint lifestyle would
look and feel like. (In rough terms, a three-acre-footprint is a higher standard of living than the average citizen of India has, but with only one-tenth
the consumption impact of an average U.S. citizen.) The project demonstrated that with three acres as a base of support, a person can consume
enough food to remain healthy, but items like wine, beer, cheese, butter,
and meat aren't feasible, and only appeared in the more consumptive six-
acre lifestyle. Likewise, air travel and transportation by taxi are not part of a
three-acre footprint. Telephone use, medicine, medical insurance, small
appliances, and computer use are available to the three-acre consumer, but
only in small, shared proportions.[3]

Still, Merkel observed that participants adapted quickly to a three-acre
footprint, with little discomfort. "Just like going overseas or moving to a new
town, once the culture shock is over, the new life is just the new life," he
says. What if resource scarcities and rising prices begin to shrink the
bloated American footprint of about thirty acres? Conceptually lopping off
four-fifths of that footprint, Merkel insists, "With careful choices that reduce our mobility needs and housing size, a six-acre option could look like
a typical North American lifestyle, only downsized, with less clutter and
less waste."[4]

Another very interesting experiment in the deliberate, creative reshap-
ing of one's lifestyle is the Compact, a group of Northern Californians of
various incomes who pledged not to buy anything new in 2006 except such
things as food, health/safety items, and underwear. "We are a group of individuals committed to a twelve-month flight from the consumer grid," an-
nounces the group's Web site. One of the group's founding members,
Sandy Clark, explains why he joined the Compact. "My wife and I decided

we valued time with each other and with our daughter more than things, and peace of mind more than things." Not mincing his words, he says, "It helped that I hated advertising. We eliminated it from our family as far as we could in a society where you are forced to see and hear advertising against your will—more effective than the old Soviet propaganda machine and twice as invasive. Try this sometime as a thought experiment: just picture the face of Stalin wherever you see an ad that you can't turn off or throw away!"

Here are a few of the actions the Clarks have taken, with encouragement from their Compact colleagues: "Watching PBS, DVDs, and using TiVo have helped with the TV ads, and CDs or the iPod cure the radio jabber," says Clark. "We started looking for activities that involved spending little money—and no money for things. Recreational shopping was out, camping was in. Walks and parks were hip, movies at the multiplex became uncool. Games became a great pastime with friends. A $40 trip to the movies pales in value comparison to a good $40 game, and that's if you buy them new. A great game lasts a lifetime. We create more, work on the home more, travel more. We also got rid of a car. My wife started taking public transit. It's only fifteen minutes longer and she doesn't have to drive. Instead, she reads an extra book a week. Believe it or not, we went from 38,000 miles a year to 3,800"—a tenfold reduction.[5]

Seeing the enthusiasm and passion of the Compact members, my own children, and so many others who are happy just above and below the poverty line, I'm continually reminded that creating one's life can be far more of an adventure than just buying it.

➤ How High-Income Households Can Help Save the World

An article in Forbes online magazine quantified how much money a person would need, to live "well" in various cities of the United States. The Web site features a calculator that compares your income with the minimum amount necessary. Living well includes: a primary residence of at least 4,000 square feet; a second home in the country or on the beach; a few upscale cars like a "sporty new BMW 325i sedan and a capacious Lexus RX 330 with front-wheel drive"; dinner out once a week at a "pricey" local restaurant; three vacations a year; prep school and an upscale college education, such as Harvard, for the kids; and a token 1 percent savings rate. This kind of lifestyle requires a bare-minimum annual income above $200,000 a year, depending on where you live.[6]

I live in the Denver area where the cost of living is slightly above the median, and the Web site's calculator coldly informed me I was $171,428 short of living well. "Try to lower your expenses by removing some items you might not need," the Web site so kindly advised. If I were living well, I'd be giving my girlfriend Bill Blass silk dresses for Christmas, which would be great, but I might be so busy making money I wouldn't be able to grow my own cut flowers for personalized summertime bouquets. Instead, I might have to pay a thousand or so a month for lavish flower arrangements changed weekly by some designer babe in a Mercedes station wagon. I might stop being an advocate for open spaces and parks that have public amenities like tennis courts anyone can use. Tax cuts that favor the wealthy might seem a little more reasonable to me if I was living well, even if those cuts reduced health care for lower-income people and public funding for state colleges and public high school teachers.

I apologize for being glib here. The basic point I want to make, as diplomatically as possible, is that living large takes a larger bite out of the environment (and often one's sanity), because of large houses and yards (or "grounds"), limitless consumer goods, frequent flying, and so on. The ecological footprint of a high-income lifestyle can amount to 50 acres or more per person—certainly, far more than anyone needs, and several times the impact of, let's say, a Manhattan apartment dweller who buys green products and takes the subway or a bus to work. Even the expectations and salaries of low-income Americans are huge compared to the rest of the planet's residents, but the perceived needs of a *wealthy* American are without historical precedent, except by royalty. (To get your global rank in wealth, go to globalrichlist.com. Even with my "taking the year off to write a book" salary, my income ranks in the top 7 percent.)

I believe that America's many, many wealthy households (there are now three million millionaire households) can and will be a leverage point for significant cultural change. What if those in the top 10 percent of our economy focus their intelligence on social equity, civil rights, and the design of green products? What if they lead the way in the installation of solar energy on their homes; drive only the most technologically advanced, fuel-efficient cars; and invest in the stocks of wind energy, heat pumps, and alternative fuels? What if it becomes hip in the living-well circles to steer the economy toward high-tech, well-run public transit, and livable cities like those they've seen in Europe and notably green U.S. cities? What if those who are now "living well" work with such groups as Nature Conservancy to preserve private land as contiguous biological habitat? What if the wealthy lead the way back to a society of active citizens again—not just passive consumers? The wealthy, along with the rest of us, can change the direction of our culture, and of history. They can easily consume half as many resources as they do now in favor of other forms of wealth, such as generosity with their time. This won't require "cutting back," but merely living more efficiently and mindfully. (For example, simply living in an urban area rather than the suburbs is at least a third more energy efficient). They can mentor an underprivileged kid, help coordinate a network of community gardens, or work with their neighbors to create a neighborhood recycling system.

➤ Investing in a Sustainable Future

Marie and Steve Zanowick didn't set their sights on being "rich," but like many other American households in which several people make high-echelon salaries, theirs is very secure financially. What distinguishes them from many a high-consumption household is the way they spend and invest their money. Marie is an environmental engineer with U.S. EPA, now at a grade level that pays about $100,000 a year. Steve is a computer software designer who makes about $150,000. Says Marie, "We both come from large families, and we both were influenced by parents with very frugal values. I was raised on a small dairy farm in Wisconsin where eight of us shared a 900-square-foot house, and believe it or not, one bathroom! We found great value in having a large garden, and being out in nature. My father would come home from work (he was a farm safety inspector) and say, 'I saw a huge stand of asparagus and lots of wild raspberries on my way home,' and we'd all pile in the car and pick gallons of fresh, wild food." The family also spent a few weeks every summer fishing and camping together at a Minnesota lake—a tradition that Marie's family continues. In fact, it could be said that the values of Marie and Steve's upbringing are what they value the most.

"We sat down early in our marriage and asked ourselves, "What did we learn from our parents that we should pass along to our children?" An appreciation for nature was high on that list. "My nine-year-old daughter will sit and watch a squirrel eat nuts for half an hour, partly because we don't have a TV. If she instead watched nature shows, she'd get the impression that behind every tree, there's a litter of baby foxes and a bald eagle perched on the highest branch. Anything less would be boring."

Marie and Steve aren't heavily invested in the stock market because they don't want to put their energy and focus into following all the ups and downs of companies. Instead, they spend their money in ways that bring them greater satisfaction and just as much security. To give a few examples, they've recently bought land for their retirement years in British Columbia, and have also purchased other properties to pass along to their kids. Says Marie with a smile, "A Canadian realtor found out we were interested in land and said he could show us some great properties on golf courses and in fancy suburban neighborhoods. But what was more important to us was having direct, walkable access to town and knowing that our water supply was clean and reliable."

They've just completed the construction of a greenhouse as an addition to their current home, to augment the produce they grow in their garden. Rather than going to the big chain furniture stores to buy a much-needed bed, they hired a furniture maker to handcraft a Mission-style bed made from oak. "That bed will last a few hundred years," says Marie, proudly. Since they decided not to adopt a child despite being very tempted, they send monetary support to two orphanages. And rather than pay large premiums for long-term health care for their retirement years, they prefer to invest in preventive measures. "Steve spends about $200 a month for massages, and we each pay attention to what we eat and how much we exercise. We're confident we can stay healthy rather than paying a fortune to be sick."

5

The Bonds of Social Capital

The More We Spend, the More We Have

Resonant relationships are like emotional vitamins, sustaining us through tough times and nourishing us daily.
—Daniel Goleman

Oh, the fun of arriving at a house and feeling the spark that tells you that you are going to have a good time.
—Mark Hampton

Happiness is perfume you can't pour on others without getting a few drops for yourself.
—Ralph Waldo Emerson

Our survival depends on the healing power of love, intimacy and relationships. As individuals. As communities. As a country. As a culture. Perhaps even as a species.
—Dean Ornish

It's inevitable that our society will once again give higher priority to belonging and lower priority to *belongings*. The reason is simple: our current way of life often leaves us feeling used up, and lonely. On the way to becoming world-class, gold-medal consumers, many assumed that social connections were so basic they didn't require much effort. After all, relationship challenges on TV usually resolve themselves in twenty-three minutes or less, and we expect the same in our own lives. We buy into a richly advertised paradigm that says products are socially advantageous—we smell sexier, or have that distinctive sparkle of success. But the sparkle is fading from a lifestyle that consumes so much time and human energy—leaving fewer opportunities for genuine connection. Now we see that many of the products we work so hard to buy actually *isolate* us from other people—for example, the iPods, video games, and Visa-funded fantasy vacations that take us (temporarily) to other realities; houses so large we sometimes can't *find* family members; and automobiles that carry us on solo journeys where we desperately dial numbers on our cell phones.

According to a study conducted by the National Science Foundation, summarized in *American Sociological Review*, one-fourth of Americans say they have *no one* they can discuss personal problems with—more than twice the number in the lonely hearts club in 1985. The typical American has lost one of his or her closest friends, it seems, since even the average number of confidants has fallen from about three to about two. Says Lynn Smith-Lovin, a Duke University sociologist who helped conduct the study, "The image of people on roofs after hurricane Katrina resonates with me, because those people did not know someone with a car . . . We're not saying people are completely isolated. They may have 600 friends on Facebook .com (a popular networking Web site) and e-mail 25 people a day, but they are not discussing matters that are personally important."[1]

Sociologists like Robert Putnam, author of the book *Bowling Alone*, believe a downward trend in the quality of social connections began in the 1960s, when TV became the national pastime, families began to split apart like billiard balls, and the shortest distance between two points was suddenly jammed with traffic. Putnam estimates that each additional ten minutes in commute time decreases civic involvement by 10 percent, partly because we're too worn out to engage socially. His research indicates that Americans go on 60 percent fewer picnics now than we did in the 1960s, and that families eat dinner together 40 percent less than they did in 1965. Donations of blood have fallen in proportion to the drop in membership in clubs like Boy Scouts, church-related groups, labor unions, PTAs, and organizations like the League of Women Voters and Elks clubs.[2]

Although other connections are springing up—from Internet chat rooms to conventions of people who are all devoted to the same product or celebrity—Putnam makes a distinction between active involvement and token membership in social networks. For example, the American Association of Retired People (AARP) is a huge and expanding organization—second in size only to the Catholic Church. But what responsibilities and commitments are required of members, other than paying annual dues? We don't form lasting friendships or feel a strong sense of belonging in groups like these. Still, Putnam believes that Americans have reinvigorated their civic life before and can do it again. As entrées to active social involvement, he and his colleagues in the Saguaro Group make note of indicators like these:

Indicators of Social Capital

- How many of your neighbors' first names do you know?

- How often do you attend parades or festivals?

- Do you volunteer at your kids' school? Or help out senior citizens?

- Do you trust your local police?

- Do you know who your U.S. senators are?

- Do you attend religious services? Or go to the theater?

- Do you sign petitions? Or attend neighborhood meetings?

- Do you think the people running your community care about you?

- Can you make a difference?

- How often do you visit with friends or family?[3]

Those who score high on these types of surveys are more likely to be what author Malcolm Gladwell calls "connectors." In Gladwell's book, *The Tipping Point*, Paul Revere is the classic connector: a man who personally knew most of the revolutionary leaders along his thirteen-mile, midnight ride through Boston neighborhoods in 1775. Because he was respected and trusted by his compatriots, he successfully rallied a rag-tag but resolute army that defeated the British at Concord the next day. (History tells us that the simultaneous ride of William Dawes, in another direction, was not as successful. Apparently, Dawes wasn't as revered as Revere.)[4] But we don't have to be historical icons to take advantage of social connections. The wealth of social capital also becomes apparent when we share information about resource efficiency in our houses, about which computers are more reliable, or which friend of a friend is looking for a partner. Social capital is the "glue" that binds communities together, creating cultural norms, energetic networks, and reservoirs of trust.

When freely and wisely spent, social capital lowers crime rates, makes schools more productive, and helps economies function better. Contracts, leases, and schedules operate more smoothly. In socially abundant communities and nations, individuals don't have to earn as much money to be comfortable, because quality of life is partly provided by the strength of social bonds. For example, two farmers who share machinery with each other avoid having two combines on adjoining farms, credit union members and insurance carriers can share pools of financial capital, and job-seekers can find work more easily—substituting networking for possible bankruptcy. (More jobs are found by word of mouth than by reading the classifieds.)

As the aptly nicknamed baseball player Yogi Berra once said, tongue-in-cheek, "If you don't go to your friend's funeral, he won't come to yours." When social capital is squandered or remains unspent, the results can be dismal; the bonds and agreements that keep life humming along smoothly begin to unravel. Though we're trained to think that individuality is our most valuable trait—that we need to be strong and smart enough to be successful in a cutthroat world—this money-bound mentality often severs authentic connections between people, leaving us feeling confused. We're hard wired to rely on each other, yet we're also supposed to compete with each other and make it on our own. . . .

Consideration and kindness are sometimes thought to be expendable—we just don't have time for them. For example, this morning I had an appointment with a guy who wanted to look at my basement apartment, currently for rent. I kept up my end of the deal, making sure I was available to show him the space. But the potential renter was a no-show, disrupting my focus and energy as I kept listening for the doorbell to ring. When it becomes normal to break appointments—and relationships—without warning, daily life requires more effort. Part of the problem is the breakneck pace of our society. In a world of instant everything, we try to find instant intimacy—for example, we resort to "speed dating" and Internet intrigues that often go south by the second encounter. We think we can judge a person's character overnight (often literally), but solid relationships take time to build.

When the disappointment of a broken promise is replicated a million times over, every day, the Golden Rule gets turned upside down: Do unto others as they did to you, man. Self-esteem plummets and aggression proliferates; relationships that could be richly rewarding become toxic and draining. Like a social plague, whole societies become infected with mistrust and insecurity. Stark evidence that social capital is being swept away in America is that one of every thirty-two people is now either in prison or on parole. (Certainly these are "clubs" whose memberships are more beneficial when they are *small*, and I believe that only the empathy and healing of social bonds can shrink them.)

➤ The Healing Power of Social Connection

Philosopher Martin Buber's work distinguishes between two kinds of social connection—what he calls I-You relationships and I-It relationships, explained in his 1923 book *Ich und Du* (I and Thou). In the I-You relationship, an unwavering, holistic bond of trust exists between an individual and key aspects of his life, including other people, other living beings, and whatever that person perceives God to be. In Buber's view, when we experience life from a perspective of I-You, we enter a sacred realm of authenticity and oneness. We make and keep commitments to "be there" without pretense or judgment, on a playing field of mutual caring, respect, and responsibility. In this way, we create the priceless relationships that make life worth living.[5]

On the other hand, in I-It relationships, people are misperceived as objects, valued only for what we can *get* from them. The ego is in the center, surrounded by things and people it tries to manipulate. Instead of being at one with the world, we become detached and isolated from it. If people or other living beings are no longer of use, we just throw them away. For example, when a huge school of fish is perceived as huge profits, it doesn't matter if that particular species is an endangered species—the fish are just objects that exist for our benefit. We assume there are always more objects to exploit.

The analytic I-It approach to life makes us strangers in our own world, and is a primary reason why many feel a sense of emptiness. We strive to connect with a Higher Power we can sanctify rather than objectify—a being who won't let us down, and to whom we are devoted. I believe we can and must bring sanctity to our *everyday lives* by creating I-You relationships, treating even the food we eat or a masterpiece painting with great respect, wonder, and connection, because the people who grew healthy food or created the painting "speak" through it. By changing the way we regard the world, the "me" in each of us becomes a much wider "we," and we feel interconnected and complete. Even in a world filled with contradiction and superficiality, we find True North.

A wealth of scientific evidence now supports what we've known in our hearts all along: Without strong social and spiritual connections, we wither. We need to elevate love and connection to a higher priority even if that means we make less money and spend less time worrying about it. Researchers say it's a matter of life and death. Dr. Dean Ornish, author of *Love and Survival*, says, "Study after study has shown that people who feel lonely, depressed and isolated are three to seven times more likely to get sick and die prematurely than those who have a sense of love, connection, and community in their

Nadine Lightburn reads to her husband of fifty-eight years, John, who is legally blind but still very interested and active in world affairs. Credit: Jonathan Castner

lives."[6] One study looked at men and women who were about to have open-heart surgery. "The researchers asked two questions: 'Do you draw strength from your religious faith?' and, 'Are you a member of a group of people who get together on a regular basis?'" Those who said no to both questions were dead within 6 months, compared to only 3 percent of those who said yes to both questions—a seven-fold difference in mortality."[7]

After many years of hands-on medical work, Ornish concludes that the real epidemic is not just physical heart disease but also emotional and spiritual heart disease. Social support makes us feel valued and loved, feelings that enhance our health, but conversely, "Anything that promotes a sense of isolation can lead to illness and suffering." The reasons why are tangible: for one thing, isolation increases the likelihood we'll smoke, overeat, or fail to exercise. Furthermore, says Ornish, "Bacteria, viruses and other microorganisms must penetrate through our immune, neuroendocrine and other defense systems, and these defenses are measurably enhanced by love and relationships." Social connections also reduce stress, the universal Grim Reaper. For example, when you're low on cash, one of the most stressful things going, it sure helps to have a friend throw you a lifeline. When you're sick, maybe another friend will take care of your kids for a few days until you feel better. Ornish has observed an especially strong correlation between the love of parents and good health, in part because parental relationships have such a long span: nutrition before and after birth; coping (or not really coping) styles developed when young—such as anxiety, anger, and optimism; spiritual values and practices; and parental support and love in one's adult life.[8]

In a Harvard study in the 1950s, students were randomly chosen and asked to describe their relationship with their mother and father—whether "very close," "warm and friendly," "tolerant," or "strained and cold." Thirty-five years later, results were conclusive. All of the participants who rated both parents low in warmth and closeness had diseases in midlife (including coronary artery disease, high blood pressure, duodenal ulcer, and alcoholism), whereas only 47 percent of those with warm, close parents had the target diseases.[9]

Our health is even boosted by the unconditional love of pets. In a study of heart attack victims who now had irregular heartbeats, six times as many people died if they *didn't* have a pet. Many other studies show similar results. Says Dean Ornish, "If some new drug showed a six-fold decrease in deaths, you can be sure that just about every doctor in the country would be prescribing it. Yet when was the last time your doctor prescribed a pet or supportive friend for you?"[10]

➤ "Good Chemistry"

Social emotions travel on chemical pathways in our bodies. Writes Daniel Goleman in *Social Intelligence*, "A hundred men and women wore devices that took readings of their blood pressure whenever they interacted with someone. When they were with family or enjoyable friends, their blood pressure fell; these interactions were pleasant and soothing." On the other hand, in a group of British health-care workers who had two different supervisors on alternate days, the more controlling supervisor caused spikes in blood pressure, whereas the presence of the second, more empathetic supervisor did not.[11]

In *Love and Survival*, Dean Ornish cites other clinical evidence of social chemistry: A doctor at Stanford Medical School studied women with breast cancer who were randomly assigned to one of two groups. Each group received conventional medical care and, in addition, one group of women met together for ninety minutes once a week for a year, to express their feelings about their illness. "In the safe and supportive environment, they could discuss their fears about topics like being disfigured, dying, or being abandoned by their friends and spouse," writes Ornish. The results were dramatic: The women who attended the weekly support group lived twice as long as the others. After five years, only those in the support group were still alive.[12]

The chemistry of intimate relationships is more immediate. For example, an attractive woman "turns a man on," literally, when she meets his gaze directly; his brain secretes the pleasure-inducing chemical dopamine. (If he looks but she doesn't, there's no chemical release.) If they later become intimate, her massaging hands relax him, lowering his blood pressure and releasing the antistress hormone oxytocin. His metabolism downshifts, reports Goleman, from the "ready-to-run mode that primes large muscles for running, to a restorative state in which nutrients are stored and the body recharges."[13]

What would you give up to experience ongoing good chemistry like this at work, in the neighborhood, and at home? Would you give up stress, fear, and the need to control others? Of course you would, if you could. Would you cut back on the amount of work you do, the amount of time you spend acquiring and pampering possessions, and trade it for honest relationships? Maybe not, because you may be so wrapped up, so defined, by the so-called good life that you can't find a way down. However, many believe that social engagement is worth far more than money can buy, and given the choice between "your money or your life," you *might* just choose life and love. Whenever we're lucky enough, and open enough, to have real wealth like this in our lives, I believe we should always choose to be lovers, not fighters. And I speak from experience, having been both.

Daniel Goleman tells the joke about a couple that's only had one fight in their entire marriage—and they're still having it. In my younger days when I was (even) less mature and still had some frustrations to work out, a friend once good-heartedly referred to my not-yet-ex-wife and I as "the Bickersons," because we couldn't seem to balance the energy in our relationship, despite many wonderful moments in our early years. I'm confident that our kids came through okay, and hopeful they find relationships that are more enduring. For the past six years, I've felt, and returned, the love of a remarkable woman. It's commonly said that attraction between the sexes boils down to sex objects and success objects. While this assessment does have some degree of anthropological truth, it tells only part of the story. Such relationships may well be I-It in nature, regarding people as objects. In my maturing years, I see that the most compelling features about a partner are kindness, independence, and humility—and Susan has them. To see her caring for a newborn grandson is to see how warm she is. In those moments when loving energy sparkles in her eyes, I melt.

I met her when she came to a party at our community house. Seeing her across the room, I said to myself, "I wish I could sit next to that good-looking woman—I wonder if she's single." As luck would have it, that very seat was empty, and I dusted off my courtship skills. In an instinctual display of plumage, I gave her a copy of a book I'd recently coauthored, *Affluenza,* and invited her to tour the neighborhood garden and orchard where I spend so much time. The next day, I brought her an artfully arranged box of ripe tomatoes, basil, and cut flowers from the garden. From my perspective, my charm had won her over, though she gives much of the credit to the basil.

Of course, it helps that we each have our own nests, about half a block apart. The truth is, I may not know everything there is about being a slob, but I *am* an American male and that's a start: An American male artist-type, who gardens with abandon, stares at computer screens for hours at a time waiting for the right words to self-assemble, has his share of opinions (maybe you've noticed?), and vacuums every three months whether it needs it or not. But maybe I have redeeming qualities. Let's just say I've learned the value of cuddling, and of listening, and that I've taken a chance on opening up. Marital researcher John Gottman observes that happy, stable relationships have about five positive interactions for every negative one, and as I was outlining this chapter, Susan and I agreed that we meet that criterion pretty well. Life's good.

The longest-running relationship I've experienced personally is the sixty-three-year love affair between my parents. Though my father passed on five years ago, my mother still wears the wedding ring he gave her three weeks before he shipped out for Europe, to take part in the Normandy invasion. They met at a sorority party and he was one among several other suitors until he climbed the fire escape of an antique building where she was in class and asked her to wear his fraternity pin. "He was a smoothie," she recalls. "He was intelligent, interested in things, and had a good sense of humor." What she really thought was "sharp" was when he and a few friends made and sold sandwiches to campus sorority girls, who weren't allowed out after ten at night. They raised enough money to go to Cuba for spring break. "That's when I realized he had a sense of adventure."

So did she. After their quickly rearranged wedding, he left to "shake down" the ship on which he was second-in-command. She followed him by train to his port of departure, astonishing him by showing up to say goodbye. She recalls, "It was against the rules—no civilians were allowed, especially women, but I talked an officer into taking me out to the island, and I really caused quite a stir. They were all lined up for dinner, and some of those men were coming back from the war and hadn't seen a woman in months. If I'd had two heads and three left feet, I would have looked good to them. But the important part was that I sent my love along with him."

From those romantic beginnings onward, their marriage was rich in mutual respect. I don't remember a single shouting match between them, though my sister and I made up for that a few times. Dad steadily became successful in his career, but the emphasis was on frugality, family, and faith. "We didn't need to spend a lot to be happy," says Mom. One night, Dad came home when a Cub Scout meeting was still in progress. He showed interest in what we were doing and, as always, he paid attention to us as individuals. Says Mom, "The other den mother told me, 'You're lucky to have him for a husband.' That's the way I felt, too," she says. "Wherever he went, he was *there*."

Dad's company sent him to Mexico City where they lived for ten years, immersed in learning and living a completely new culture. After retiring, they went on thirty or more Elder Hostel adventures—from theater tours in England to educational seminars on Indian reservations. "The one disagreement we had," she recalls, "was about him giving up smoking. Although he didn't smoke in front of me, he'd smoke when he was out playing golf." One of my most poignant memories is how she took care of him in his last days, as lung cancer slowly ate away his life. She'd be up at four in the morning to give him his pain medicine, and they spent seven months in their Tucson home knowing their days together were coming to an end, and making the most of each day.

Before he died, he took her to the bank, the car mechanic, and other places she'd need to know about. "This is how you pump gas," he told her. "This is how I've been watering the lemon tree." I was lucky to be at their house the week before he died. Although he and I had gone back and forth about the environment for years, he conceded that global warming was a reality, symbolically giving value to all my environmental efforts and convictions. "Write something good," he told me, putting his now-frail hand on my shoulder.

➤ Making Connections Wherever You Are

"He's the fullest, wealthiest man I've ever known," says my friend Patricia (you met her in the "Personal Growth" chapter), referring to a remarkable man she's known since her early days in an orphanage for girls. "Some of the priests at the orphanage seemed lonely but Father Reynolds (I'll call him that) was different. His life mission was to have a positive affect on girls who were having problems at the orphanage. Initially it was the ones who were giving the nuns fits—probably free spirits, like wild ponies, who needed a mentor to help them survive," she continues. "The nuns would rule with an iron fist out of necessity, but Father Reynolds helped steer them through the choppy waters. He had a little money he inherited from his parents when they died, and if one of his girls got into a tough place or needed a little spending money at college, he'd be there for them, like an anchor. He learned to speak Spanish, and when one of his girls got pregnant, he escorted her to Mexico so she could make peace with her parents.

"When I visited him recently at the retirement home where he now lives, I saw how his life mission had come into full blossom: on one whole wall of his little apartment—the centerpiece of his home—were dozens of pictures, radiating out from a central picture like spokes on a wheel. They were pictures of the fifty girls whose lives he's enriched. 'This is Angelina,' he told me, 'she was a tough little girl when I first met her, but now she's happily married, as you can see, living in Virginia.' He went through quite a few of the photographs, and I could see how appropriate the title 'father' was for him. He didn't have biological children, but he had fifty children-of-the-heart who continue to enrich his life—he gets calls from one or another of them every few days, inviting him to attend the graduation ceremony of their granddaughter, at their expense—or to ask his advice about what to get a master's degree in, or just to say hello. Three of his girls actually live in the same town that he lives in." Patricia concludes, "He chose a path of integrity that makes his retirement years so abundant—all these connections with people that are so significant in his life."

Stories like these remind us that everywhere we look, compassionate people are lending support and making connections—that's what we do best, really. I was up at 5:30 A.M. this past summer when my next-door neighbor Phil Lohre raced across the front lawn and directed an ambulance to the front of his house. I didn't want to be a nosy neighbor but I did want to be available if my friends needed help, so I stood on my front porch as the crew rolled Phil's wife, Julie, out on a gurney. I found out later that day that she'd had a seizure and had a tumor in the front of her brain.

The first thing that occurred to her is that she had to write her three children a letter with her best life lessons, love, and wisdom—just in case. The kids—who I've watched grow from beans to beanstalks—were at summer camp a thousand miles away, but Julie and Phil decided to fly them home the next afternoon. "We realized that we aren't separate from them," she says. "They were important to our decision-making process." As the Lohres began their intensive research on the science of Julie's condition, Phil was her first strong pillar of support. Julie is a nurse-practitioner and is very well versed in health science, but the details of the various treatment options were extremely complex. Phil's note-taking and sharp intellect helped the pair equip themselves with the right information. For example, they opted not to have a separate biopsy done since the tumor would have to come out in any case, whether it was benign or malignant. They flew to New York for a second opinion, and kept their wits about them as they gathered information. "Without Phil's support, I would have felt overwhelmed," says Julie.

Neighbors began cooking meals for the Lohres, old friends brought perennials to plant in Julie's garden, and Julie began to shift into a different mind-set. "I started to look at life's priorities in a totally different way," she says. "While I waited for a few weeks to have the surgery, I wanted laughter and music in my life, and I wanted to avoid labeling. Yes, I had a brain tumor, but that shouldn't prevent me from still feeling good . . ." She began to slow down and reassess where her time and efforts were going. Her son, Will, asked if she'd play pool with him. "Normally that would be something that would go on my to-do list—'spend quality time with Will'—but that afternoon, I STOPPED and played pool with him. We had a great time! I found out how good he was, who had taught him to play, and how they sometimes cheated, just a little. When we slow down and look at things differently, we see there's an underlying rhythm and vividness to everything." She gets out a card that her daughter Lisi had made for her: "Wherever you are and whatever you do, we will be there with you."

As a precaution, after the tumor was removed, Julie was scheduled for thirty-one low-dose radiation treatments over a six-week period—a huge effort, especially since she couldn't drive. Twenty different people offered to drive her to the hospital and wait for her—at least a two-hour commitment. "The support I got from people was awesome!" she says. "I felt like I was being carried by the positive energy people gave me." She made each trip to the hospital into a productive healing session. For example, when I took her, our discussion was about visualization. She wanted to clearly and decisively instruct her immune system what to do with all uninvited cells in her body, and we talked about sending them to a virtual compost pile. Julie's prognosis is excellent, and no doubt all the intentional thoughts and support have played a key role.

➤ Spending Social Capital in the Neighborhood

I lived in a rural mountain town for twenty years and rarely interacted with my neighbors, who were scattered throughout the valley in cabins. But when a blizzard hit, our vehicles would get stuck in snowdrifts, and we relied on each other to dig them out. Sometimes the power also went out, and in each little house, families were sitting around woodstoves telling stories the way humans always have. In our little cabin, we always had piles of firewood cut and split, and we'd get out the candles and pop popcorn on the stove. By the end of the storm, we became a closer family in a more supportive community. It felt great.

The question is, why did it take blizzards and power outages to strengthen natural bonds between people? In many of America's neighborhoods, we've become strangers on our own streets. What can we do to bring those streets back to life? The process of reinventing a neighborhood might begin when you walk out your front door and just say hello to someone you've seen before, but never met. After preliminary conversation, the topic of neighborhood security comes up, and maybe you comment how valuable it would be to compile a list of the names, addresses, and telephone numbers of everyone on the block. "That way, if someone gets hurt or just needs help moving a dresser, he can call one of us," you say. Your neighbor, whose name is Shawn, agrees, adding, "Maybe we could set up a neighborhood e-mail listserv, to provide a forum for news and opinion, and a digital bulletin board for babysitting exchanges, discussion groups, and carpooling . . ."

Coincidentally, while the two of you are talking about homeland security at the neighborhood scale, another neighbor—Marion—comes by with her own idea for getting neighbors together—a community picnic in her large backyard. She prepares a homemade flier and takes it door to door to forty-four houses on the block, explaining to those who are home that her intention is to help create a friendlier, livelier neighborhood. All but a few neighbors seem interested, and many of them show up at the barbecue, which includes musical talent from the neighborhood, humorous name tags, and locally grown food.

The next day you notice neighbors knocking on each other's doors, following up on conversations, dropping off recipes, and arranging help with lawn watering or pet-sitting while people are on vacation. In the months that follow, a discussion group, book club, a few carpools, and a food co-op form. Matt, a sociology professor, uses the new e-mail listserv to suggest a work-share program enabling neighbors to trade skills like dry walling and landscaping, to save money and continue building community. Sarah, the young woman with the German shepherd, joins him to help coordinate the project, and she also spearheads a community cleanup of the vacant lot at the end of the street. While they pick up McDonald's wrappers and newspapers, she has an idea: Maybe the absentee owner of the lot would let them have a community garden there. After all, the lot's been vacant for the last fifteen years, and he would get a tax deduction for it.

These first few neighborhood-building efforts result in a new way of thinking about your neighborhood. You begin to think outside the boxes of your houses to envision a more productive and useful community. With a

Neighbors at Tierra Nueva Cohousing Community in Oceano, California, had a party to celebrate the resilience and social wealth of their neighborhood. Credit: Magdy Farahat

handful of successes behind you, you organize a meeting at the elementary school one evening, to talk about visions for the neighborhood. This is an important step because it formalizes neighbors' intentions to cocreate a place that is supportive and strives to be sustainable. You stand up and report, "Since our first community picnic, I've watched less TV, saved time and money by carpooling with Frank, and helped remodel Jerry's garage, where he will park an old pickup truck that's available for any of us to borrow. Aren't these the kind of things that good neighborhoods should be about?" One young adult, Liz, decides to return to the neighborhood to live near her family and friends. The elderly widow, Nancy, rents her the apartment that her late husband created by remodeling the garage into a cottage. So, now Nancy can afford to stay in the neighborhood—and Liz can, too.

Gradually, your neighborhood gets a well-deserved reputation for being a great place to live. Crime is almost nonexistent, property values go up, and turnover goes down. At a barbecue near the community garden one evening, Marion comments, "It's funny—when we focus just on ourselves, the world shrinks and our problems seem huge. But when we learn to focus on other people, the world expands and our own problems seem smaller. As our world expands, so does our capacity to care."

6

Time Affluence

How to Save Time, and Savor It

The bad news is time flies. The good news is you're the pilot.
—Michael Altshuler

I'm not sure people are meant to work full-time. Life is more complicated than that. We human beings need time to think, make music, weave baskets, play with kids and dogs, bond with each other, and care for friends and family. Those of us with demanding jobs that continually spill over into our personal lives often don't have the time for those things while we work full-time.
—Carol Ostram

Every morning I awake torn between a desire to save the world and an inclination to savor it. This makes it hard to plan the day.
—E. B. White

Whether it's the best of times or the worst of times, it's the only time we've got.
—Art Buchwald

Time is a natural resource. Like oil or copper, there's only so much of it available—eighty-five years for each of us if we're lucky, divided into twenty-four-hour (sometimes frantic!) parcels. When some new, time-consuming activity comes along, like deleting endless spam e-mails, creating new passwords we'll soon forget, or waiting in line for three-dollar gas, we don't usually ask ourselves where the time *comes from* to do these extra things. The truth is, time is often borrowed from important life functions, such as maintaining strong relationships or cooking healthy meals from fresh ingredients. The more time we need to borrow, the less is available for the things that make us feel great.

In the essay "Wasted Work, Wasted Time," social commentator Jonathan Rowe compares the resource of time to water that's been diverted for commercial uses. Water and time are judged to be useful—economically—only when they are channeled from their natural flows to become part of the market. But Rowe counters this standard economic evaluation. "Water left in a river or aquifer is working all the time. It sustains fish, forests, wildlife, and ultimately humanity," he writes. "So it is with time. When we aren't working for or spending money, we often are doing more genuinely useful things, like working on a project with our kids or attending a town meeting, or fixing a banister for an elderly neighbor. We might just be sitting on a front porch or stoop, providing watchful eyes that help keep the neighborhood safe."[1]

Nature gives us time, but our current work-and-spend lifestyle takes it away. We draw down reserves of time just as we draw down an aquifer or bank account, making constant due-date payments for activities and commitments that keep us too busy. "The market has been claiming more and more of the nation's time just as it has been claiming more of nature," Rowe continues. "Never before in history has a society expended so much time and energy on work of dubious value—pitching junk food to kids, for example—while neglecting so much work that really needs to be done. Push junk at kids and you count. Give your time to them and you don't."[2] Rowe echoes Henry David Thoreau's sentiments of 160 years ago: "If a man walks in the woods for love of them half of each day, he is in danger of being regarded as a loafer. But if he spends his days as a speculator, shearing off those woods and making the earth bald before her time, he is deemed an industrious and enterprising citizen . . ."[3]

➤ Where Time Goes

The market relies on consumer time as well as consumer dollars. It assumes that we'll take the time to read the instructions to assemble the fan ourselves that we bought at Target, that we'll teach ourselves how to operate the new computer from Best Buy, that we'll maintain our health so we can be more productive workers and also raise future employees-of-the-month. But our busy lifestyles don't leave much time to do all this unpaid work. "Those hours we spend puzzling over the options of medical insurance, long distance, and investment plans—and then dealing with disputes over bills—are hours not available for other things," concludes Rowe.[4]

With credit cards in our pockets and 20 cubic feet of cargo space in our huge vehicles, we spend a large portion of our time hunting and gathering consumer goods. My least favorite time-consuming consumer activity is penetrating the packaging on products intentionally designed for a short lifetime, such as disposable razor blades. When I recently bought an electric razor to curb the flash flood of disposable blades, I opened its package with trepidation, wondering how many have died opening plastic-encased packaging with sharp scissors and knives! (I also wondered how much energy went into the manufacture of my new "speed shaver," and why razor blade *sharpeners* have not yet come into the market. Why can't we have blades that last at least as long as refrigerator leftovers?)

I'm fascinated by all the time that's embedded and programmed into our products. A microwave dinner, for example, appeals to us because it takes only a few minutes to prepare; yet it took nature millions of years to produce the oil for the plastic wrapper and make the soil that grew the trees for the cardboard tray. The packaging for that frozen lasagne is programmed for a cooking time of about four minutes, a shelf life of maybe six months, and a landfill dead time of centuries. In a sense, isn't packaging insulation from time, enabling and promoting a system of long-distance, energy-rich transportation and storage? Packaging makes buying local products unnecessary, and also prevents the buyer from assessing the quality of an individual product; one packaged item is assumed to be the same as another. As I wrestled with the thick plastic that encased my new razor, I resented the fact that they were making the money but I was spending the time—first the work-time to afford the razor, then the shopping time to buy it, and finally the fluster-time to actually hold the product in my hand—which in the end malfunctioned and had to be returned.[5]

For the alleged convenience of such short-time products as razor blades, computer software, paper towels, tape dispensers, batteries, and all the rest, how many hours do we spend prowling supermarket and store aisles in search of replacements? How many salespeople and friends do we talk to about these products, and how many consumer reports do we read on the Web? How much "hidden" time do we spend in the car and at work, to obtain that product? For example, one of the silliest inventions in recent years is prescrambled eggs that you heat up, no muss, no fuss, in a microwave. You save about five minutes by not having to crack a few eggs, stir them up, and cook them yourself. But the prescrambled eggs cost about twenty times as much as fresh eggs do—about twelve minutes in working time for someone making an average salary.

We're discovering how costly consumption really is, in time as well as money—hurrying through our best years partly to overcome the hidden costs of these disposable, poorly designed products. The most effective weapon against all the packaging, payments, and pretense is to fill our time with things that last; and the truth is, quality usually takes time to obtain or achieve. For example, to really take care of our health takes time, just as learning to play the piano does, or reading stories to our kids. Yet all of these uses of time can substitute for consumption.

➤ The Time Costs of Excessive Spending

We tend to think about time only when face to face with it—eyeball to eyeball with a deadline or unachievable to-do list. Yet author Jerome Segal takes a wider look at time, pointing out that we work from New Year's Day to March 10 just to pay for our cars, which lately have become a full sixth of the average household budget. On an average income, we spend about two minutes working per mile of annual travel.[6] And the average American then spends more time *in* the car than he or she does for activities like reading, having conversations, exercising, or having sex.

Social critic Ivan Illich once evaluated car travel in a slightly different way: When we add the time spent in our car (an average of 445 hours a year) with time spent to purchase and maintain the car, we're going less than five miles an hour. (Compared to the average human pace of 3–4 mph, in which the walker gets exercise). Even the *actual* speed of the average car amounts to less than 30 miles an hour, including stoplight respites, where in nonhybrid cars the motor is turning but the wheels are not.

Partly because people think "time is money," our world is teeming with time thieves, lurking like pickpockets at a mall. For example, a bank or insurance company that installs an automated phone tree not only steals the jobs of employees but robs customers of their time, too, as they listen for the right "branch"; press 3 for account questions, 9 for more options; listen to the Muzak for ten minutes; and finally hang up in frustration. According to a recent survey conducted by Harris Interactive, the typical American will spend six months of his or her life sitting at red lights, eight months opening junk mail, one year searching for misplaced items, two years trying to return calls to people who aren't there, four years cleaning house, and five years waiting in line—all activities that relate at least in part to our lives as consumers.[7]

Certainly, there are opportunities to save *years* of time in the above categories by rearranging the details of one's lifestyle. Author and Simplicity Forum chair Vicki Robin proposes that we can gain time and improve our lives by rethinking the "time cost of stuff," to change our priorities and enrich our lives. Robin offers the example of a young single person who makes $20 an hour yet can't seem to make ends meet. Here's why: From $800 a week she earns, she needs to subtract weekly transportation costs of $20, the portion of her upgraded car payment that relates to her new job—$25 a week, restaurant lunches at $30 more than brown-bag lunches, $25 a week for clothes appropriate for work, monthly seminars to improve her chances for advancement—another $50 a week, and then income taxes for another $125 a week.[8]

So she has $525 in her purse as she begins to consider the actual *time* she spends on work-related activities: ten hours a week just getting dressed, fed, and out the door in the morning; and another ten hours a week to recover from the workday; three hours a week for the monthly training sessions; seven hours for work-related reading; three hours a week for the monthly seminar; and ten hours, easily, for "dribs and drabs" of unpaid overtime—an extra half hour a day at her desk; weekend calls and a steady stream of e-mails and text messages. Dividing the $525 she's got left by eighty actual work hours, the young professional is really making $6.50 an hour. Writes Robin, "A new car at $6.50 an hour becomes over three thousand hours—a year and a half on the job. A daily "double tall skinny" latte ends up costing over hundred hours a year—over two weeks of work." She concludes that any $6.50 item must be worth more than an hour with a friend or with a good book, or why bother with it?[9]

Thoughts like these make us wonder how to recover some of that work-related time. In the book *Your Money or Your Life,* Robin and coauthor Joe Dominguez lay out a financial strategy that will enable conscious consumers and investors to retire years early.

➤ Taking Back Our Work Time

Many others are asking a similar question about regaining time before retirement, including John de Graaf, who edited the anthology *Take Back Your Time,* in which Vicki Robin's "time cost" thoughts, above, appear. He is also national coordinator of the organization Take Back Your Time, and has thoroughly documented the American syndrome of overworking. (He has many suggestions for what to do about it, too. See www.Timeday.org.) De Graaf notes that 57 percent of employed adults say they don't always leave work on time, and less than one out of five are "very satisfied" with their current work/life balance.[10] "More than half of Americans say they'd be willing to trade a day off a week for a day's pay a week," says de Graaf.[11]

A full third of U.S. adult employees don't use all of their vacation days— 574 million vacation days were left on the table in 2006! Why? Because overwork has become "normal" in America. We can't afford to lose our jobs because house payments are huge, the standard of living is inflated, and health-care benefits are linked with work. Although employers are convinced that longer hours mean more productivity, countless studies link longer work hours with carelessness and injuries. "Job stress and burnout costs the U.S. economy more than $300 billion a year," estimates de Graaf.[12]

John de Graaf has become politically active on the work-time issue, meeting with politicians such as Barack Obama to find political support for legislation that his organization advocates. This proposed legislation would amend the Fair Labor Standards Act to grant three weeks of time off for anyone who's worked at a job for a year. Says de Graaf, "Unlike 96 other countries in the world, the U.S. has no law governing vacations." He's had a close look at European work standards, observing first-hand how the French, Germans, Dutch, Swedes, Italians, and other Europeans *make* time for living. "Their national policies ensure things like guaranteed maternity leave, minimum annual vacation time, and part-time opportunities with benefits. And the results are plain to see: they have much lower stress. In France, for example, it's not just the red wine that leads to lower risks of heart disease, but the long, leisurely meals that create healthy bonds of friendship."[13]

The French are setting the pace when it comes to slowing down work commitments. Many French labor unions have negotiated with employers workweeks as short as 35 hours, and the average French employee also enjoys 39 days of vacation, compared to 14 in America. "On average, Europeans work 350 hours less than Americans overall," says de Graaf. There have been occasional experiments with reduced workweeks in the United States, such as the well-documented, and well-loved, six-hour day at the Kellogg Company, which lasted from 1930 to 1985. With two hours more of discretionary time, Kellogg employees transformed the lifestyle of Battle Creek, Michigan. Families and neighborhoods benefited from the extra time; schools included curricula about the "arts of living," and parental involvement in schools— such as "room mothers" in the classrooms—increased. Parks, community centers, skating rinks, churches, libraries, and YMCAs became centers of activity. Kellogg workers recall that the balance of their lives shifted from working to living. What to do with their time became more important than what to buy with their money.[14]

California's Paid Leave Law of 2004 goes one step further than the federal Family and Medical Leave Act of 1993, which provides up to twelve weeks' unpaid time off to care for babies or sick family members. The California law provides partial payment for up to six weeks time off, but the catch is that it's 100 percent employee funded. It appears that until employees' voices are once again unified in their demands for time, overwork will continue to be a defining American and Canadian characteristic.

◆ Time to Care ◆

A Policy Agenda Proposed by Take Back Your Time

- Guarantee paid leave for all parents for the birth or adoption of a child. Today, only 40% of Americans are able to take advantage of the 12 weeks of unpaid leave provided by the Family and Medical Leave Act of 1993.

- Guarantee at least one week of paid sick leave for all workers. Many Americans work while sick, lowering productivity and endangering other workers.

- Guarantee at least three weeks of paid annual vacation leave for all workers. Studies show that 28% of all female employees and 37% of women earning less than $40,000 a year receive no paid vacation at all.

- Place a limit on the amount of compulsory overtime work that an employer can impose, with our goal being to give employees the right to accept or refuse overtime work.

- Make Election Day a holiday, with the understanding that Americans need time for civic and political participation.

- Make it easier for Americans to choose part-time work.

- Provide hourly wage parity and protection of promotions and prorated benefits for part-time workers.

www.timeday.org/

Some courageous employees are willing to challenge the rules of work-time as individuals. When newspaper reporter Carol Ostram and two co-workers first proposed a job-share arrangement more than ten years ago, their editor vehemently declined. Ostram explained that she loved journalism and could do a better job if she was able to decompress occasionally; and that there were other parts of her life that she could no longer put "on hold"—such as caring for her mother and elderly aunt, and spending more time with her partner. But the editor stood firm in a work culture that employs many a workaholic.[15]

A few years later, after a change in management, the three employees pitched the idea again, agreeing to pay some of their own health and dental benefits and to guarantee that two of the three writers would always be available in heavy news weeks. They had learned that their idea was less marketable as "family time" and "worker satisfaction" than getting managers what they needed. "We got our job share, finally, because newsroom managers wanted desperately to hire someone with specific skills for another position," says Ostram. "The money wasn't in the budget, but we noted repeatedly that the job share would be a way to 'gain' a position. It might have gone a lot more smoothly for us if we'd figured out earlier that it wasn't about *us*." Each job was scheduled as four months on, and two months off, an arrangement that soon began to bring each person's life into blossom.

"Susan, for example, suddenly found time for herself," Ostram recalls. "She painted the inside of her home, began exercising, read voraciously, and still had time to volunteer at her children's schools. She and the kids romped at the beach, and she reveled in spending time with them while they were still young enough to want to do that." Each of the three found that they became more energetic, more likely to be effective when they interviewed people. "We would come back armed with Great Ideas," says Ostram, "and with the energy to shape them into Great Stories." In fact, the job sharers soon earned kudos from bosses and helped establish the newspaper as a great place for working women.

As for the editors at the newspaper who had originally opposed their job share proposal, one took an early retirement and moved to a small town in Idaho. Another got so stressed and busy she forgot to pick up her little kid after summer school. "She was so horrified at what she'd done, she changed her life, her job, her hours," says Ostram. First she took some much-needed time off. Later, she came back part-time—in a job-share.[16]

Lore Rosenthal, a Maryland sign language interpreter, is another example of a person choosing to shorten her workweek. Says Rosenthal, "I recently reduced my hours from thirty-two to twenty-eight hours per week. I told my boss I needed that extra hour a day, to go work out or do something healthy. To my delight, she granted my request! I am now a ⅞ employee; I still qualify for full benefits, health insurance, 401(k), profit share, annual leave, sick leave, and holiday pay. I immediately went out and joined Curves, an exercise class. I decided to make my health more of a priority and work/money less of a priority." Lore's fellow workers are glad she made the switch. When their boss observed that at even thirty-two hours, Lore wasn't having physical problems but those who worked forty hours were, the standard workweek became thirty-two hours. This was also a quality-of-life enticement to keep the interpreters from going to work for other employers.[17]

John de Graaf proposes a phased-in retirement plan that can deliver many of the time-rich benefits Ostram and Rosenthal experience. Says de Graaf, "At 55, an employee might cut back to thirty-two hours a week and receive 20 percent of his pension. Then at 60, he'd go to twenty-four hours a week (or else work 60 percent of the year); at 65, to sixteen hours, and at 70 he might choose to retire." Such a program would have multiple benefits, he points out: It would reduce fiscal pressure on pension systems, open up spaces for new workers, retain older workers as mentors, allow older workers to find hobbies and interests gradually, and help retirees to avoid the depression that sometimes follows the sudden loss of connection with workplace associates.[18]

➤ Time for Quality

Quality in products and experiences takes time, but it also *provides* time. For example, if a person has takes the time to eat quality food, he or she may live longer. However, this presents another possible challenge: Having lots of time available but not knowing what to *do* with it. Seventy-nine million baby boomers are now in the process of learning how to "cope with leisure" in their retirement years, since working has kept many of them so busy they didn't have time to cultivate hobbies and skills. What they come up with might result in great value for our society. (No doubt there will also be mountains of snack food consumed in front of the TV.) High-quality leisure time requires creativity. We need to know ourselves well. What do we like to do? What are we good at? Do we want to fill our time, or just kill it? When we retire, we have to actively learn new things about ourselves and about the world. As people retire, it's a setup for feeling as if we've missed the boat if we're not constantly out spending the money we've saved. Yet to me the more important values to have "saved" are calmness, curiosity, skills, a sense of humility, and self-worth. These will help ensure that time is of greater value than money.

Linda Breen Pierce distinguishes between "dead" time and "live" time. Ten minutes spent getting dressed for work is perceived as less time than ten minutes chatting with a friend, she suggests; and half an hour stuck in traffic is no comparison to half an hour walking in a beautiful neighborhood. Prison inmate Donny Johnson may never again have any of those experiences, but he converts dead time into live time as well as he can while *doing* time at Pelican Bay Prison in California. Using a paintbrush made from plastic wrap, foil, and strands of his own hair, he paints little abstract prison masterpieces on postcards. Recently twenty of the paintings sold at a gallery on the "outside" for $500 apiece. Although drug abuse and aggression were challenges for Johnson (he's serving three sentences for murder), creativity hasn't been. The colors in his palette come from M&M's ordered from the commissary, which he soaks a few at a time in salvaged plastic grape jelly containers. "Skittles also work," he told a *New York Times* reporter, "but I end up eating them all."

Advertiser H. Jackson Brown Jr. once wrote, "You have exactly the same number of hours per day that were given to Helen Keller, [Louis] Pasteur, Michelangelo, Mother Teresa, Leonardo da Vinci, Thomas Jefferson, and Albert Einstein," yet in our world of overconsumption (which several of these luminaries foresaw), the way we use time has a direct bearing on our personal ecological footprints. For example, my neighbors Jim and Beth Davis have now climbed all fifty-three of Colorado's 14,000-plus-foot mountains, and are now going after the thirteeners. Other than a little gas and lots of trail mix, that passion hasn't consumed anything. These experiences give them greater pleasure than products do, and are a great example of how information, curiosity, experience, skill, and time can substitute for consumption in the new American lifestyle.

My sister, whose photographs appear in this book, has always loved to shop. She once told me that she only liked to take walks when they included shopping destinations along the way. But she recently discovered that she doesn't need to buy and own things like well-crafted clothes and jewelry if she instead takes great photographs of them. It's the inherent qualities of products that stimulate her—the colors, patterns, shapes, artistry, and materials. Digital photos, made of ethereal bits and bytes, don't take much of a bite out of the environment.

➤ Time to Let Go

"Time is God's way of making sure everything doesn't happen all at once," goes the amusing and ponderous saying, but it often seems this celestial strategy isn't working! You dart out of your house and dive into the car because you're late for work, but as you're backing out, something under the hood makes a terrifying, screeching sound, accompanied by blinking red lights on the dashboard. The neighbor flags you down to complain about dog poop, and the kids appear in the driveway right on schedule, having missed the bus. Throughout the day, work deadlines hover over your desk, bills have to be silenced, the dinner groceries have to be hunted and gathered, and a doctor's appointment needs to be stressed over and finally canceled at the last minute. Many days, it feels like everything *is* happening all at once. "I just don't have time" is the standard lament, and it's literally true. We *don't* have time—it has us. (Think about the word "deadline," or the phrase "drop-dead date.")

But imagine the long-awaited summer vacation in southern Colorado, when you're finally able to let time spread out a little. What a relief! Camping in a place like the Great Sand Dunes, mysteriously deposited by nature near a red-tinged mountain range, you can leave your watch in the glove compartment and let all life's gears wind down. After all, what real difference does it make if it's three or four in the afternoon? When you let time take a break, reality is simplified to three remarkable events: sunrise, high noon, and sunset. No worries! It becomes too much of a chore to keep track of the day, let alone the hour. When even brushing your teeth becomes enjoyable, you're back in sync with real time. Cooking breakfast—an eight-minute, every-second-counts stunt back at home—becomes a decompressed, mindless opportunity to combine colors, smells, textures, tastes, and sounds of nature with daydreaming, and meandering conversation. If the pancakes burn, cook some more—there's plenty of time.

"The modern mind," writes Wendell Berry, "longs for the Future as the medieval mind longed for Heaven."[19] Berry argues that we've been conned into believing that the present is something we need to escape because it's just not good enough. We can't be here now because we don't yet have enough money, enough gadgets, or a large enough house. We're not yet powerful enough or "happy" enough to live in the present. The truth is, if we're satisfied with what we have in the present, we're less likely to be obedient consumers, so the supply-side of the economy has invested trillions to engineer dissatisfaction into our shell-shocked psyches. Leisure, love, and laughter can best be had in the future, we begin to believe, but we can't put our fingers on where that disturbing idea came from.

My not-then-ex-wife, Julie, and I sat on top of a huge sand dune, wriggling bare feet into the cool sand beneath the hot surface. I realized how badly I needed a "mindwash." Maybe I could enter one end of the vacation all grimy—like a car entering a carwash—and emerge from the other end as a calm, centered human being. About half a mile away, our kids were doing mindless, joyful gymnastics on a sand bunker near the creek—we could hear them very faintly, laughing, screeching; doing handstands and somersaults. Completely in the present, they were, completely at the Sand Dunes on a sunny Wednesday morning—or was it Thursday? Hypnotized by snow-capped mountains in the distance, I wondered how much time the huge dune we sat on *contained*, if it somehow became the grains in a gigantic hour glass.

Historians tell us the impetus for subdividing time into units smaller than hours was the unbearable longevity of Christian sermons in the Middle Ages, which often droned on for two hours or more. In self-defense, churchgoing tinkers manufactured smaller sand glasses to measure half-hour and quarter-hour time periods. (The Egyptian sundial and water-drip timepiece—both invented about four to five thousand years ago, preceded the sand glass, invented in Europe around A.D. 100) But the world's most familiar face—the clock—didn't emerge until the thirteenth century, in Benedictine monasteries. Since the sixth century, Saint Benedict's cardinal rule, that "idleness is the enemy of the soul," had echoed through the somber stone hallways of Benedictine orders, and now the elders had an unerring instrument to keep idleness at bay. Saint Benedict's well-meaning preoccupation with orderliness may have transformed the social order of our species, nothing less.

By the late fifteenth century, the clock had come out of the cloisters and become the central feature of the town square. The newly emerging bourgeois class, a vigorous, mercantile bunch of folks, quickly adopted and replicated the clock, correctly sensing that it could make them rich. Not that country folk readily surrendered to synchronization—it took a few hundred years for the clock to midwife the industrial revolution. But the die was cast. The gears were already in motion.

Until the clock came onto the scene, medieval folk adjusted the rhythms of work and leisure to natural cycles. They organized their lives by the calendar, a tradition- and ritual-oriented device. Calendar cultures commemorate ancient legends, historical events, heroic deeds of gods, and the phases of Moon, Earth, and Sun. What the clock brought was a schedule-regulated culture. We became hungry for the future, obsessing about human productivity per unit of time. We became Charlie Chaplin in *Modern Times*, hanging desperately to the gears of the clock; and later, the soccer mom, speeding frantically across town to pick her kids up at three different ball fields.

A week into our schedule-free vacation, time and Colorado had worked their magic. Slowly climbing a boulder-filled trough towards the sky above Crested Butte, I was right on the verge of Fundamental Knowledge about time, because I was *in* it. I knew consciously that time is the sun's course across the sky, yes, but it was also the gradual, relentless erosion of the very mountain I was climbing. Time was what separated me from Julie, who moments ago had gone back to camp because of the thunderheads brewing in the northwestern sky. Time was the day-by-day aging of my own body, moving relentlessly toward the aches, pains, and, hopefully, wisdom of old age. It was the meteorites we'd seen last night, streaking from hundreds of thousands of years away—and it was stars that weren't even there anymore. It was lupines and delphiniums bursting into living color every summer, and it was the western tanager's migration from Colorado to Guatemala and back—I knew all this from thirty-six years of living.

But subconsciously, as the clouds whipped ominously overhead, I knew something much more basic, and humbling. Sure, clocks all over the world would continue to spin mechanically through their daily cycles, and when I got back, the meetings and deadlines would drag me back—against my will—to that rhythm. But right at that moment, I was unhurried, square in the center of calmness. Right at that moment, time was on my side.

7

The Stocks of Wellness

Preventive Pathways to Health

A man's health can be judged by which he takes two at a time—
pills or stairs.
   —Joan Welsh

There are more overweight people in America than average-weight
people. So overweight people are now average. Which means you've met
your New Year's resolution.
   —Jay Leno

You gotta eat green stuff to make sure you're pretty on the inside.
   —Takayuki Ikkaku

Be careful about reading health books. You may die of a misprint.
   —Mark Twain

The benefits of being healthy cascade through all other aspects of our lives: finances, relationships, discretionary time, ability to work effectively and play passionately, and so on. When we're healthy, things seem effortless. We have the energy to do what matters most; we can more readily tap into values like clarity, security, connection, caring, and a sense of purpose. Stress levels are lower, bones are sturdier, and senses are sharper. We don't fuss over ourselves as much—taking this medication, stressing about this ache, or making an appointment to see that specialist—and we give our time more freely to others.

We also don't have to dwell as much on what we need to *buy* to feel happy, because feeling good generates its own value. Certainly, the times come when each of us is not as physically vigorous as we'd like to be, but the nice thing about health is that if given a chance, it comes back! There is also a healthiness of mind, a wisdom and contentedness that ideally is deepened by many years of healthy decisions. "Old age is like everything else," said performer Fred Astaire. "To make a success of it, you've got to start young." Let's take a look at how health-related decisions affect our bodies in day-to-day activities. See if you can guess what the activity is as you read. Which sets of physical responses will you choose today?

1. The heart shifts into high gear and blood pressure rises as the body speeds oxygen and glucose to muscles and into the bloodstream for emergency fuel supplies. Platelets in the blood become more "sticky" to aid clotting in case of a wound. Adrenalin surges, increasing your strength and speed. Eyes widen and jaws clench. (road rage)

2. Heart rate and blood pressure increase: often there's a noticeable "flush" in the chest, neck, face, and ears. Nipples become erect and muscle tension increases throughout the body. Erections occur in the penis in males and clitoris in females, and the vagina becomes moist. As excitement moves toward climax, respiration rate increases and various hormones are released that create a sense of euphoria. (sex)

3. Heart rate slows, brain blood vessels dilate, and blood flows away from major muscles. The brain focuses on gathering more information as cuts and edits per second demand your attention—in case the information has survival value. Brainwaves resemble a state of hypnosis; the rest of the body goes limp. (watching TV)

4. A state of deep rest is attained, opposite to the stress response. The body produces lower levels of cortisol and higher levels of serotonin, reducing feelings of fear, anger, anxiety. Muscles relax, blood flow to the brain increases; brain wave patterns include increased alpha wave activity, an indicator of a relaxed state of awareness. (meditation)

5. General metabolism increases, the rate of breathing increases, as do urination and the levels of fatty acids in the blood and gastric acid in the stomach. Neural activity is elevated in many parts of the brain, fatigue is postponed and physical work that involves endurance is enhanced—but not fine motor coordination. Overuse can result in symptoms that resemble a panic attack. (excessive coffee consumption)

6. Blood sugar skyrockets and the body tries to bring it back. The pancreas pumps out a big blast of insulin, and blood sugar levels crash.

This dip in blood glucose stimulates hunger and produces irritability. Over the years, this repetitive cycle wears down the pancreas, potentially resulting in diabetes. (eating starchy or sugary foods like white bread or candy bars)

7. Blood flow increases to the brain, the nervous system is stimulated and morphine-like substances are released, that have a positive effect on mood. Endorphins and adrenalin produce antidepressant, anti-anxiety effects and a general sense of "feeling better." (vigorous walking or other exercise)

➤ Preventive Pathways to Health

We may not feel like we're in direct control of things like interest rates or deployment of troops to the Middle East, but we *can* make decisions that directly affect our health. Though we tend to think of the new high-tech drugs, joint replacements, and heart bypasses as the most significant medical breakthroughs, even more significant are natural ways to meet our basic needs and *avoid* the expensive high-tech interventions—(and all the pain that precedes them); such things as diet, exercise, emotional connections, avoidance of stress, avoidance of toxic substances, and a reasonable relationship with bacteria (there are ten times more bacteria in and on each of our bodies than there are human cells, so let's relax a little). These preventive approaches can provide wellness—not just partial recovery—for a fraction of the cost of high-tech, after-the-fact miracles.

Says Dr. Dean Ornish, director of the Preventive Medicine Research Institute, "Every man and woman who can avoid coronary bypass surgery by changing diet and lifestyle saves $30,000 immediately, and there may be additional savings because half of coronary bypasses clog up again. An angioplasty costs $10,000 and more, and cholesterol-lowering drugs can cost $1500 a year per person . . ."[1]

During my ongoing, thirty-year experiment with moderate exercise and a whole foods diet (limited refined foods and chemicals, very little sugar), I've saved quite a bit of time and money by not being too sick to get out of bed (except once), not needing second opinions, or even first opinions, and not having to wait in line at the pharmacy for prescriptions. I have my blood tested every year, with good results so far (I'm knocking on my hollow, wooden head with one hand as I type with the other). I'm not trying to be or even *appear* to be a superhero; I'm just sharing years of observation about habits that have definitely enriched my life. Believe me, there's plenty of other things I've screwed up along the way! I'm certain that part of being healthy is *thinking* of ourselves as healthy. If I'm a walking placebo (*and* if I make daily offerings like exercise, stress-busting, and good food), my mind somehow directs the interactions in my body toward positive ends.

Radical Simplicity author Jim Merkel's four-tiered approach to low-cost, high-return health care is similar to mine. At the base of his pyramid is a commitment to be an empathetic person who helps others when they need it; one day they may help you. (The social connection alone has proven health benefits.) Second, says Merkel, "Treat the body well, eating healthy organic food, exercising, reducing stress, being in nature, and having a spiritual practice." Third, know how to heal yourself with herbs and natural remedies, and last, get a high-deductible, catastrophic illness plan for the worst case.[2]

Dean Ornish has worked with many people whose new-leaf lifestyle changes led to rapid, dramatic improvements in quality of life:

> *Paradoxically, many people find that it is easier to make big changes in diet and lifestyle than to make small, gradual ones . . . When people make comprehensive lifestyle changes, they often feel better and have more energy immediately. Blood flow to the brain improves, so they think more clearly. Blood flow to sexual organs improves, so potency often increases. These changes often occur within days or weeks. On a deeper level, many people report that their relationships improve, and they often rediscover inner sources of peace, joy, and well-being.*

> *When we change our diet, meditate, exercise, quit smoking and increase our intimacy with other people all at the same time, we may find that we feel so much better so quickly, that it reframes the reason for changing diet and lifestyle: from fear of dying to joy of living . . ."[3]*

Ornish has collected years of data focusing on the connection between lower rates of heart disease and healthy lifestyles. But the benefits reach far beyond heart disease to the prevention of arthritis, Alzheimer's, cancer, depression, and everyday assets like good eyesight, and significant reductions in colds, headaches, and flu. In fact, healthy lifestyles offer far more than the absence of disease; they deliver a higher baseline of *wellness*—a gladness to be alive. That's the real wealth.

Though we should be aware of ailments in our family history, it's the everyday choices we make that determine if we crawl or spring out of bed each morning. I think of health as an investment portfolio built up from various sources—what we eat, how active we are, whether we make strong emotional connections with others, whether we steer clear of drugs, and so on. We can bank health just as we bank money, and over a lifetime, we *might* save enough to reach that fabled hundred-year milestone. (If so, let's hope we've got a damn good pension.)

➤ Steps in the Right Direction

My own health strategy is focused on feeling alive and well today—I'll cross the hundred-year-old bridge when/if I get there. One of the things I've actually done right in my life is to be uncompromising about daily exercise. In the last thirty years (about eleven thousand days), I've done at least half an hour of aerobic exercising on all but a few hundred days at most. I've never been a marathon runner, long-distance bicycler, or weightlifter; I'm just consistent in my moderation. In that time period, I'm sure I've covered 25,000 miles under my own power—the equivalent of a journey around the world. I really don't get out there because I think I "should"; the fact is I do it because it makes me feel good. It gives me lasting energy, and I guess it also helps keep the doctor away, since in those eleven thousand days, I've only waited—and waited—in doctors' offices a handful of times. I've never resorted to prescription drugs in that time period, except antibiotics a few times, which haven't worked that well anyway. (I usually use raw, organic garlic instead, that works for staphylococcus, streptococcus, and boosting the immune system.) I even stay away from over-the-counter drugs—with their artificial colors, additives, side effects, and chase-one-symptom approach—except for the occasional ibuprofen or Tylenol in a pinch. I can't deny that I've swallowed my share of vitamins and multiminerals—probably more than was necessary, since I eat well.

My immune system is much stronger when I exercise. I sleep better, enjoy sex and physical activities more, and don't get upset over small things. Does an unwavering thirty minutes a day subtract anything from my life? Not at all—it's built into the top third of my to-do list—the third that actually gets done. Sometimes, before a conference or retreat that starts early, I need to get up a little earlier to exercise, but if I *don't* make that effort, I get bored and fidgety during the meetings. If my day includes an early flight that prevents walking that day, I often just walk up and down the concourse a half an hour's worth, taking the stairs rather than the escalator. When I'm not feeling well, I make an extra effort to exercise, to keep from getting worse.

Dave Wann is the coordinator and official scapegoat in the Harmony community garden, where organic produce fuels his exercise. Credit: Noah Bryant

The most prevalent obstacles to regular exercise are perceptual—people often think that moderate exercise makes them tired. But I've found that exercise is a net energy *producer* because it feeds oxygen to the body and burns fuel we've stored by eating well: fats that come from vegetable sources (such as olive oil and nuts), and carbohydrates from whole grains, fruits, and vegetables.

People also perceive they don't have time to exercise—it's a lower priority than something else—but I find the time even if I'm out walking after dark or with a parka on. I just tell significant others I'll be home half an hour later. Since I get energy and clarity from this moderate exercise, I'm more effective with my time the next day. I've also heard people say they don't have a scenic or safe place to walk, but what about the school playground or track, or a safe, quiet neighborhood somewhere along their commute or errand route? My friend Marie, a mother of three children, keeps a pair of athletic shoes in her car. "If I have a little time before picking one of the kids up, I take a walk rather than go shopping, which used to be how I would kill time—and waste money," she says.

James O. Hill, cofounder of the America on the Move program, encourages people to walk an average of 10,000 steps per day—a cumulative

5 miles. According to Hill's research, residents in my home state of Colorado walk an average of about 6,550 steps per day, and about 16 percent of the state's population is classified as obese. By comparison, in Tennessee, where the average is about 4,650 steps per day, the obesity rate is 25 percent. More tellingly, Hill says, obesity is almost unknown among Amish men and women, who live a preindustrial lifestyle and walk an average of 16,000 steps per day, or 8 miles, just doing what needs to be done.[4]

➤ More Un-American Activities

When it comes to food, I confess to being particular—okay, I'm a "health nut." I'm not a vegetarian but the only meat I eat at home is organic and ideally, range fed. The moderation and lightness of the Mediterranean diet, described in a later chapter, comes closest to what I've practiced for years. Especially in the summer, a lot of the food I eat comes right from the garden or a nearby farmers' market, and I can feel the energy it brings me. I'm especially glad about several dietary decisions I made years ago. For example, giving up coffee was by no means a sacrifice because for the few years I was a user, it gave me occasional, mild panic attacks, acid reflux, insomnia, stained teeth, and no doubt bad breath. In fact, though I've been to a doctor only a handful of times in the last thirty years, two visits were in response to fake heart attacks that were actually heartburn, courtesy of the greasy, aromatic bean.

Switching to green tea gave me steady endurance and staying power, and reduced my stress levels. Similarly, giving up "soft" drinks thirty years ago wasn't a sacrifice but a welcome avoidance of vague paranoia and nervous queasiness from all the sugar, additives, and acids. It felt like each Coke or Sprite put another half-inch of flab on my stomach, which I'd have to work to get rid of. Yet soft drinks are now the nation's most widely consumed "food," rising in sales by more than 60 percent between 1977 and 1997. In that same time period, the prevalence of obesity more than doubled. Every time I've taken a sip of a soda out of curiosity, my taste buds scream, "Stop, this isn't food!" A glass of high-quality juice is far more refreshing, or even just a glass of water with a few squirts of fresh lime for accent. The American average is a whopping 53 gallons of soft drinks a year, and for the cost of those 557 12-ounce beverages, I could afford a lot of limes.

Just so it doesn't seem like I'm a total grump when it comes to food, maybe it will help if I remind you that dark chocolate and I have formed a strategic alliance. What a great arrangement, that the antioxidants in high-quality dark chocolate lower my blood pressure and elevate my libido at the same time. Although I can't routinely keep gourmet ice cream or healthy snack chips in the house (they're gone within minutes), I consider them pleasant indulgences when I do eat them. An important aspect about healthy food is what the gourmet chefs have known for centuries: fresh, well-grown food tastes great. When your taste buds slough off all the junk food grease and relearn to appreciate the natural sweetness in fruits, vegetables, and grains, sugared cereals and candy taste too sweet. And Andy Warhol's favorite soup is way too salty.

Over the years I've studied the effects of food on myself and on others, observing how eating well helps people reach their best potential. One example is Appleton High School for developmentally challenged students, in Wisconsin. Police officers routinely patrolled the halls of that school to prevent fighting between teachers and students—some of which latter carried weapons. But several years later, the atmosphere was completely different. After just a few food-related changes, the students are now "calm and well-behaved," according to a counselor at the school. Says the school's principal, "I don't have the vandalism. I don't have the litter. I don't have the need for high security." What changes did school administrators make? They replaced vending machines with water coolers, and replaced foods high in fats and sugar (such as hamburgers, French fries, and soft drinks) with fresh vegetables and fruits, whole-grain bread, and a salad bar.[5]

When Stephen Schoenthaler, a professor at California State University, supervised a similar change in meals served at 803 schools in low-income New York City neighborhoods, the number of students passing final exams rose from 11 percent below the national average to 5 percent above.[6] Because of results like these, more than four hundred school districts in twenty-three states now serve regional fresh produce at school lunches, feeding close to a million students food that meets their nutritional needs better as well as helps family farmers stay in business.

The same effect has been demonstrated in workplace cafeterias, prisons, and my house (I lost 700 pounds and my IQ doubled. Just kidding—my IQ is still low.) But I do know this: The value of food extends far beyond its price tag. It's worth it if we pay slightly more for reliably high-quality food because we get more *value* from it. Healthy food provides satisfaction for days—in the way we feel and function—rather than just gratification and "fun" for a few minutes. Good food equals good mood. Data from many different sources demonstrate one reason why that is. Research at the United Nations Food and Agriculture Organization and elsewhere showed that since the 1980s, the vitamin and mineral content in beans has fallen by 60 percent, in potatoes by 70 percent, and in apples by 80 percent. These decreases have occurred in produce from conventional farms that don't replenish their soil with cover crops, compost, and organic wastes.[7]

"To stay healthy, humans need some 50 different minerals that we can't produce ourselves," reports Marco Visscher in *Ode* magazine. "Popeye would have to eat 200 cans of spinach today to get the same amount of iron as he got from one can 50 years ago," he adds. Similarly, we'd need to eat ten slices of white bread today to get the same amount of nutrients that used to be in one slice. Will an apple a day—with less vitamin A—still keep the doctor away? It doesn't look like it; Americans visited doctors more than a billion times in 2004.[8]

➤ Drowning in a Sea of Junk Food

According to the latest Centers for Disease Control data, about a third of Americans are classified as obese, another third are overweight, and the numbers are rising. The connection between lifestyle choices and extra weight couldn't be clearer. Many physicians and scientists believe our children will be the first generation in a century or more to have a lower life expectancy than their parents. For example, childhood obesity expert Dr. Brian McCrindle of Toronto warns that diseases related to being overweight, such as heart disease and diabetes, will "totally swamp the public health care system."[9]

What we eat is largely determined by culturally and psychologically based habits, often very difficult to break. In a recent *New York Times* series, reporters conducted in-depth interviews with populations at highest risk for diabetes—a disease that now afflicts one in every eight people living in New York City. One resident of East Harlem explained that in his culture, when a guy eats a salad, he's considered a wimp. "They make fun of you: What are you, a rabbit?"[10]

Another man, when asked how his blood sugar readings were doing, lowered his eyes and said, "They've been a little high. I started eating Frosted Flakes. What can I say? I like them. You can't always be eating things without sugar. Sometimes, you have to take a chance."[11] The stakes are extremely high, yet the urge to "be good" to oneself often wins out. From the time we're infants, whenever things are going badly, someone gives us a cookie, and in effect we learn to reward ourselves for feeling bad! The results can be catastrophic, as N. R. Kleinfield writes in one of the *New York Times* stories:

Begin on the sixth floor, third room from the end, swathed in fluorescence: a 60-year-old woman was having two toes sawed off. One floor up, corner room: a middle-aged man sprawled, recuperating from a kidney transplant. Next door: nerve damage. Eighth floor, first room to the left: stroke. Two doors down: more toes being removed. Next room: a flawed heart.

As always, the beds at Montefiore Medical Center in the Bronx were filled with a universe of afflictions. In truth, these assorted burdens were all the work of a single illness: diabetes. Room after room, floor after floor, diabetes. On any given day, hospital officials say, nearly half the patients are there for some trouble precipitated by the disease.[12]

Obviously, diabetes is so much more than an inconvenience. As many war veterans lost lower limbs in 2005 to this disease as American soldiers did to combat injuries in the entire Vietnam War. What's the primary cause of blindness in American adults? You guessed it.

"If current trends persist, the work force 50 years from now is going to look fat, one-legged, and blind, a diminution of able-bodied workers at every level," says Dr. Daniel Lorber, an endocrinologist in Queens, New York. "Nursing homes are going to be crammed to the gills with amputees in rehab. Kidney dialysis centers will multiply like rabbits. We will have a tremendous amount of people not yet blind but with low vision . . ."[13] Yet we Americans continue to hit the snooze alarm, because we don't know how to wake up from a lifestyle bulging with dysfunction. As former President Clinton told a conference of state governors, "To beat obesity, you've got to consume less and burn more. There is no alternative. And to do that, you've got to change the culture."[13]

It's ironic to realize that we humans, who dominate the planet, have lost track of what we should be eating. Culture and tradition teach people about nutrition, but when cultures unravel, focusing more on wealth than health, we end up eating from boxes, cans, and depleted soil. Meanwhile, gorillas know precisely which leaf to eat to get rid of which parasite, which fruit will add more endurance to their diet, or which type of decaying bark helps their digestion.

The good news is that junk food is beginning to go the way of tobacco (Already, 99.99999 percent of gorillas don't smoke). Responding to the obesity and diabetes epidemics, New York City has banned artificial trans fatty acids, and Chicago and Los Angeles are following in the Big Apple's footsteps. In New York, that means that twenty-five thousand restaurants, bakeries, and food-prep businesses will have to steer clear of the partially hydrogenated oils found in shortenings, margarine, and frying oils. Mc-Donald's, Kentucky Fried Chicken, and Dunkin' Donuts will have to change their lardy recipes. This is by no means a mission impossible—already, Wendy's has switched to a new cooking oil; Crisco now markets a shortening without trans fats; Frito-Lay has taken trans fats out of its Doritos and Cheetos; and Kraft has reformulated Oreos. The question is, are these foods salvageable to begin with?

Nutrition activists at groups like the Center for Science in the Public Interest advocate these next steps:

- Require chain restaurants to declare the calorie content of soft drinks and all other items on menus and menu boards.

- Require the Food and Drug Administration to put warnings on the labels of nondiet soft drinks to stating that frequent consumption of those drinks promotes obesity, diabetes, tooth decay, osteoporosis, and other health problems.

- Require all schools to stop selling soft drinks (as well as candy and other junk foods) in hallways, shops, and cafeterias.

- Levy a tax on foods that contain excessive fats and sugar, similar to the tax on cigarettes.

A significant voluntary agreement was recently signed between the Alliance for a Healthier Generation, whose PR icon is Bill Clinton, and five of the country's largest snack food producers. Students must bid farewell to fatty French fries, ice cream, candy, cupcakes, and potato chips, now banished from school vending machines and lunch lines.[14] At the same time, they can say hello to better grades, better friendships, and a greater interest in what life can offer.

➤ Avoiding a Prescription for Disaster

As you get out of your car, two bright headlights come hurtling toward you. You're astonished at what happens next: a monster SUV smacks into the back of your car, instantly converting it into a totaled two tons of trash. And the driver, you soon discover, sleeps right through the collision! He had taken a prescription sleeping pill after his second-shift job, which "kicked in" a little early. About thirty million people in the United States routinely take sleep medications, according to the American Academy of Sleep Medicine—a 50 percent jump in the last five years. Between 2004 and

2005, advertising expenditures for sleeping pills increased fivefold, from $60 million to $300 million. The advertising paid off for pharmaceutical companies, if not always for the troubled sleeper, who spends five or more dollars extra per night to battle insomnia. (Collectively, Americans shell out $2 billion annually to "purchase" sleep).[15]

Increased use of sleeping pills has also increased the frequency of strange reports about people having sex while still asleep, and forgetting events that occurred while they were supposedly awake. For example, a neurologist at Massachusetts General Hospital in Boston said a colleague who had taken sleeping pills could not recall advising residents on rounds the next morning. Is that guy also forgetting which patient is having which surgery?![16]

A professional woman who lives near Denver resorted to Ambien to try for a good night's sleep, but within a few hours she was sleep-driving on a street in her neighborhood, dressed only in a thin nightshirt in twenty-degree weather. She bent the fender of a parked car, urinated in the middle of an intersection, got violent with police, and later confided to her lawyer that she didn't remember any of it. She wasn't drunk, she was in a trance of overmedication.[17]

Hasn't society reached an epidemic state when, according to federal data, half of all Americans took at least one prescription drug within the last month, and one out of five took three or more? Isn't there something we could do with the $270 billion a year spent for prescription drugs that are chock full of side effects, if *preventive* health measures at all levels (individual, industry, government) became a national mission?

What sort of risks will we take to sleep, reduce depression, or decrease the odds of getting diabetes? What pills will we swallow under a banner that says, "In technology we trust?" There's far more to it than the gruesome side effects that TV ads caution us about to reduce their liability. According to a recent article in the *Journal of the American Medical Association*, one hundred thousand deaths occur in America every year from bad reactions to prescription and over-the-counter drugs. Those aren't side effects, they're *end effects*. And there are often preventive alternatives to the pills.

Walter Willett, an epidemiologist at the Harvard School of Public Health, puts it this way: "Our studies have shown that with healthy diets, no smoking and regular physical activity, we could prevent about 82 percent of heart attacks, about 70 percent of strokes, and over 90 percent of type 2 diabetes. The best drugs reduce heart attacks by about 20 or 30 percent, yet we put almost all of our resources into promoting drugs rather than healthy lifestyles and nutrition."[18]

A big media splash recently unveiled the results of a large clinical study testing the effectiveness of a drug called Avandia to prevent diabetes. After a three-year trial, an impressive 62 percent fewer people on the medication developed diabetes. For about $120 a month, many of the twenty-one million Americans with type 2 diabetes—and the estimated fifty-four million who have a prediabetic condition—can reduce their risk. The GDP will go up, and certain pharmaceutical stocks will be good investments. But the irony is that an equally impressive clinical trial by the National Institutes of Health revealed that with 5 to 7 percent reductions of body weight and thirty minutes of exercise a day, 58 percent fewer people developed diabetes.[19]

Let's see . . . one approach costs $1,440 a year, puts a burden on public health-care systems, and carries high odds of side effects, such as heart disease. The other approach is free and has various personal and social benefits in addition to cutting the risk of getting diabetes: A more healthy, proactive lifestyle will also reduce risk of heart disease and cancer, reduce the number of sick days used at work, and increase productivity and general vitality. Which approach would you take if you were at risk?[20]

Similarly, when an anonymous blogger who has been off and on antidepressants for about eighteen years went to renew her subscription, she discovered that a one-month supply was $90. "If I thought I was depressed before," she wrote, "having to pay $90 to feel better will only make me *more* depressed." So she started swimming three times a week, and will be bike riding when the weather permits.

➤ Playing Doubles at Age 96

It seems that somehow, our society has lost the will and skill to thrive! Unless we *use* our bodies and minds, they begin to atrophy. Ask the centenarians who are still active, curious, and . . . *alive,* but who have seen many others falter. There have been some great studies of the world's oldest people in recent years, and these super-seniors have many insights about what it takes to be healthy

A woman named Margaret, profiled in a great *Time* magazine cover story, recently renewed her driver's license at the age of ninety-six so she could continue to be designated driver for her seventy-something friends—and also to get to the tennis courts two or three times a week, where she plays doubles matches. She lives in a two-story house but prefers to use the bedroom on the second story to get extra exercise going up and down the stairs. She wears a baseball cap with a Harley-Davidson logo on it, and maintains emotional ties with many people—knitting blankets, sweaters and baby booties for family members, friends, and a charity for unwed mothers. No wonder she's pushing one hundred—she has the right stuff: attitude, activities, curiosity, a sense of challenge, and connection with people.[21]

Here are a few lessons we can learn from people like Margaret:

• Advice from the Centenarians •

- Keep your mind sharp—for example, one super-senior has made entries in a diary for the last twenty years before he goes to sleep. "My head is filled with all the things I want to do tomorrow," he says. Stay curious about things that are going on in the world—especially hopeful things. One researcher reported that super-seniors are less depressed than most people in their sixties. Another points out that daily exercise keeps blood flowing to the brain.

- Be a stress-buster by doing yoga, meditating, and joining support groups. Emotional stress plays a role in many illnesses, making arteries constrict and blood clot faster, which may cause a heart attack. A study led at Johns Hopkins University found that men with high levels of anger and stress were three times more likely to develop premature heart disease than were men with low stress levels. Stressful people are more likely to smoke, overeat, drink too much, and work too hard.

- Avoid refined carbohydrates like white rice and candy bars, instead eating foods that contain complex carbohydrates like whole wheat and brown rice, fruits, vegetables, other grains, and legumes. (One study found that the average Seventh Day Adventist, who is largely a vegetarian and avoids caffeine, tobacco, and alcohol, lives four to ten years longer than does the average American.)

- Eat foods that contain antioxidants—cinnamon; blueberries; kidney, pinto, and black beans are especially good. In a war against the "terrorists" that promote aging—the free radicals—antioxidants prevent cellular damage in general, and specifically atherosclerosis, Alzheimer's, and cancer.

- Avoid being around toxic materials, including antiseptic soaps that destroy natural, health-supporting microbes.

- Maintain a weight level that doesn't put a strain on your vital organs. Said one researcher, "I haven't yet met a centenarian who was obese." The legendary centenarians of Okinawa practice *hara hachi bu* which literally means eating until they are only 80 percent full. (On average, Okinawans have high life expectancies, but when they move to other cultures, their lifespan plummets.)

- Have a sense of purpose, what the Japanese call *ikigai*—"that which makes life worth living." Many centenarians are gardeners whose garden "needs them," or are mentors in social networks. Okinawans maintain a strong sense of community, making sure that each member is respected and feels valued.

- Have a personal belief system or religion that sets you free from fear and stress, have a sense of belonging in the universe, and have faith that life knows what it's doing.

- Says one centenarian, "I try to stay off the highways, limiting my exposure to other older people who sometimes step on the accelerator rather than the brakes; nervous people in a great hurry who don't look in the rearview mirror; and chemically impaired people who drive on roads that appear to them to be sideways."

See "The Secrets of Long Life" by Dan Buettner, *National Geographic*, November 2005; and "15 Ways to Live Longer," Forbes. com, http://www.forbes.com/2006/04/28/cx_vg_0501featslide2_print.html.

8

The Currency of Nature

Balancing the Biological Budget

A thing is right when it tends to preserve the integrity, stability and beauty of the biotic community. It is wrong when it tends otherwise.
—Aldo Leopold

To me a lush carpet of pine needles or spongy grass is more welcome than the most luxurious Persian rug.
—Helen Keller

Nature does nothing uselessly.
—Aristotle

Given a chance, a child will bring the confusion of the world to the woods, wash it in the creek, and turn it over to see what lives on the unseen side of that confusion . . .
—Richard Louv

Nature is not just window-dressing, not just a backdrop for our busy lives; it's where we live and what we *are*. It's what flows in our arteries and endocrine systems, and it's the whole-grain cereal that gives us energy to start the day. Interwoven with everything we do, nature directly meets our needs for air, food, fresh water, materials for shelter and products, beauty, recreation, serenity, nutrient and waste recycling, disease prevention, flood control, climate regulation, and many other quintessential values.

But sadly, the more sidetracked we get chasing possessions and the money to buy them, the poorer we become in other forms of wealth, such as connections with nature. When natural systems are healthy, they spin off benefits far more valuable than gold, or $100,000 bills. For example, the world's predator insects, such as ladybugs, naturally control far more pests than expensive, environmentally destructive pesticides do. Why not spray less and let colorful little allies like these proliferate? Why not use knowledge about how nature works, to meet more of our needs?

The truth is that humans used to value nature as the greatest and most sacred wealth of all, but now it's being traded for convenience, comfort, and perceived security. In our current way of seeing the world, the environment is just a collection of problems; we won't protect it until we correctly see nature as a collection of *solutions*—a regenerating form of wealth we literally can't live without. If we let it, nature can take care of us, energize and delight us, free! In research studies, when people view slides of nature, their blood pressure counts fall; and when those with ADHD spend time in nature, the results are often as effective as if they'd taken the widely used drug Ritalin. A classic ten-year study reported in *The American Journal of Preventive Medicine* documented that hospital patients with a view of trees went home sooner than did those who viewed a brick wall. In a similar study, Michigan prisoners whose cells overlooked farmland had 24 percent fewer illnesses than did those whose cells looked into the prison courtyard.[1] Many universities now offer degrees in "horticultural therapy," including Michigan State, Kansas State, University of Maine, and University of Cincinnati.

Describing positive questionnaire results from more than a thousand wilderness trips (both adult and child), Robert Greenway says that 90 percent of the participants felt an increased sense of aliveness, well-being, and energy; 76 percent of all respondents reported dramatic changes in quantity, vividness, and context of dreams; and 77 percent described a major life change upon return (in personal relationships, employment, housing, or lifestyle).[2] Nature's hard wired into our genes, and into the human nervous system. Humans are blessed with what E. O. Wilson terms "biophilia," the urge to affiliate with other forms of life.

In our high-tech world, we often turn away from biophilia, considering ourselves *above* other species. In my opinion, each animal or plant is the very best at being that particular species, but no species is "better." Whenever I begin to think humans are somehow superior, I remember how various animals headed for higher ground before the imminent 2004 Asian tsunami. I think about the 176-year-old tortoise that recently died, possibly transported from the Galapagos Islands to England by Charles Darwin in 1835. (And we think 77.6 years is old.) I recall a newspaper story about how dogs can smell cancer in humans: In repeated experimentation, not only did dogs conclusively demonstrate a 90 percent success rate in identifying human patients with biopsy-confirmed cancer, they were also able to detect cancer incidences a full year before medical technology did.

One very charming example of biophilia occurred recently in San Francisco Bay when a fisherman spotted a whale in great distress, weighed down and entangled in hundreds of pounds of crab traps and fishing lines. The fisherman called an environmental group that sent a crew of divers, and although a single thrash of the whale's fin might have been lethal, the rescuers worked patiently for hours to cut her loose. When she was free, she swam around in joyous circles like a dog let off its leash. Then she returned to each diver, one at a time, to say thank-you with a gentle nudge. Hearing stories like these makes us smile, because more than anything, at our very core, we want life to thrive! It really doesn't take more than a walk in the park, past an ecstatic baby in a stroller, to make my day. But in our world, we have fewer and fewer of these direct, outdoor experiences, for several reasons—we don't give ourselves time, nature isn't at the edge of town anymore, and we're simply out of the habit of *being* in nature.

➤ Last Child in the Woods

For the most part, mothers want us to be happy, right? When they used to tell us, "Go outside and play," it wasn't just because they were sick of us, but (also) because the components of nature and the way they fit together are the most instructive and enjoyable curriculum on the planet, no tuition necessary. These days, though, parents aren't as likely to urge their kids to go outside. Unfortunately, both kids and adults often perceive "outside" as a place that *lacks* stimulation and is also dangerous.

The engineered planning of towns and cities often reduces nature to concrete water channels, manicured petunia beds, and rectangular soccer fields, removing the rough, wildish edges that kids like the best. Many American schools have reduced or eliminated outdoor time, even as the epidemic of childhood obesity spreads. In fact, as Richard Louv points out in *Last Child in the Woods*, education boards in a dozen or more states have "outlawed" recess because they consider it less important than national test rankings, it presents perceived liability issues, and it has the potential for violence on the playground. On some school playgrounds that do allow outdoor play, signs read, "No Running!" Tracking the origins of what he calls "nature-deficit disorder," Louv has observed many other obstacles to natural play, including municipal and homeowner association laws. For example, building codes prohibit or inhibit the construction of tree houses in some towns, some cities forbid climbing on trees in parks, and many of the country's HOAs (there are now nearly a quarter of a million) frown on basketball hoops and skateboard ramps in driveways.

Add to these restrictions the specters of "stranger danger," DUI-heavy traffic, and "ecophobia" (the fear of spiders, skin cancer, mosquitoes, snakes, Lyme disease, and poison ivy) and you've trained kids to retreat indoors to their video games, TVs, and computer screens. My friend Marie held her ground when her son kept asking for the latest video games: He could only play games that didn't involve killing, and he had to buy them with his own money. But this teenager knew how to play more than video games; he did a research paper at school on violence in video games, and thus, he convinced her, had *no choice* but to do the research . . .

Richard Louv cites a study documenting that in 2003, the average American devoted 327 more hours to electronic media than in 1987. But Louv asks a probing question—very relevant to the theme of this book: "What *drives* us to virtual reality?" He believes that lack of time and the changing patterns of our cities and towns are key reasons, but that fear—a spell being cast by the news media—is the main reason.[3]

And I believe there's still more to it: kids (and adults) don't value or understand nature because it's not an action-packed commodity sought after by their peers. Nature is subtle, not in-your-face like virtual reality, and we need to be taught to slow down and appreciate its subtleties and interconnections. We need mentors who can lead us back to nature. Louv interviewed a camp counselor who was awakened by an inner-city girl when she had to go to the bathroom. "We stepped outside the tent and she looked up. She gasped and grabbed my leg. She had never seen the stars before. From that moment on, she was a changed person. She saw everything, like a camouflaged lizard that everyone else skipped over. She used her senses. She was awake!"[4]

➤ Lost Child in the Woods, Found

When I was four or five, I wandered with a young friend into the woods near our house. My recollections of that distant morning include splotches of bright sunlight projected through the trees onto the dark forest floor, the earthy fragrance of leaves and rich Illinois soil, and knowing what it must feel like to be a butterfly. We fluttered farther and farther away from our yards, clueless that back home our moms were beginning to panic. After an hour or more of frantic searching, someone drove to the other side of the

• How to Reduce "Nature-Deficit Disorder" • in Kids, and Adults

In personal activities:

- Protect "nearby nature," such as a creek behind your house or a little woods at the end of a cul-de-sac.

- Plant a shade tree in your yard to reduce air-conditioning loads an average of $80 a year, reduce pollution, and absorb storm water runoff. Property values are 7 to 25 percent higher for houses surrounded by trees.

- Become a more effective recycler to conserve natural resources; consider green alternatives to standard products like cleaners, personal care products, clothes, and building materials.

- Become a habitual walker who observes the cycles of nature at the park or in neighborhood yards.

- Let your thumb turn green, maybe starting with a single plant—maybe your favorite variety of tomato.

- Learn about nature! For example, about "biomimicry," which applies the designs of nature to products and designs. Instead of viewing predictable mainstream movies, rent such brilliant live-animal films as *March of the Penguins, Winged Migration, The Wild Parrots of Telegraph Hill* . . . or the great series, *Life on Earth,* that explains all the incredible variations in species.

- Institutionalize the benefits of nature, moving nature "from the recreation column" to the "health column."

In medicine:

- Conduct research on the benefits of exposing children to nature instead of pharmaceuticals.

- Incorporate the health benefits of nature into medical and nursing school curricula.

- Encourage pediatricians to prescribe nature time for stress reduction and as an antidote to child obesity.

In education:

- Assure that every school utilizes nearby nature; create partnerships between schools, farms, ranches and public parks. Example: a Saint Paul magnet K-4 school partners with a 320-acre ecological education center and habitat restoration preserve located across the street, to link cognitive development and science scores directly with hands-on nature experience.

In government:

- Launch programs like Connecticut's "No Child Left Inside" initiative, designed to reintroduce children to raise public awareness of underused Connecticut state parks and forests. Through partnerships, increase contact with nature. Example: persuade AARP to create a "Take a Child to Nature" program.

Based partly on Richard Louv interviews and Richard Louv columns in the *San Diego Union Tribune*: http://gristmill.grist.org/story/2006/3/30/11527/6491; http://www.signonsandiego.com/news/metro/louv/20060926-9999-lz1e26louv.html.

forest and found us near the highway, still in the throes of discovery and exploration. I seem to remember that everyone was very agitated, insisting that we'd gotten lost and could have been killed! But we didn't see it that way. All we had lost was a sense of time, and a sense of imposed boundaries.

About fifty years later, I experienced a similar, unbounded feeling in a Costa Rican rain forest north of San José. I've always thought of myself as a nature guy—a backpacker and fanatical gardener who's learned about the cycles and meaning of nature by observing them directly—on switchbacked mountain trails or in rich garden beds teeming with vegetables. But I wasn't prepared for what I encountered at Rara Avis, a biological reserve that is true, undeveloped wilderness. I was like that delighted young preschooler again, fluttering into the woods in search of anything. My girlfriend had gone home and I stayed in a casita without electricity for eight days by myself, drifting further and further from the pace of life back home, where the president was sending the first troops to Iraq.

The story of that experience begins with a rigorous three-hour, tractor-drawn wagon ride over boulders and potholes, the exact opposite of "luxurious" (probably a little like having a baby in an earthquake). But the other travelers and I somehow survive it, and within minutes of arriving near Waterfall Lodge and its outlying casitas, the forest begins to speak to us! A

The three-hour ride to Rara Avis biological reserve is no picnic, but it is well worth the effort. Courtesy of the author

tiny, strawberry poison-dart frog hops across the trail; his bright red skin contains toxins so strong that he has no predators. He just hangs out in his territory—he needs no more than 100 square feet—and waits for females to come to him. What a life!

A little farther up the trail, a boa constrictor wraps around the trunk of a small tree, in no hurry to get out of our way. Instead she relies on her camouflage, ability to constrict, and (maybe) trust in humanity. A regiment of leaf-cutter ants ascends the trunk of a 100-foot-tall tree to prune its leaves, increasing by a third the light that reaches the forest floor. The leaf fragments they bring back (like surfers carrying bright green surfboards) are composted underground to fertilize the fungus crop they find so tasty—an operation that puts nutrients back into the soil. En route, some ants become snacks for birds and other insects, so their niche provides several basic resources the rain forest needs—sun, soil, and food. Thousands of other species make similar contributions, weaving the rain forest together like a tapestry. Creeping over the forest floor toward the shadows is a Monstera vine, which "knows" that by climbing the tallest trees that cast the darkest shadows, it will ultimately bask in full sunlight.

Rara Avis is like a 2,500-acre lungful of fresh air—a masterpiece of biological abundance that provides undisturbed habitat for 362 different species of birds! Twenty different species of orchid were recently counted on a single fallen tree. In a way, this virgin parcel of land is a living self-portrait—the rain forest is *painting itself* in the bold colors and shadowy nuances of its many species; for example, the red, green, yellow, orange, turquoise, and black of a keel-billed toucan (called a "flying banana" by another traveler); the dark, iridescent blue of a morpho butterfly; and the dappled red of a stained-glass palm.

I walk down to dinner one evening in the foggy twilight and my flash-light beam falls on the orange and black stripes of a coral snake. I'm star-tled, knowing she's poisonous, but fascinated that she's slithered into my life. As I bend closer to get a better look, she retracts from the path into the bushes, like the scene in the *Wizard of Oz* where the Wicked Witch's striped sock melts away under the house that smashed her. With the hair on the back of my neck still bristling, I step gingerly from one stepping stone to another, watching the miniature headlights of fireflies hovering in the descending darkness, lit only by a rising crescent moon.

After dinner in the big log cabana, biologist Amanda Neill explains why she puts her energy into studying a single species of rain forest flower: the bright red gurania, or jungle cucumber. "Think what might happen if the taxonomists mistakenly lump two similar species together," she says. "We might assume that there are plenty of these—don't worry about saving their habitat—when really there are only a few of each species left, that have traveled a billion years to get here."

The sense of ecological urgency in this blond-haired thirty-year-old woman mixes well with her sense of delight. Even in her narrow niche of study, she's traveled widely—to Ecuador, Belize, Peru, now Costa Rica—to study the taxonomy and ecology of her focus species. In effect, she's found her own symbiotic niche in the rain forest, trading her skills at cata-loging and protecting the gurania for the privilege of living a month at a time under the lush, protective canopy of the rain forest.

That night, when the cicadas, tree frogs, trogons, owls, howler mon-keys, and hundreds of other species all join the chorus, the forest sounds like a smoothly running factory—*Taca, taca, taca . . . sissit, sissit . . .*" Given that the mission of each call is to be heard among a symphony of other calls, there are all varieties of pitch and syncopation—creating an incredi-bly rich and complex symphony. Over the eons, rain forest species don dif-ferent colors and improvise different shapes so all nutrients will be used, and all niches occupied. (They utilize information and design rather than superfluous resources, an important lesson for our civilization.) In the morning I'm awakened by a cuckoo clock that turns out to be a bird with a very complex, mechanical-sounding call. I count the hours, groggily, but even in half-sleep, I know it can't be nine o'clock already . . .

➤ Waking Up in the Rain Forest

On a remote jungle trail toward the end of my retreat, I'm dressed only in shorts and rubber boots. I've taken off my T-shirt to feel the rain forest on my skin, despite the warnings that deadly fer-de-lance snakes could strike from overhead branches and vines. I'm thinking, "Remember this moment. Remember the way you feel, right now, as howler monkeys growl like lions way off in the distance, and the sun filters through the dense foliage onto your stupefied, grateful face."

Sure, we can read about the rain forest and see it on TV, but until we spend quality time there, letting ourselves slow down, we don't really grasp what tropical biology is all about. It struck me on that Costa Rican rain forest retreat that we overconsuming humans need to somehow absorb these colors, this bold brilliance, into our hearts, and revalue nature's wealth all over the planet. There's so much more to life than the gray of concrete and the drab green of paper currency! My feeling is that until we acknowledge the butterfly, orchid, rose, maple, and wisteria colors inside each of us, we can't feel truly at home in *ourselves*. We can't see the deficiencies of our economic system clearly enough—that it isn't programmed to preserve nature, or to optimize human potential. Until we launch an unwavering mission to Planet Earth, we'll keep postponing the homecoming until there's not much left to come home to. In that rain forest, I saw and felt complexity-in-balance, and realized how far *out* of balance our industrial complexity is—infantile and clunky by comparison, with only thousands of years of experience as opposed to billions. Rather than cooperating to make the overall system sustainable, our industrial species compete to attain their own, narrowly defined goals. The name Rara Avis comes from a medieval poem containing the phrase *"Rara avis in terris."* The phrase means, literally, "a rare bird in the world"—or figuratively, something new and fresh happening in human civilization. And so there is!

➤ The Zen of Gardening

What's the opposite of a suicide bomber? Maybe a community gardening activist—like a Green Guerrilla—lobbing a benign grenade filled with seeds and fertilizer onto a vacant lot. The mission of the New York City–based Green Guerrillas is to "help people turn vacant, rubble-strewn lots into vibrant community gardens that serve as outdoor environmental, educational, and cultural centers." About twenty-five years ago, I became a green guerrilla in my own yard, and what I learned along the way changed my life.

Growing vegetables and fruits taught me the value of filling time with something that feels *right*. I'd spend Saturday planting vegetables and digging a new plot in the crazy quilt I called a garden; then Sunday morning,

I'd just want to do more of the same. Getting so much exercise and good food taught me what it felt like to feel *great*, and I wanted more of that feeling. (My then-wife customized a T-shirt for me that read "Mr. Vigor," which I wore proudly as I ate organic broccoli or battled slugs and hailstones.)

I learned what a passion is about—something you did whether or not it seemed like a good idea to others. I noticed, though, that people would tour my little garden and comment on how much work it must be; then the next year, they'd call with questions about how to start their own gardens. It's not that we gardeners are trying to be "old fashioned" or unsocial with our time, more that we are reviving a skill we can take with us into the future—a pastime that doesn't cost money but saves it, while also delivering wide-ranging health and environmental benefits. If I eat a sweet pepper or a handful of raspberries as I work, I can count on an energy boost that lasts for hours, because that food is still charged with life as I'm eating it. Rather than traveling an average 2,000 miles to my mouth, it's more like two feet. The fuel savings are huge. The food that comes from my garden also doesn't require pesticides, but rather skill—again, a great energy-saver and environmental bonus. Gardens create habitats, absorb storm water to reduce flooding, and give us something to take care of—a basic, primordial human need.

In the book *The Zen of Gardening,* I wrote, "In the garden, life's struggles, snags and snafus decompose into rich, black earth. I see and feel things happening—things that are real, not just white-knuckle policies and commercial blabber. As I plant seedlings or hoe a sturdy crop of basil, I don't think about operators who are 'currently busy helping other customers.' I can touch, smell, see, and taste where I live; I know about Golden, Colorado, partly by making horticultural deals with it. I learn what it can provide and what I can coax from it, as my knowledge and skill continue to expand. In the garden, life and death dance before my eyes every day, and I come to a better understanding of my own health and mortality. The garden literally brings me back to my senses."

When the garden becomes a lifestyle, we begin to rethink where we spend our time, energy, and money. We go out to eat less, partly because what comes out of the garden is vastly superior to what comes out of a typical restaurant's kitchen, and partly because we just want to keep working in the strawberry bed or planting the broccoli seedlings. It occurs to us in a flash of insight that time isn't money—it's *life*.

So consider these passages to be an uncommercial for gardening. Turn off the tube and take a few gardening classes. Start small, with a raised bed or two. I guarantee you'll like it, or "double your time back."

Although nighttime temperatures often fall below freezing in the Harmony cold frame, baby lettuce plants announce, "No worries." Courtesy of the author

➤ The Nature of Heaven: Adventures in the Great Beyond

One of the many people Richard Louv interviewed for *Last Child in the Woods* was a twelve year-old girl who commented, "I really think there is something about nature—that when you are in it, you realize that there are far larger things at work than yourself." I know what that girl meant. I remember a suddenly-spring day at Hampstead Heath in London (where I was an exchange student), wading barefoot in a shallow stream, mud squishing between my toes. Although my learned reaction to the squishiness was, "yichh," I realized in a flash of insight that mud isn't really dirty—in a sense, it's the essence of clean—the place where life originally came from and where it ends up. What I hold sacred is life itself, and that includes even the life that teems in soil and squishy mud. The incredible beauty and complexity of living things assures me that everything's all right; that I'm part of something that goes on and on. There's no need for fear, and no need to hurry.

I do have a strong suspicion that there's an afterlife, but I'm not convinced we each carry personal identities with us up some cosmic escalator like beat-up pieces of luggage. Instead, what I think may happen is that after a transition period at the Pearly Gates (while our luggage is inspected and gratefully acknowledged), departing souls melt back to a wavelength

• Ten Rules of Thumb for Those Seduced by Gardening •

1. *Go easy on yourself.* Gardening is best practiced without shame, doubt, regret, envy, or dread. The only good garden is a no-guilt garden. As Diane Ackerman says, "Weeding can attain the status of a holy war. My philosophy is: Forget winning, cultivate delight." Just as we leave our muddy boots at the back door, we need to leave stress and guilt at the garden gate. Any garden that yields knowledge, health, and no-worries recreation deserves a shot at something less than perfection.

2. *Garden strategically, just for fun.* Rather than single crops, grow recipes! As you stretch across multicolored rows of lettuce to weed the icicle radishes, think tossed salad. Prepare the soil for pie, not just strawberries and rhubarb. You can even set target dates for serving the recipes, such as roasting red, white, and blue new potatoes for the Fourth of July; midsummer night's pesto; or strategically planted salsa for autumn football parties.

3. *If at first you don't succeed, keep planting.* Wipe the slate clean by burying the evidence or hauling it to the compost pile. Your Brussels sprouts may be covered with aphids from stem to stern, but nobody needs to know that. The spinach looks anemic? Now you see it, now you don't.

4. *Garden with all your senses.* You may not be able to see a billion microbes in a handful of soil, or smell subtle chemical messages constantly being sent from plant to plant, but you can see a glow on the leaves of a healthy stand of chard. You can smell the richness of a well-rotted bucket of compost, taste the season's first crunchy snow peas, feel the feathery leaves of an asparagus plant, and hear the leaves of an apple tree rustling in an autumn breeze.

5. *Harvest the intangibles.* This may be the most important rule of all. It's not just food we're after, but knowledge, serenity, and a sense of purpose. Remember, what gardens do best is help gardeners grow.

6. *Fertilize the soil, not just the plant.* Gardens aren't factories, they're ecosystems that are constantly at work. Mulching a tired-looking crop with rich compost brings health not only to that current crop, but also to the surrounding soil and therefore the crop that follows it—to the system as a whole.

7. *Never make the same mistake twice.* (In my case, never make it more than half a dozen times.) As insurance against repetitious errors, keep a logbook. Or at least tell your spouse or gardening colleague about the initial mistake, so if you do it again (and again), you can blame it on them.

8. *Remember that gardening is a race we should never expect to really win.* We can appear to be in the lead from time to time, however—if we're willing to neglect the housekeeping, our career, and our personal hygiene.

9. *Remember that the best garden ever is always in the future.* Garden for the years to come as well as the present. Build next year's soil, nurture the roots of trees and perennials for future years.

10. *Watch the gardens of your neighbors.* Pay particular attention to the older folks to find out what grows best in your neighborhood. Kneeling in lush, hand-crafted beds, they leave paving stones behind themselves so the rest of us can find the way.

Adapted from *The Zen of Gardening* by David Wann (Fulcrum Publishing, Golden, Colorado, 2003).

---

that courses through all of life. And I strongly believe that if Heaven in whatever form *does* exist, it's not just a comforting, unknowable fable, it's biology and physics. If it's made out of reality rather than fiction, we should be able to make contact with it, with all our expanding, awesome technologies, from spectroscopy and astronomy to magnetic resonance imaging.

Just for the fun of it, let's say we *do* retain our identities in Heaven. One day as you listen to the car radio, you pick up a staticky message from some deceased air traffic controller trying to get in touch with his daughter. As the frequency gets sharper and reaches listeners from Delaware to Darfur, there's great rejoicing on Earth! Holy wars cease when we learn that all of life—and death—are governed by natural law that treats everyone equally. But then (this is the cynic in me and in many of us), I'm imagining that some of the more enterprising folks here on Earth might see a huge new market opportunity. "Even you angels will be much more *blissful* if you have communication links with family members you've left behind, won't you?" they coax. "Won't videos from home make you feel more *secure* about your reputation back on Earth . . . ?" These masters of public relations will make even angels feel insecure, and, in the end, Microsoft and AOL, Wal-Mart and Target will trade digital uploads for heavenly balls of energy.

The fact is, we don't *know* the nature of that other side, or other frequency. Sometimes I wonder if our brains have learned to filter it out (despite vivid glimpses during near-death experiences) because it's not critical for dealing with more immediate survival issues here on Earth, like saber-toothed tigers and broken fuel pumps.

But we *do* know that nature is fundamental to our survival, and that it needs our help, now. Standing in my galoshes and shorts in that Costa Rican rain forest, I was completely amazed; completely in the moment. A shiny blue dragonfly with a body about the size of a clothespin decided to orbit my head three or four times, showcasing its remarkably shiny, helicopter-like wings. By that time, I'd become completely open to everything the rain forest had to offer. At least temporarily, I'd gained a wider, more holistic sense of self. "I" was not enclosed by my skin, but extended out into the infinitely patterned rain forest and beyond. I remember thinking as the dragonfly hovered comically around my head, "That's *me*, saying hello to myself!"

9

Precious Work and Play

Going with the Flow

I once gave a talk at an elementary school to third graders, and told them there are a billion people in the world who want to work and can't work. A girl raised her hand and asked, "Is all the work done?"
   —Paul Hawken

The point of life is not to slave away for years until the age of 65 and then say, "Phew, Glad that's over!" Rather it is to make sure that we do not die with our music still in us.
   —Lance Secretan

It's impossible to enjoy idling thoroughly unless one has plenty of work to do. There is no fun in doing nothing when you have nothing to do. Wasting time is merely an occupation then, and a most exhausting one. Idleness, like kisses, to be sweet must be stolen.
   —Jerome K. Jerome

There was bad news and good news for Michael Penkala, who had camped in line for *two days* to buy the newly released Sony Playstation3. The bad news was that he had to be taken to a hospital with gunshot wounds after two thieves held him up while he was waiting. The good news? Wal-Mart publicly announced he'd receive a free Playstation3 as soon as one became available. Woo-hoo! At hundreds of Best Buys, Wal-Marts, and GameStop stores all over the country, the release date was a violent video game come-to-life. For example, in Connecticut, a buyer walked triumphantly out of a store with a new PS3 that five masked men promptly made off with. In Kentucky, a passing car opened fire on buyers waiting in line; and in California, two GameStop employees reported a fake robbery to cover up their own theft. The list goes on and on; stampedes and near riots broke out all over the country—police fired pepper pellets at unruly shoppers, and multiple stabbings occurred just like in the games.[1]

Let's hope the new console is somehow worth all the pain and police time! I suppose I should suspend judgment until I sit down with one of the games (not likely)—but the PS3 frenzy tells us one thing: Millions of Americans are willing, as always, to take risks to PLAY. There's further evidence of that in Cleveland, where resolute, wet-suited surfers challenge the murky waters of Lake Erie, even in the dead of winter. Writes a *New York Times* reporter, "Cleveland largely turns its back on Lake Erie, lining the coast with power plants, a freeway and mounds of iron ore to feed its steel factories. The shore is especially deserted in winter, when strong winds and waves pummel the land." Clearly, somebody had to put those polluted waves to good use, and forty-four-year-old Bill Weeber, known as Mongo, stepped forward with his surfboard and companions. "Surfing Lake Erie is basically disgusting," he admits, "but then I catch that wave and I forget about it, and I feel high all day."[2]

As author and adventurer Diane Ackerman observes, play can be much more than diversion. Humans as well as most other animals evolved not only through war games but courtship games, socializing games, hunting games, and games that sharpen the senses. The more an animal needs to learn to survive, the more he needs to play, she maintains. Who knows what skills crows learn when they play tugs of war with twigs? Maybe it's just for sheer enjoyment, which also has survival value. Says Ackerman, "A crow may swing upside down on a branch, monkey style, or play drop the stick— flying down fast to catch it. One researcher saw a crow invent a log-rolling game in which it balanced on a plastic cup and rolled it down a hill."[3] (An oversized version of that game might just work on the TV show *Fear Factor,* if it was filled with rattlesnakes.)

"Play is a refuge from ordinary life, a sanctuary of the mind, where one is exempt from life's customs, methods, and decrees," writes Ackerman. "The playground can be as big as the Grand Canyon, as fluid as the ocean where dolphins swim, as crowded as a jazz club."[4] For my talented friend Phil Lohre, a Colorado or Alpine ski slope is the perfect playground. "Being at the top of a ridge with the sun setting and fresh powder below is totally exhilarating," he says with a smile that reveals many memories. "On the way down you experience a freedom of openness, a feeling of great challenge, and occasionally, a heroic wipeout that sprays your equipment all over the hill. But most of the time, you look back up and say, Wow, those are my tracks? I did that?"[5]

Phil's passion for skiing spans thirty years or more. In fact, in his twenties, he considered competing professionally on the freestyle mogul circuit, but an appointment with the Foreign Service popped up first. He got hooked on skiing in his teenage years. "At that age, you go as fast as you can until you fall down," he recalls with a laugh. "Your speed gets away from you, you catch a tip, and the next thing you know you're cartwheeling down the hill. But one day I was skiing at full speed, to the point where I usually crashed, and I *didn't* crash. I realized that I'd jumped to a new level of proficiency, and that's what I'd been working for."

In each of the sports Phil has played competitively—including hockey, basketball, softball, soccer, and Ultimate Frisbee (now known widely as "Ultimate")—the game is the center of the universe while it's being played. "Going onto the field, you enter a sacred space. You can leave all your worldly anxieties behind and just be totally immersed in the game. Whatever you've done in the past is irrelevant; the present is what counts. You feel a sense of urgency as you work intently with your teammates to execute strategies and tactics, because time is always a factor." One of Phil's favorite feelings is the satisfied exhaustion that follows a game. "When the game's over and you've given it everything you have, you come away with memories, experiences, and a deeper camaraderie. You feel high as a kite."

Phil has played Ultimate for twenty-five years and been a key member on various championship teams. In 2000, his team went to Germany as U.S. national champions. "I remember looking down the line at my six teammates and thinking, 'solid, solid, solid . . .' Our sense of confidence and teamwork was awesome, and the sense of fitting and belonging was something I'll never forget." His team won the world championship that year, and then went to the semifinals four years in a row. But despite the thrill of winning, it's the *playing* that really does it for him—those transcendent moments when he loses himself in the game. Winning may be the frosting on a cake made from ingredients like skill, focus, fun, and teamwork, but when opponents and teammates want *only* the frosting, Phil becomes less interested. In fact, he first became involved in Ultimate because of its informality and emphasis on the joys of playing. "There was no coach barking at us; we coached ourselves. The idea was to play hard, have fun, and get to know each other. Sometimes, I think we all take winning too seriously, at the expense of enjoyment."

Now, as a high school coach in various sports (as well as a teacher of academic subjects), he emphasizes teamwork. "My goal is to give them tools so they can work together and *improve* together. Instead of throwing the disc to the star player all the time, I encourage them to throw it to whoever's open so they all learn new skills, build confidence, and have fun as a team."

➤ "The Peak Justifies the Climb"

Certainly, we make the effort to climb, fish, or play Ultimate *partly* because of a potential prize—reaching the peak, pulling out a five-pound trout, or scoring the winning point. But the real reward—available to amateurs as well as masters—is that we're *out there*, interacting with others and challenging ourselves to reach our highest potential. When we watch sports on TV, the biggest challenge may be whether we'll personally polish off a whole pizza. We aren't using our senses; we're not risking exciting, high-payoff strategies; we're not getting the ball to a pumped-up teammate who's ready to do something with it. We don't receive the rewards of physical conditioning and we're often clueless about the intricacies of the game. By default, what we're left with is whether our favorite team wins or loses. Residents of Ashbourne, England, still stage an annual match of "mob football," a spirited forerunner of soccer and football, played for at least seven hundred years. Anyone willing to risk getting trampled is welcome to play. Traditionally, the game started at a midway point between two towns. Players tried to kick, carry, or throw an inflated pig's bladder to a goal marker in the opposing town, and no doubt there was much merriment afterward, in the pubs of both the winning and losing teams.[6]

In our more "civilized" times, the mob only watches. Though watching sports in person is often more energizing than on TV, the escalating cost of tickets is one reason (among many) that American savings rates have gone negative in recent years. Typically, the players on a star-studded team make more money than a majority of the fans in a packed stadium, combined. Meanwhile, back at the ranch house, a family has just invested three hours of sitting in their "home theater" watching a losing game. Watch out—the whole evening could go up in smoke. Unless, that is, the game is about something more than winning, like being together as a family, or being immersed in the sport itself. Let's say we know enough about the sport to be fascinated with its strategies, or maybe we go outside at halftime and throw a football around with our son, rake leaves, or talk with a neighbor. Think how much postgame depression and sports-induced suicide can be avoided if we take the hyped-up games on TV a bit less seriously, not letting them become addictions that substitute for life itself.

The Evergreen Cougars, including Libby Wann, take the 1997 state high school title after a double overtime. © Dennis Schroeder/*Rocky Mountain News*

Psychologists tell us it comes down to *involvement*. From long-term studies of human behavior, psychologist Mihaly Csikszentmihalyi finds that the more expensive and energy consuming our leisure time equipment, the more detached we are from the activity itself. Despite incredibly intricate camera work and awesome television technology, our huge-screen TVs don't take us any closer to reality. In fact, many times, we are only half-present as we watch, suspended in an ether of *virtual* reality, with distant voices calling us back to reality—where we could be feeling *alive*. Hobbies like playing music with friends; playing amateur sports such as softball, bowling, and skill-intensive fly-fishing; reading a great book; or conversing at a dinner table make us happier, because we *participate* in them. (The root meaning of the word "amateur" is "I love," not "I'm not very good".) These activities require less expensive equipment and consume less energy, but demand a lot of *psychic* energy and focus. Teacher Phil Lohre not only coaches sports, but also offers an elective class in card games that his grandmother taught him—hearts, spades, and bridge—all of which involve teamwork, concentration, and involvement.

In Csikszentmihalyi's research, U.S. teenagers only experience *flow* about 13 percent of the time while watching TV, compared with 34 percent while doing hobbies and 44 percent while playing sports and games. Yet these same teenagers spend at least four times more of their free hours watching TV. What's going on—is it hypnosis? We adults, pioneers of an electronic generation, don't seem to be faring much better. "Instead of playing music," says Csikszentmihalyi, "we listen to music by billionaire musicians. We spend hours each day watching actors who pretend to have adventures."[7]

We're socially conditioned to believe that passive relaxation yields the greatest happiness, and that consumption and possessions help us relax. We imagine them to make our lives so convenient, so easy. By using various machines, media, and consumer products, we believe we can remove "distractions" like cooking, walking, and even *thinking*, so we can fully relax. But there's a critical difference between passive relaxation and restorative relaxation. We all need time to unwind, and we are usually refreshed by the beauty of nature on a hike, a depth of calmness when we meditate, or the sense of gratitude and delight we get from playing with our kids or the dog. I think of these activities as restorative and creative relaxation. But when we are simply under the spell of commercial stimuli on the tube or at the mall, we aren't creating ourselves but rather allowing ourselves to be *created*. We aren't aligning our actions with our values, but aligning our *in*actions with someone else's values.

➢ Getting Unstuck: The Playground Is *Us*

Residents of the average American household will spend about a quarter of a million dollars over the course of their lives, trying to entertain themselves—with tickets, electronic toys, sports equipment, vacations, and all the rest.[8] (Of course, a very affluent American household could spend that much in a single year.) The question is, what sort of *value* do we get from these expenses—what exactly are we trying to buy? And what percentage of those expenses results from social pressure and commercial persuasion? Not only do we want to have fun; we also want to *appear* to be having fun, because of its social currency. We want to tell stories about sports and vacation adventures because everyone else is telling their stories. In effect, we buy leisure partly in self-defense.

However, in a less consumptive lifestyle, the most valuable leisure equipment is free—our minds and bodies. The equipment we were each issued provides almost infinite opportunities for play, from sex to sudoku. The leisure industry can't sell us our own bodies, and though our minds are often easier targets, we can develop the natural equivalent of pop-up blockers if we work at it. Industry-sponsored media love to portray the American lifestyle in terms of what we buy and own, but a more centered, calmer American lifestyle is now digging out from the avalanche of hype that just about smothered us. Millions of people, including some of my friends and me, are getting their fun and entertainment from activities that don't cost a dime. Instead of *buying* entertainment, we are creating it.

For example, organic gardening gets a huge exclamation point in my life because of its many intrinsic rewards. I burn calories digging soil, turning the compost, and gathering organic materials to grow high-quality food; in turn, the food gives me more energy. It just makes sense. In the neighborhood garden, I work with friends to devise strategies to beat the heat or outwit invasions of villainous insects. (The challenge is similar to a video game, only real; and the solutions use martial arts approaches rather than handheld missile launchers.) In the garden, we constantly use all our senses—including the climactic experience of tasting a fresh peach or a salad of juicy tomatoes and basil—all within prescribed rules that avoid the use of hazardous chemicals. It's a game you can eat. Skillful gardening is as challenging as golf or downhill skiing but instead of costing $50–$100 a day, it yields an ongoing income. The time span may be seasonal and the feedback slow and steady—a drawback for those addicted to constant hits of stimulation—but for me, and many others, slow time is luxury time. What's the hurry?

For Gary and Patricia, nothing beats a day spent on a photographic adventure, either in the city or out in nature. They love to forage for images on hikes and seasonal explorations. Instead of taking along credit cards, they bring lightweight cameras and tripods. Instead of mindlessly obeying advertising images, they create their own images with skill and curiosity. At the end of the day, they bring weightless digital treasures back to their computer lab to see what beauty, mystery, whimsy, and irony they've captured.

Creative sewing gets Susan's recreational juices flowing. Since her early days, when her grandmother taught her to sew on a treadle sewing machine, she's learned how to create just about anything with fabric: a wedding dress for her daughter; a slipcover for a long, sectional sofa in her son's family room; silly Halloween costumes for skits at work; and stuffed animals like the two-foot-tall, jagged-toothed Tyrannosaurus rex that now prowls her grandson's bedroom.

For Jan, contra dancing is a great way to end the week. She loves the lively jigs and reels that have survived from another time, and the nonverbal communication and customary exchanging of dance partners. Her steps, skips and twirls connect her with the kaleidoscopic pattern of the whole group. Even though I myself have been left scratching my head at such events—wondering where I was supposed to turn—I understand the giddy appeal of being in motion in this conspiracy of joy.

How many people do you know who have a trapeze in their high-ceilinged living room? Edee and Bob also stay in condition by taking

Gary Galger and Patricia Lynn Reilly love to spend their time lost in the deep play of looking for great photographic images. Credit: Gary Galger

turns balancing each other on their outstretched legs—an exercise in trust and coordination, and also an impressive parlor trick at parties! Once the Michigan state pogo stick champion, she claims to be able to bounce no handed and one legged at the same time, though I haven't confirmed that one yet. She's the queen of ceremonies and celebrations, recently orchestrating a wacky neighborhood parade complete with streamers, noisemakers, and a marching band of kazoos. We carried cloth banners and pulled toy wagons decorated as floats, and Edee marched beside us in a drum majorette outfit, blowing a whistle as cadence. Says Edee, "Parades are like fresh flowers. They are momentary splashes of color and energy and then they're gone." Bob's passion is designing and building things, preferably out of salvaged materials. I've watched him over the course of ten years, remodeling houses, building handrails for elderly neighbors, crafting artful sand containers to prevent falls after a snow, and making sturdy compost bins and cold frames for the community garden, enabling something to be grown every day of the year, even in Colorado's erratic climate.

In a single generation, we've forgotten that conversation is an art. You set up unspoken "rules," as you go; you find areas of common interest, you entertain each other with stories and jokes, you comfort each other, all free. John de Graaf explains how we've abandoned gatherings around the table: "Think about it. Who has informal chats at the kitchen table? How often do we use our dining room tables for company or our coffee tables for gatherings with neighbors? 'Having people over' has been reduced by nearly half in the last forty years. Instead, we're eating fast foods alone in our cars."[9]

What happened to charades and scavenger hunts—which bring people together, don't cost anything, and are uncomplicated fun? What happened, I think, was they fell out of style because there's no money to be made. Nobody advertises profitless people-games that don't require products. In a world of affluenza victims, public relations professionals—who create the image of our lifestyle without our permission—don't promote self-created, free recreation. However, in our style-oblivious neighborhood, Nancy orchestrated a great scavenger hunt recently, leaving intriguing clues to go to various locations, like, "How exciting when told, A surprise this cabinet will hold." (The storage box for packages left by the mailman.) On our team, we sent the kids ahead, telling them to find each clue and bring it back to headquarters, where we sat drinking beer. In a pinch, we sent adult members into action—on the run, of course, because the other teams were right on our tail. Who needs reality shows when reality is even better?

Sometimes the universe itself is playful. I *love* it when a belly laugh washes over me from out of nowhere, as one did in a Mexican fishing village a few years ago. I was sitting in the shallows of the surf, trying to put on a pair of flippers to go snorkeling. But every time I made the attempt, another wave mischievously knocked me over, and the joke carried me to a wonderfully humble place that made even the seagulls cackle. It was hilarious how small I was compared with the ocean!

Dawn, who tells stories about swimming with whales and dolphins, tells another story of what happened when a blue jay attacked a robin's nest in her backyard, knocking the baby birds to the ground: Dawn quickly built a nest out of a breadbasket and dried grass, lashed it onto a tree limb, and carefully tucked the fallen babies into it. Mama Robin, who watched the whole scene, quickly abandoned the old nest and moved into the new one to take care of her family. Dawn swears that Mama returned the following summer, landing on her windowsill to say hello.

Other friends of mine are learning to speak Spanish, largely for the challenge; volunteering to do ecological restoration; and becoming knowledgeable about citizen involvement in the political process—from caucus through election night. The fine line between play and work begins to dissolve when we enjoy doing things that are also useful.

➤ The Puzzle and Paradox of Work

I've reached some nice heights performing music, sometimes becoming so involved that it seemed like someone *else* was singing and playing guitar. When I was back in college playing in an acoustic band, I considered trying to convert that passion into a living, but then I imagined all the smoky bars we'd have to perform in; all the people talking, laughing and drinking beer while we played our best songs. Instead, I decided to try kneading another passion, writing, into a profession. In my late twenties, I wrote a novel that sprouted from postadolescent convictions and was *almost* published. One of the book's themes is—guess what—finding meaningful work in a top-heavy, money-obsessed economy. The main character, Josh Watkin, needs to find work quickly, since his wife is eight and a half months pregnant. With the goal of retaining deed to his soul while still making a living, Josh fills out dozens of job applications, each of which seems to have unacceptable linkages with the Growth Machine he despises. In one chapter, he feels existential anxiety about the prospects of finding good work:

> The phrase "reason for leaving" may ring a bell as three words that always appear on a standard job application. They want to know why you'd rather be "here" in this job than "there" at your last one. The underlying accusation, of course, is that you were fired, but even if you weren't, they give you a box about the size of a cornflake to explain why you did leave, when really nothing shorter than a book could tell the story.
>
> Your "reason for leaving" doesn't have to be an honest one, but it had better sound like everybody else's reason or you're automatically out. Be careful what you put in that box! Don't try to explain in ten words or less that "We need jobs that use our equipment—our bodies—rather than machines, because obesity is becoming an epidemic." Don't say, "We need jobs that don't extract and auction off every last square foot of land and every last particle of soil," or that, "We need jobs where we don't lose our dignity; where our voices are heard and our creativity is challenged but not used up; we need work that's meaningful and important to be doing; where we can feel human, alive, and energized." Don't even try to summarize that you "want to feel fulfilled." It might be honest but it sounds way too earnest in today's wound-up, cynical world. Do yourself a favor: just put down "money" and you're on your way.

I guess I didn't follow my own character's advice: the money hasn't for the most part been my reason for leaving the jobs I've left. I simply wanted bigger challenges, doing work that I believed in. Admittedly, I was a product of my times: In 1970, 79 percent of college freshmen said their goal was developing a meaningful philosophy of life. By 2005—after the spread of affluenza—75 percent said their primary objective was to be financially very well off.[10]

Studs Terkel begins his epic book of interviews, *Working*, with the sentence, "This book, being about work, is, by its very nature, about violence—to the spirit as well as to the body." The book is a search for daily meaning as well as daily bread, for recognition as well as cash. One of the people he interviewed, editor Nora Watson, says, "I think most of us are looking for a calling, not a job. Most of us, like the assembly line worker, have jobs that are too small for our spirit. Jobs are not big enough for people." Other people from all walks of life concur: "I'm a machine," says the spot-welder. "I'm caged," says the bank teller. "A monkey can do what I do," says the receptionist. "I'm an object," says the model. "I'm less than a farm implement," says the migrant worker.[11]

Commenting on the way work often dominates our lives, essayist Bob Black writes, tongue-in-cheek, "Free time is a euphemism for the peculiar way labor, as a factor of production, not only transports itself at its own expense to and from the workplace, but also assumes primary responsibility for its own maintenance and repair."[12] True enough, but sometimes we luck out—always in a give-and-take kind of way, of course; no job is perfect. Advertiser H. Jackson Brown Jr. suggests, "Find a job you like and you add five days to every week."

Yet, a large and very diverse mix of variables determines what work will make us happy. We crave work that has meaning beyond the paycheck; that challenges our creativity and aptitudes; that gives us a sense of being recognized and remembered; that connects us with people; that's safe and secure, both physically and fiscally; and that doesn't strip away all our energy. Much of our enjoyment of work depends on who we are and how we perceive the world. For example, when asked what they were working on, one proverbial stonecutter replied, "I'm cutting this rock into slabs that are two feet by two feet by six inches." The second stonecutter had a wider view: "I'm helping build a cathedral." The question is, are we building enough cathedrals? Is our economy moving in a direction that provides great jobs?

Personally, if I were going to work in a car factory, for example, I'd rather it be a factory that manufactures hybrids, safe and durable cars. Traveling salesman Peter Gilbert recently donated his 1989 Saab 900 SPG to a museum after a million miles of service; I'd want to be part of that assembly line or engineering team! If I were going to work as an investment counselor, I'd want to steer clients toward investments that are good for people as well as the environment—so-called socially responsible investing that now screens trillions of dollars. It's up to each one of us to *know* why we should or shouldn't feel proud of the work we do. Brooklyn fireman Tom Patrick, another worker in Terkel's book, comments: "The firemen, you actually see them produce. You see them put out a fire. You see them come out with babies in their hands. You see them give mouth-to-mouth when a guy's dying. That's real . . . It shows I did something on this earth."[13]

Good work affects much more than the size of an individual's house. People whose goals and values are more intrinsic agree with statements like, "I want my work to provide me with opportunities for helping other people and increasing my knowledge and skills." For example, a surgical doctor makes great money and also saves lives, learns something new every day, and uses his or her training and skills to meet one unique challenge after another. However, these days, physicians in general are often told exactly how much time they can spend with each patient. The waits are long and the doctor visits short when cash becomes more important than caring. Says one European neurologist, "They're applying the logic of machines to people. Lots of doctors are frustrated—they want to have time to treat the person, not just the disease."[14]

In fact, according to Dr. Daniel Goleman, "Surveys find signs of burnout in 80 or 90 percent of practicing physicians—a quiet epidemic." On the positive side of health care, there is a resurgence of doctors who choose to make house calls rather than seven-figure incomes; and there's also an increase in classes offered to medical students dealing specifically with patient-doctor communications and empathy.[15]

By choosing good work, we contribute to a world that, with luck, produces more biological, economic, and cultural assets than liabilities—or at least stays even. A culture improves largely by the work of its people—employers, employees, activists, and caretakers. Certainly, not all work that's important is salaried. For example, a recent study by Salary.com calculated that a stay-at-home mother or father—who works an average of 91.6 hours a week as a de facto housekeeper, day-care teacher, cook, computer operator, laundry machine operator, janitor, facilities manager, van driver, chief executive, and psychologist—would earn $134,121 a year if paid for all of the work, including overtime—an amount similar to a top ad executive, marketing director, or judge. Is any work more important than this?[16]

➤ Good Work

Though many regard the word "employment" with the same disdain that economists give to the word "*un*employment," Mihaly Csikszentmihalyi's research demonstrates that we often achieve a greater sense of "flow" at work than in leisure time. (A recent Pew Research Center poll found that employed people are as likely to be "very happy" as retirees.)[17] One reason we lead the world in average hours worked per week may be that work is sometimes more like a game than the American version of leisure. Work usually has clear goals and rules of performance, just like in a game. It provides challenges and feedback, encourages concentration and lack of distractions, and, ideally, matches the worker's skills with the task to be done—all aspects that characterize flow. It can also offer social connections and a feeling of accomplishment.

World-acclaimed viola player Geraldine Walther has been in the flow of music since she was seven; she always knew that playing violin and viola was her passion. She is the newest member of the Takács string quartet, considered by some music critics to be the greatest string quartet in the world. When I heard the group perform a few months ago, I was swept away by their playful, buoyant intensity. The concert seemed to fill me up; to heal whatever needed healing. As I listened, I felt I could *be* what they were playing—their sense of celebration burst through the music and inspired me. The next day I called the group to request an interview with Geraldine (Jeri), because I wanted to ask her how this musical magic came about.

Over lunch, she tells me she's recently left the San Francisco Orchestra, where she played for thirty years as primary violist, because she wanted to challenge herself. "I had a comfortable job with the orchestra, and the salary was great," she says. "I knew that I could have coasted indefinitely, but music is such a central part of my life; I needed more." By accepting the new job with Takács, she hadn't taken the easy road—string quartets are widely known as the riskiest venue in classical music. "There's nowhere to hide," Jeri says with a smile. "But the guys are so expressive and so generous; they help me be the best I can be. I feel like I can't let them down . . .

"Each performance is like an improvisation—I don't know exactly what's going to happen, but then we find a way to stretch individually and stay together at the same time. We'll feel someone *about* to do something different and we each make minor adjustments—it's a fantastic feeling . . . I lose myself in it. She adds, "I consider it a joy, privilege and responsibility to be playing in this group."

I ask her how the audience connects with the energy of a given piece. "There seems to be a *cycle* of energy. We feel the attention and the involvement of the audience; everyone wants and expects us to play as well as we can, and we don't want to waste their time." She mentions a certain movement in a Bartók piece, which the composer meant to be amusing. "The audience always laughs when we come to that part—the humor comes across."

First crafted in the 1500s, violas are slightly larger than violins, often providing harmony. According to violist Geraldine Walther, "Some say the cork is the first violin, the cello is the bottle, and the wine is the viola and second violin." Credit: Susan Benton

Jeri's work connects her intimately with her colleagues, demanding that she rise to her highest potential. It also connects her to audiences all over the world that are uplifted and empowered by the music. Clearly, hers is good work.

Teri Rippeto also had a youthful realization about the kind of work she wanted to do. "I always had curiosity about food," she tells me. Her Aunt Judy was a mentor, teaching her at a very young age how to can fruits and vegetables. "Canning is from your heart," she says, "and that's the most beautiful and most important part of cooking." In fourth grade, Teri won a 4H blue ribbon for her chocolate chip cookies, and thirty-five years later, she runs a restaurant, Potager, with a staff of nineteen and a customer base that includes the mayor of Denver—and me, of course. I'm particularly impressed with her emphasis on serving the freshest, highest-quality food she can find. She's a regular at the well-known Boulder Farmers' Market, whose vendors grow all the organic produce they sell. The meat she serves is local and grass fed; lobster, scallops, and clams are express-mailed by a friend in Maine; and fresh fish is delivered by an airport courier right to her restaurant.

Quality comes first, but Teri's next priority is to cook with vegetables, fruits, and herbs that are locally grown and in season. In mid-December, I didn't expect she'd still be preparing seasonal dishes from local sources, but she surprises me. "On the menu right now are dishes with locally grown potatoes, winter squash, onions, garlic, fresh salad greens grown in cold frames and greenhouses, Jerusalem artichokes, beets, and cold-hardy leafy greens like kale, chard, collards, and mustard greens." She is so passionate about the *meaning* of food that last year she mailed a monthly newsletter to 1,500 people, with staff-written articles about knowing where your food comes from, the health benefits of organic produce, and how to use what's in season to create gourmet meals. Her sous-chef teaches classes on healthy cuisine at Boy's and Girl's Clubs, and she wants to become involved with gardening programs at local elementary schools. When I ask her if she considers her work "play," she says she wouldn't go *that* far—but without a doubt, her work shows that the time we spend making a living can enrich lives.

The Algonquin Hotel in New York City recently celebrated the ninetieth birthday of one of its most revered employees, Hoy Wong, a gentleman originally from Hong Kong who, in his fifty-eight years of bartending, has served drinks to celebrities like Marilyn Monroe, Bob Hope, and Judy Garland. Once, when the Duke of Windsor ordered a "House of Lords martini in and out on toast," the veteran "Mr. Hoy" had the expertise to serve him a martini with a lemon twist, ignited with a match. The bartender knew his trade. "After he drink, he liked it," Wong said proudly. "And he had a second one." Says the Algonquin's general manager, "He never misses a day. If the weather's bad he shows up early. It's just really an honor to work with someone like Mr. Hoy." The hotel showed their respect for him by inviting 350 friends and admirers to a party in his honor. Mr. Hoy's good work is about doing his job well, with pride.[18]

One of my pet peeves (in addition to the term "pet peeves") is dealing with sales people, government workers, and others who distance themselves from their work, essentially becoming prisoners of their paychecks. They do the work just well enough to get by, as if they are worthy but the work is not. As an aspiring writer who spent seven years in the computer control room of a sewage treatment plant, I learned firsthand that pride in one's work is not about social distinction but self-esteem. No matter what the job is, it needs to be done well or not at all.

➤ Making Work More Playful, and Play More Purposeful

What can we learn from athletes, musicians, and other masters of play to help work be more enjoyable? Interestingly, in some cases monetary rewards become an obstacle to enjoyment. In research with two groups to observe the effect of extrinsic rewards on behavior, one group received money for solving a puzzle and the second group did not. The group that was paid stopped playing after the first game, while the unpaid group continued to enjoy the puzzle for its own sake. Researcher Edward Deci concludes, "Rewards seem to turn the act of playing into something that is controlled from the outside: It turns play into work."[19] If we want work to be more like play, it seems we need to emphasize the joys of challenge and creativity, as well as the social value of what we are doing.

The money's important, but so are other, more intrinsic rewards. Athletes tell us that the winner doesn't always "take all." In both work and play, the greatest value comes from qualities like peak performance, involvement, pride, respect for others, and continuous learning and improvement. These values make life worth living, regardless of trophies or salaries. If we're relatively content in both work and play, extrinsic rewards become less important. It seems we need to devote more time to teaching and mentoring children that there's more to life than working and spending. I believe we need to learn, again, how to *reconnect* with activities that challenge us—for example, how to cook, build a table, or be politically active. We need to breathe life into workplaces so even menial jobs can be enjoyable, by offering more opportunities for autonomy, more employee-defined challenges, more emphasis on quality and the "story" of the product or service, and more direct feedback on work performance (as opposed to just quarterly, numerical score sheets).

Can workplaces become kinder, gentler, and more soulful? There seems to be a movement to bring "spirit" into our offices and places of business—which essentially means treating employees with greater respect (leadership from the heart, not just the head) and working together to create meaning in the product. The annual Business and Consciousness Conference is now one of North America's largest events, and books like *Reawakening Spirit at Work* and *Chicken Soup for the Soul at Work* are being used as texts in business seminars all over the country. Business leadership coach Lance Secretan points to SAS Institute, the largest independent software company in the world, as a good example of spirit at work. The company shuts its offices promptly at five o'clock, recognizing that people have lives outside of work. They also provide other work-life amenities, such as "Free Breakfast Fridays," soda fountains and snacks in every breakroom, on-site childcare centers, employee health-care centers, fitness centers, and wellness programs. Staff turnover is 3 percent in an industry that averages 20 percent, and a few years ago they received 27,000 applications for 945 job openings. The bottom line is that SAS saves an estimated $50 million a year in recruitment and training costs.[20]

"Getting a life" includes both work and play. We've become world champion consumers partly because our culture doesn't know how to enjoy leisure; instead, we try to buy it. Writes author Susan Ertz, "Millions long for immortality who do not know what to do with themselves on a rainy Sunday afternoon," and psychologist Milhaly Csikszentmihalyi would agree. "The popular assumption is that no skills are involved in enjoying free time, and that anybody can do it," he says. "People are unhappiest when they are alone and nothing needs doing. In our studies, people who live by themselves and do not attend church find Sunday mornings to be the lowest part of the week, because with no demands on attention, they are unable to decide what to do."[21]

Priceless moments await us in both work and play. Both are interrelated with the other assets this book presents: creating a rich sense of self, using time well, maintaining great health, learning from history, and so on. However, to become more satisfying, it seems that work and play need to be better balanced. Right now, work dominates the lives of a majority of Americans, leaving little time for learning *how* to play. Most economists, philosophers, moneylenders, and media moguls assume that we need constant growth to create more work and perpetuate an ever-expanding standard of living. This assumption—that jobs and growth are the backbone of the economy—is systemic in tax structures, educational planning, healthcare coverage, and insurance plans. Maybe it's time we rethink what we want the ultimate product to be. Do we want limitless economic growth, or satisfied people?

◆ Creating Playful Work and Purposeful Play ◆

Overall goals:

- Reach for values that move satisfaction from the "end product" (winning, output, high salaries) to the everyday *process* of work and play.

- Elevate play (not just leisure) to a higher status in American culture.

- Strive for cultural consensus on "what work needs to be done." For example, as many people now work in the recycling industry as in the automobile industry, and recyclers outnumber the mining industry workers three to one. To become a less consumptive, wasteful society, we also need better minds and more workers in the fields of renewable energy, healthy food, and green design.

A Few Strategies:

- Offer greater flexibility to choose part-time work. Workers should be able to choose shorter hours if they are more satisfied with free time than they are with higher income. For example, 36 percent of the Dutch labor force works part-time (34 hours or less per week), and those part-time workers are legally entitled to a proportional share of pay, bonuses, holidays, and other benefits.

- Increase opportunities for lifetime learning and life enrichment classes at universities, churches and other institutions, where adults and children can learn new skills (e.g., cooking, carpentry, film appreciation, civic involvement).

- Watch for personal signs of dissatisfaction at work, such as: apathy, feeling overwhelmed by deadline pressure or workload; project procrastination; a toxic relationship with your boss; withdrawal from friends and family members; sleeplessness; increased smoking, drinking, or caffeine consumption; increased physical symptoms such as headaches, colds, exhaustion, ulcers, or heart condition. Change jobs if necessary.

- Increase the use of tools that help students and job applicants find work that aligns with their passions and aptitudes.

- Provide management approaches that make work more like a game, with clear rules, continuous feedback, and teamwork; (e.g., the "total quality management" initiatives of the 1990s emphasize quality circles in which each employee is trained in all aspects of the business).

- Give greater emphasis to quality and the "story" of a product or service, to enhance both worker and consumer satisfaction.

- Emphasize healthy lifestyles that optimize both play and work; e.g., many workplaces have improved the quality of food in cafeterias; have implemented employee outings that are active and healthy; and have built "high productivity" facilities where employees have more individual control over temperatures and air quality and where atriums, sunspaces, and indoor forests bring nature into the workplace.

- Hire human resource consultants like Barbara Brannen (letsplaymore.com) who intentionally bring play into the workspace with "appreciation programs," "moments of laughter," and projects in which employees perform charitable functions together. Fear is replaced by pride as a motivator, leading to higher productivity and greater employee satisfaction.

Public and
Cultural Assets

10

The Real Wealth of Neighborhoods

Designing for People, Not Cars

When we build our landscape around places to go, we lose places to be.
    —Rick Cole

The loss of a forest or a farm is justified only if it is replaced by a village. To replace them with a subdivision or a shopping center is not an even trade.
    —Andrés Duany

The 20th Century was about getting around. The 21st Century will be about staying in a place worth staying in.
    —James Kunstler

The only way you run into someone else in LA is in a car crash.
    —Susan Sarandon

Imagine "zooming in" with satellite imagery all the way to the roof of your house or apartment. Beneath that virtual roof, sitting at your computer, you're effectively hooked up to a consumer-support system. Not only is your Internet cable an umbilical, but also the natural gas lines, pipes that carry water in and wastes out, electrical wires, telephone wires and waves, streets, postal trucks and delivery vans. These days, just about everything we need to be champion consumers is delivered right to our homes—except of course the money to buy it all, and the ethics and values to make sense of it. The fact is, beneath that zoomed-in roof, you may not be as healthy as you'd like. Maybe you spend so many hours browsing on the Web (and we can see what you're looking at) that you neglect other important aspects of your life.

You may feel isolated from people in your well-equipped castle, disconnected from nature, or short on time. Your diet of fast food and ready-to-eat meals conveys an abundance of calories but not much in the way of energy. The evening news upsets you and your stomach rumbles from job-related stress and unpaid bills. The relaxation you need may not happen since you're not sleeping that well lately. You're a mess! (We all are, really, because the culture we've created is off balance.) Like all of us, you want your home to be a place of comfort but it sometimes feels more like a house of detention.

Maybe it's time to think differently about the way you live. For example, by literally thinking "outside the box" of your house or apartment, you can tap into intrinsic assets your neighborhood and town have to offer. Instead of consumption, you can have community. Though the housing market in general is sagging in 2007, the quest for housing alternatives is going strong. In every large metro area and many smaller ones, there are now "new urbanism" projects and traditional neighborhood developments where these kinds of features are part of the design: stores and public buildings; parks in central locations; narrow, traffic-calming streets; shade trees; front porches; small yards and common open space; and functional alleyways. The idea is to create a sense of place and encourage interactions among neighbors, just as in the well-designed neighborhoods of a hundred years ago, which often become a town's flagship neighborhoods. Like Denver's Washington Park neighborhood, which has a great park as a centerpiece and restaurants at the fringes, these neighborhoods are as strong as the bricks and hardwoods they're made of. I lived in Wash Park for a few years, and I admired this sturdy, functional place.

There are also many examples of neighborhoods codesigned by the people who will soon live there. Since 1989, two hundred "cohousing" neighborhoods have been built or are in the planning stages, and I've lived in one of them for ten years. As described in chapter 5, there are even ways to give *existing* neighborhoods extreme makeovers, creating community culture out of what used to be just a collection of houses and streets.

I believe that neighborhoods and communities offer the best counterweight to the corporate dominance that takes away our voices. Whether or not we realize it yet, the grassroots power we collectively wield in our communities can tilt civilization in a more sensible, peaceful, democratic direction. Neighborhoods can be places where Americans make the transition from "me" to "we," getting our priorities straight and becoming citizens again.

Writes mainstream real estate columnist Blanche Evans, "Homes are about more than houses—they are about proximity to jobs, services, community resources, schools, parks, dining, entertainment, friends, and family . . ."[1] Three-fourths of Americans now say they'd give up their dream homes to live in great neighborhoods. Yet the habits of privacy and "the good life" are deeply ingrained in our generation. Many people don't know where to look for a neighborhood rich in real wealth. Or if they already live in one, they don't take advantage of it by getting to know their neighbors, being active in local politics and places of worship, helping to make improvements in the school system, or learning about the history and natural characteristics of the place they live in.

Where we live is one of the most tangible indicators of what we value. So the question, "What makes a neighborhood great?" is really asking, "What do we value the most?" There are many annual lists of Best Places to Live, most of which place the familiar categories near the top: jobs, crime, property values, cost of living, low taxes, and average commute time. Other qualities often considered are average income in the neighborhood, average education level, and average number of divorced residents. Toward the bottom of many a list are access to public and cultural amenities and health considerations.

These familiar lists seem to evaluate neighborhood assets largely in terms of income, appearance, and exclusivity—what we have rather than who we are. However, writer/editor Jay Walljasper looks at places through different lenses. "Cities can rank quite high in these categories and still be dreary, soulless places," he believes. "Indeed, such qualities sometimes diminish the spirit of a community, as the push for a narrowly individualistic vision of the Good Life results in economic inequality, environmental degradation, social fragmentation, and lousy public services. A good place to live ought to offer more than just high salaries and low crime rates."[2]

Walljasper looks for great spots to "sip latté, watch foreign films, and browse used-book shops." In ranking the ten most enlightened towns in America, he and his team looked for communities "showing the way to a better future" and gave Ithaca, New York, and Portland, Oregon, the highest rankings. Access to preventive, alternative health care was important; as were strong evidence of civic involvement; diverse spiritual opportunities; homes that are affordable to the town's hairdressers, janitors, and teachers; a celebration of regional culture and regional products: locally baked bread, locally grown produce, local artists; and governmental policies that reflect the specific needs of a place, such as Portland's promotion of downtown development.

➣ Where Do You Live?

We use the question, "Where do you live?" automatically, without really thinking about it. Sometimes the question just means, "How far do I have to drive to get there, and how long will it take?" Too often "where you live" means where you park your car, consume energy, watch three or four hours of TV a day, generate four pounds of trash, and argue with your spouse. Hopefully, in *your* case, it means something far more magnificent: where you have your best relationships, and your most creative ideas. Where you feel the most content and energized. Where you *come to life*.

Ideally, where you live is about a *place* and not just a house. A place where neighbors know and value you enough to be there for you if you need help, and where you can meet the universal human need to offer your own support and caring. A great place to walk, because a thriving pedestrian population results in healthy neighbors, cleaner air, human-scaled architecture, and lower crime. A great neighborhood creates less stress and offers more "social capital" and trust than a typical neighborhood; and it creates less stress on the environment by using less land, water, energy, and materials. While the general assumption is that a house in the upscale part of town would always be preferable, it may not necessarily have the most value overall. To afford that mini-mansion, you may be stretching your paycheck tighter than the rubber band on a toy airplane, spending many hours vacuuming unused rooms, and climbing ladders to squeegee endless, impossible-to-reach windows.

If we think about what we need to be happy, great neighborhoods can provide many of those needs directly. We need a sense of belonging and participation, a sense of security and safety; we need healthy food, connection with the no-worries feelings that nature bestows, and activities that we enjoy, to name just a few. Think of the places you've lived, and how they met or failed to meet needs like these.

I've been pretty lucky in the neighborhood department; I've spent at least half my years in places that really supported my growth. One of them was Larchmont, a small suburb of New York City with great connections. It's connected to the ocean, by passenger rail to the city and all the culture that goes with it, and to a rich heritage that's reflected in its sturdy, sometimes opulent homes. It's linked with the Boston Post Road, developed in the 1670s from an old Algonquian Indian trail that King Charles II made America's first official mail route. President Washington traveled this road through New England on his 1789 inaugural tour.

To live in Larchmont is to be into sailing, fishing, or at least swimming. Chances are the household includes commuters to jobs in the city that are stimulating—often linked with company headquarters, entertainment, or the financial sector. And then there's upstate, a huge universe of forests, farms, and delightful small towns that don't seem to notice that New York City's on the same planet.

I learned how to drive in Larchmont, and how to play guitar (my dad brought a ukulele back from a Hawaiian business trip). I had my first job there at the age of fourteen—as a caddy at the local golf course. I kissed my first kiss, published my first poem, cut high school classes to go to Jones Beach and Greenwich Village, and watched my older sister and her friends dance to Bill Haley and the Comets' "Rock Around the Clock." I watched my parents weave a network of friends from church and people in the neighborhood. We didn't have a large yard, but my mom loved to take care of her azaleas and rhododendrons.

I went back to Larchmont a few years ago after thirty-five years away, observing again how great communities meet needs. I parked at my old house and spent a few hours walking through the old neighborhoods—even sneaking across the corner of a backyard the way I used to on my way to elementary school. I was a time traveler, on a spring day somewhere in my past. The dogwoods were in full bloom and the houses still echoed with the voices of my friends. Munching a classic hot dog from the same stand I went to as a kid, I analyzed this place through the eyes of a filmmaker (I'd recently produced several programs on sustainable communities). My old hometown had great bones: well-designed pockets of public space in each neighborhood; a great school; and big, old hardwood trees that forested the whole village. In fact, I recognized a few familiar cracks in the heaving sidewalk in front of my old house, created years ago by wandering oak tree roots (A grown-up kid would notice). The same steel steps and stone walls were still securely in place at my elementary school, and I wished the school was open (it was a Sunday) so I could try to retrieve a baseball card I'd flipped under the school's metal threshold forty years earlier. (A coat hanger *might* possibly get it, and I just happened to have one in my suitcase.)

I tested a standard indicator of a great community, walking from my old house to the business center in a little more than five minutes, which makes it quite possible to pick up a quart of milk without burning a quart of gas, and say hello to neighbors along the way. A similar indicator still seemed viable in Larchmont—an eight-year-old girl could safely walk to the park or the public library. This indicator presupposes a library worth walking to, sidewalks to walk on, and neighborhoods safeguarded by the active presence of the neighbors themselves. I was tempted to try developer Andrés Duany's blindfold test, in which you assume that slow-moving cars will stop if you cross a commercial street with a blindfold on. But my faith in modern-day Larchmont didn't extend *quite* that far.

I observed with older eyes that the town offered a place for people, not just cars. I observed great parks, great attention to lush landscaping, increasing ethnic diversity, and the classic, fully functional railroad, still running right on schedule. To my delight, I reexperienced a town worth living in (if you could afford it), a town whose residents cared about its continuance. And I realized that community greatness is *built* on caring, good design, citizen participation, and a strong vision of what a community can be. From these desirable qualities flow a strong fiscal base and a satisfied population. Yet many of America's seventy thousand or more communities don't reach these goals, partly because the "factory" that builds and maintains communities (zoning regulations, building industry, government incentives, certain patterns of thinking) is out of step with what people need.

Since *Ozzie and Harriet* and *Father Knows Best* days, America's demographics and values have changed significantly, yet we are still platting and building neighborhoods and homes that assume upwardly mobile families live there with jobs in the city and plenty of time to take care of the lawn. In fact, fewer than 50 percent of America's suburban homes (where more than half of Americans now live) are occupied by traditional mom-and-pop families; more than a quarter of our houses are occupied by single people. As author Joel Kotkin points out, "Roughly three out of five jobs in American metropolitan areas are now located in the suburbs, and more than twice as many Americans commute from suburb to suburb than from suburb to city."[3] The ethnic mix of the suburbs has changed, too, enriching the culture and diversity of its neighborhoods. For example, a majority of Asian Americans, half of Hispanics, and 40 percent of African Americans now live in the suburbs.

Because it was assumed that Americans would always love our cars and never take account of how much we were consuming, builders accommodated a doubling of the U.S. population (between 1950 and 2005) with a drive-in design strategy. The idea of community was rarely part of the equation, and streets were laid out with little thought of such human needs as socializing, solar exposure, and exercise. Locating the new subdivisions on cheap farmland resulted in several dysfunctions at the same time: It not only paved and smothered the region's best agricultural land but also put miles of resource-intensive travel between our houses and our jobs, stores, and friends.

Now, we're faced with an ironic but pressing question: How do we strategically rebuild some of what we've just built to make it work better? In addition, how do we (quickly) refine the focus and priorities of new construction in the near future, because much will remain in place for hundreds of years? All new construction needs to be resource efficient, because the days of unlimited fuels, raw materials, and land are over. And it needs to enrich life rather than degrade it; to be less about buying life and more about experiencing it. The cultural components of American expansion have provided various ways to escape. The TV, automobile, and the suburb (country life without the mud) taught us we could always choose to be somewhere else. Consequently, we undervalue and underutilize where we already are.

Now that the brightness of the American Dream is flickering, making neighborhoods and villages livable and sustainable again should be a top priority. As we reshape *existing* components of suburbia, for example, we need to determine the best location for village centers, as well as who will fund their creation. Small businesses that convert existing houses and lots into stores is one source. Tax dollars invested in public infrastructure like community centers is another, and new alliances with utility companies may be a third. To avoid the high costs of adding power plants and water treatment plants, the utilities may fund capacity (including purchase and demolition of certain existing buildings) at the neighborhood scale. New, low-impact ways of generating electricity, such as large fuel cells (with pure hydrogen as a fuel source), would work well at the neighborhood scale. Such mini-power plants could supply electricity, pure water, and heat to networks of houses, generating neither pollution nor noise. This technology is still very expensive but its value may be much larger than its cost.

Instead of spending half a trillion dollars (EPA estimate) to repair and replace sewage infrastructure in upcoming years, wastewater utilities might begin to look closely at neighborhood-scaled "Living Machines" that mimic the way nature purifies sewage. Snails, fish, cattails, and other natural species live in tanks inside of greenhouses; the wastewater flows through them at a controlled speed. Because these systems perform as well or better than resource-intensive conventional treatment plants, some state environmental departments such as in Indiana have certified their use. I toured a Living Machine in Indiana, where wastes from about eighty employees at the PAWS office (headquarters of cartoonist Jim Davis's *Garfield* empire) are efficiently treated. Since decomposition is quick and natural, the facility smells as earthy and sweet as its final stage—a crop of marketable roses.

Conceivably, a neighborhood's homeowners association could become a for-profit business, leasing/owning and operating small neighborhood businesses and mini-facilities that make their neighborhoods far more sustainable. As Michael Schuman suggests in the book *Going Local*, community-owned enterprises are not only possible (the Green Bay Packers is one), but seemingly inevitable. Why not invest directly in our communities? Another force to be reckoned with is the confederation of Homeowners Associations; fifty-seven million Americans are now "citizens" of a quarter of a million private jurisdictions. What an opportunity to promote sustainability! Instead of just decreeing and enforcing what neighbors must *not* do (such as have sculptures on their front lawn or put up basketball hoops), imagine neighborhood associations that begin to encourage resource efficiency and the creation of neighborhood culture!

One very interesting example is the Norwood-Quince neighborhood in Boulder, Colorado, where neighbors are determined to make the car an alternative form of transportation. Neighborhood resident Graham Hill is leading the charge. Expert in out-of-car experiences from electric assisted bikes to Segway scooters, Hill and his neighbors have taken one step after another—often literally—to make their neighborhood people-friendly. Out of 210 households in his neighborhood, for instance, 130 have Eco-passes for the well-managed bus system. The city provides discounts for neighborhoods that participate cooperatively.

The neighbors also have excellent pedestrian access to a shopping area, open space in a nearby park, several bike-pedestrian walkways, and even a solar-lit walkway paid for by a neighborhood mini grant from the city. "We observed that many neighbors weren't walking to the Boulder Market at night because the street was too dark and seemed unsafe," explains Hill. "So we applied for a grant to install solar-powered lights with battery storage. Now pedestrians can be seen—and can see—even at night."

Forty people in the neighborhood are members in a car-share club—essentially car rental by the hour—and more than fifty have become members in an electric bike-share operation; the electric bikes are powered by solar cells incorporated into a bike shed.

The neighbors are now looking into creating better access by linking several existing pathways with easements through the edges of several private yards. To dramatize the efficiencies of muscle-power versus fossil fuel power, Hill and his colleagues staged a race between the mayor, who rode a bicycle, and the county commissioner, who drove a hybrid car. After each ran several compulsory errands, the bike-riding mayor won.[4]

➤ Boulder's Holiday Neighborhood: Not Only Sustainable, but Also Affordable

Originally settled during the gold rush of the 1850s, Boulder's gold now lies in its quality of life. Over the years, city leaders have championed a great system of bike trails, a well-used bus system, and an extensive tapestry of open space, funded through a small tax levy at the county level. The city maintains a geographical identity with a surrounding buffer of farms and ranches, and preserves the quality of its drinking water with a "blue

· What Makes a Neighborhood Great ·

Cultural Assets

• Great neighborhoods have active residents who participate in newsletters and e-mail listservs for sharing tools, tickets, civic information, and good-hearted jokes. They have discussion groups, community projects such as park cleanup or creek restoration, potluck dinners, volleyball games and skiing parties. (The neighbors of Elgin, Illinois, have a four-foot-tall, wooden Blue Tulip that makes monthly rounds from one yard to another. When the Tulip appears on your front lawn, it's your turn to host a Friday night neighborhood party.)

• Skill sharing, tool sharing, mentoring of the young by the elderly, job referrals, day care, dog care, neighborhood rosters with telephone numbers and e-mails, bulletin boards—these kinds of activities and tools encourage the creation of "neighbornets." (In Seattle, famous for its distinctive neighborhoods, Phinney Eco-Village—an existing neighborhood—has a Home Alone group, a natural health group, a peace group, and other networks. It has recently begun taking pledges from neighbors to fight global warming by driving less, not using dryers, using compact fluorescent bulbs, etc.)

• Free entertainment, like twilight conversations in the park; wine-tasting parties in someone's backyard; or spontaneous, no-pressure bike rides to a landmark in the town (an overlook, favorite bar, or ice-cream parlor).

• Sharing of life's ups and downs. (If I let you vent your frustrations as we each get home from work, I know I have a listener when I need to vent. If you show me your family album, I'll show you mine.)

• Neighbors who live in their house for years, creating neighborhood history and neighborhood stewards. (Studies show that hometowns are the most popular places to retire, despite all the literature about "where to retire." Of the thirty-five million people 65 and older who lived in the U.S. between 1995 and 2000, only 22 percent have left their homes and neighborhoods.

Physical Assets

• Community gardens on vacant lots, utility rights-of-way, and land donated/lent for tax write-offs. Also, the trading of garden produce and recipes from private gardens and kitchens, and neighborhood contracts with local growers (community-supported agriculture). Information about local growers can be found at www.nal.usda.gov/afsic/csa/.

- Transportation by proximity: location, location, location, and planning, planning, planning. Great neighborhoods need stores, parks, pathways, bike trails, and access to public transit (Some banks offer lower interest rates and down payments—often called location-efficient mortgages and green mortgages—to homebuyers).

- Slow, safe streets. Working with city governments, many neighborhoods have requested and received traffic circles, narrower streets, and so on. Studies have shown that the speed and volume of traffic often determine the number of friends and acquaintances neighbors have, with fast, high volume streets reducing that number by a factor of ten. In about twenty states "Safe Routes to School" has won public funding to improve and safeguard sidewalks, crosswalks, and bike paths that link children and their families to schools.

- A gathering place in the neighborhood: a community center or possibly an HOA-owned, formerly private residence with meeting, dining, office, and guest room space. Or at least a familiar space at a library, school, or church near the neighborhood.

line" above a certain elevation, to protect reservoirs and springs fed largely by snowmelt. Twelve percent of the electricity Boulder uses comes from small-scale hydroelectric turbines installed in the large pipes that gravity-feed water to city users. Boulder has been a victim of its own success: Its well-educated and civic-minded residents are willing to pay top dollar to live there. This has resulted in congested streets, as teachers, nurses, firemen, and merchants commute from more affordable areas. It also limits the social and economic diversity of the city.

At the Holiday neighborhood (named for a old drive-in theater that once occupied the site), the city-linked Boulder Housing Partners mandated that close to half of the 330 homes must be *permanently* affordable as well as lively, pedestrian-friendly, and energy efficient. Says Cindy Brown, codirector of BHP, "From the beginning, our goal was to create a great place to live and work for people earning different incomes and seeking different types of housing choices." By hiring a whole team of the region's most forward-looking developers (rather than just one), the city and BHP arranged diversity by design. Specific features began to appear in the plan, including a community garden and orchard, small neighborhood businesses, a pedestrian walkway, state-of-the art efficiency in building design, space for arts studios and work/live residences, and a mixture of home ownership and rentals.

Various interesting spots to work and play were incorporated on the site plan, which also laid streets out to optimize solar energy. The pedestrian "greenway" extends from one side of the development to the other, cutting through a two-acre "park at the heart" and also through a live/work cluster of residences called Studio Mews, where neighbors and visitors can watch artists and craftspeople create.

Boulder's environmentally progressive policies helped guide the neighborhood toward sustainability by design. For example, to receive a building permit, any new project must comply with the Green Points ordinance concerning building and landscape elements—from foundations and plumbing through air quality, indoor air quality, and solar energy.

Says green building expert David Johnston, primary architect of the Green Points system, "It keeps housing costs and sizes down so more people who work in the community can afford to own a house here." As Johnston points out, buildings are one of humanity's greatest impacts: "Forty percent of all the stuff we make and use in the U.S. goes into buildings, with all the associated pollution and impacts." He says. "Thirty-five percent of all the raw energy we use—the oil, natural gas and coal—is directly attributable to buildings, and 66 percent of all the electricity that's generated is used in buildings, primarily for heating, cooling, lighting and appliances. We are also using approximately seventy trillion board feet of softwood (a board foot is a one-inch board, twelve by twelve inches) in our buildings every year to build houses."

Adds John Wolff, chosen as the developer of three separate Holiday sub-neighborhoods, "Building at thirty units per acre is probably the smartest thing you can do in terms of conservation of land, water, and energy. Consider a typical suburban development of three units per acre—you need ten times as much land area for houses and ten times as much infrastructure for water sewer, utilities, and roadways." Part of Wolff's strategy is to build houses around a courtyard or community green—both to reduce the size and expense of individual lawns and create community.

The Holiday neighborhood demonstrates that the way buildings and streets are laid out affects quality of life for the whole lifetime of the neighborhood. For example, residents of the Holiday neighborhood are less likely to accumulate consumer goods because houses there are smaller than the average American home. At the Wild Sage Cohousing community (one unit of the Holiday neighborhood) some carriage houses-over-garages are as small as 600 square feet. The neighborhood will always have physical spaces in common that connect them: the large park, the walkway, and the community garden.[5]

➤ Neighborhoods on Purpose

I've had an opportunity to directly experience the full range of value that neighborhoods can offer because I helped design the twenty-seven-home cohousing community where I live, in Golden, Colorado. I used to have contingency plans for where I wanted to live in five years; maybe I'd move to New Zealand, or upstate New York, or a small town in western Colorado that doesn't feel the pace or swim in the smell of smog. But a few years ago, I stopped thinking about moving. And apparently, so did many of my neighbors—we've had only three turnovers (four if death is a turnover, and I'm sure it is!) in the last ten years.

From the original group of six households that bought our property together, all six are still here. At the meeting where we decided to buy the land, we weren't sure others would join our community. We worried that we might be out $320,000—a pretty great price for ten partly wooded acres, in hindsight. The process of building a community wasn't effortless, and we lost many would-be neighbors as we looked for land. A gem of a parcel right next to the world-famous Red Rocks amphitheater fell through, and other properties either cost too much or offered too little. I happened to be driving around one day, cruising the For Sale signs, when I had the idea of stopping by the Golden planning department to ask them what was available in

Harmony Village, in Golden, Colorado, is codesigned and governed by the people who live there. Its twenty-seven homes are all oriented to collect solar energy. Courtesy of the author

incorporated Golden—a great little community with a solid downtown area. Tucked right up against the foothills, the city was the territorial capital of the state until 1867, and has a rich historical feel to it. (Sometimes I see hobbyists panning for gold in Clear Creek.) In a place like Golden, we could be less dependent on cars. We could locate our neighborhood within this larger community, building the southwest-style neighborhood we'd been talking about for several years in meetings. What started out as a dream, discussed endlessly in living rooms and borrowed workplace meeting rooms, became a reality!

What exactly was the dream? It varied among our original households, of course, but was loosely organized around a concept imported from Denmark called cohousing (a translation from the Danish word for "living community" or "living together"). As architectural students in the 1980s, Chuck Durrett and Katie McCamant toured many Danish neighborhoods, noticing something unique about a certain kind of development. Says Chuck, "Whenever we walked into one of Denmark's several hundred cohousing communities, there was such life there—unlike most suburban or multifamily developments—such a joy and sense of interaction, that we began to comment, "This is unique. This is working. It made other housing seem more like warehousing. There were picnic tables between the houses where neighbors sat. Some would stand and chat for a minute, others would be there for longer, talking, laughing, sometimes eating, engaged.

Harmony Village has economic, age, gender, and cultural diversity. It also has diversity in personality traits: some are visionary, some excel in dealing with the details. Credit: Julia Rainer

When you walked into a cohousing community, it felt like people had a choice between as much community as they wanted and as much privacy as they wanted. In other housing projects, the choice was just privacy and . . . privacy."

Durrett and McCamant wanted a good place to live and raise a family back home in California, but they didn't see it on the market so they designed and built it themselves in Emeryville, adapting the Danish model of cohousing. They wrote the book that helped launch a small movement, *Cohousing: A Contemporary Approach to Housing Ourselves,* which explained that cohousing included clustered housing with lots of open space and pedestrian paths; remote parking to keep cars and people separate; a community building or common house that typically includes dining room, kitchen, living space, guest room, workshop, and office—shared and maintained by residents. Other shared amenities typically include such things as gardens, playgrounds, picnic areas, and recreational areas for Frisbee, soccer, and lounging. Features like these reduce the need for large private homes and yards, and increase the potential for people to meet their social and physiological needs right where they live. The word is getting out, because since McCamant and Durrett "imported" the idea, a hundred cohousing communities have been designed and built, with an equal number in the planning stages. There are hot spots for the concept in Massachusetts, Colorado, California, Washington, and Oregon, but there are enough other locations to travel across the country, east to west, and visit a different community every night—once a community in Lawrence, Kansas, is completed.

➣ Communities for the Future, Now

I originally joined a cohousing group because somebody had to save the planet. I knew that building houses closer together would use less land, and that organic gardening—my passion—was a central element in many cohousing communities Since future residents of a cohousing neighborhood participate in its design, surely our group could come up with the world's most sustainable neighborhood at lower than market costs. We learned differently, of course. Our southwestern-style village couldn't actually be made of adobe because it would take too long to build and cost too much. We couldn't generate all of our own electricity for similar reasons. But Matt Worswick, the project's architect, who lives in the neighborhood, and Jim Leach, the developer, did produce an award-winning development with great passive solar orientation and energy efficiency—with the active par-

✦ How Cohousing Neighborhoods Meet Human Needs ✦

(Needs are from Max-Neef table, see page 166–7)

Subsistence: Efficient homes with passive solar, access to garden produce, lots of home offices.

Protection: There are always meals, medical advice and other support for those who are sick.

Affection: Many good friends are a one-minute walk away. There are many parties and celebrations.

Understanding: Skills and perspectives gained from neighbors, directly, and via e-mail and bulletin boards.

Participation: Each neighbor is a neighborhood citizen, making decisions about common property.

Leisure: Gardening, playing music, and sharing community meals are some leisure activities.

Creation: Neighbors codesign new landscaping, aesthetic features, and celebrations.

Identity: Strengths, passions, and accomplishments are respected by neighbors.

Freedom: Each person "has a piece of the truth" and can safely express dissent and approval.

---

ticipation of our expanding community. Piece by piece, we're incorporating additional features that make the neighborhood more sustainable. Hybrid cars are appearing in our parking spaces, more fruit trees in the orchard, and solar panels on our roofs.

In fact, the installation of solar energy is a hot topic right now in the neighborhood. With federal tax credits and utility rebates already in place, solar-generated electricity has become very tempting. We have already installed solar panels to power the heavy-duty pump that irrigates our large garden, and now a handful of neighbors are working on how to get good prices and reliable installers for solar energy on our roofs. A core group of environmentalists and sustainability nuts are leading the quest for solar energy, and several have calculated the exact payback of systems that can deliver 100 percent of their household's electrical needs. For example, at .08 cents a kilowatt-hour, one system would pay itself back in fifteen years. After rebates and tax credits, homeowners would need to finance $4,000, and we've been discussing a self-help strategy in which our home-owners association would make loans out of funds we've set aside for long-term repairs.

In any group of people, there will be different personality types, skills, and ways of looking at things—we've always considered our neighborhood diversity a great asset in problem solving and creative ventures. My role in the solar discussion has been cheerleader. I'm not that interested in the fi-nancial details—my strength is more in big-picture thinking, but I really want to see more solar in the neighborhood, to take a stand against climate change. So when the payback calculations seemed to be stalling forward progress, I wrote in an e-mail, "Do we ask for an exact monetary Return on Investment from a new carpet, vacation, or charitable contribution? What about a thirty-year mortgage? We want quality in each of these transac-tions, but I think some of the ROI for solar is nonmonetary." I referred to some of the pondering I've doing for this book. We also get direct benefits in terms of the human needs we satisfy:

- Security against rising costs (security)

- Ultimate "free" energy and equity, just as if we paid off a mortgage (sustainability, autonomy)

- Satisfaction from being less of a consumer and more of a producer (self-esteem)

- An opportunity to take advantage of a very attractive offer WE made possible with Colorado's Amendment 37, that gives rebates for solar (political participation)

- A slightly greater chance to live in a world that steers clear of desper-ate, screw-the-future nuclear energy (empathy, purpose, cooperation)

Ultimately, I don't think these issues are completely about technology or money but the way we seek satisfaction. One kilowatt of panels, even though expensive, would make me feel good in a way that other purchases wouldn't. I do the same thing with organic apples from Whole Foods—I don't even look at the price because their value is greater than their cost differential: they make me feel great physically, keep me from getting sick, taste great, have more minerals, and support good farming in a world that really needs it. Solar panels do similar things, although I wouldn't want to eat one.

Our neighborhood has already become a community culture, and we've already begun to plan for its continuity. I envision a garden that continues to improve over the next three centuries. Because of its layout, with a community building as the central focus and walkways that interconnect the houses, it's quite possible the neighborhood culture will persist until at least 2307. The water rights we acquired a few years ago (600,000 gallons a year) will still be irrigating a garden endowed with grape vines, raised beds, greenhouses, and shade houses. Enriched with three centuries of compost and cover crops, Harmony Garden will grow some of the region's finest herbs, and be known throughout the area as a producer of high-quality pesto.

The park we saved from development by proposing that it be acquired as city open space will still provide a rest stop along the bike path that goes past the neighborhood. And that little three-quarter acre parcel will still be landscaped with native species that appreciate a little rain but can get along without it. The mission bell we imagined in early meetings and then acquired from the barn of a neighbor's parents will still be calling people to dinner and neighborhood meetings, and the artwork of many very creative future residents will join the great photographs already on the walls of our common house. The brick walkway that contains sixty-five thousand bricks that we laid ourselves will still be here, and possibly our sturdy townhouses, too. Downtown Golden will still be eight blocks away, and light rail will still interconnect Golden with the metro area. In three centuries, thousands of people will have lived here. We are just the first sixty.

11

Higher Returns on Investment

Twice the Satisfaction for Half the Resources

Efficiency is intelligent laziness.
   —David Dunham

Nature uses as little as possible of anything.
   —Johannes Keppler

When you have Enough, you have everything you need. There's nothing extra to weigh you down, distract, or distress you. Enough is a fearless place. A trusting place. An honest and self-observant place . . . To let go of clutter, then, is not deprivation; it's lightening up and opening up space and time for something new and wonderful to happen.
   —Vicki Robin

Simplicity is the ultimate sophistication.
   —Leonardo da Vinci

For all objects and experiences, there is a quantity that has optimum value. Above that quantity, the variable becomes toxic. To fall below that value is to be deprived.
   —Gregory Bateson

One of the most versatile tools we have for creating greater value from fewer resources is efficiency. In this time of great transition, we ask each other, a little desperately, *"What should we do now?"* The answer is simple: change our lifestyle to fit reality, rather than continuing to stretch reality to fit our addictive lifestyle. Although supplies of fossil fuels, minerals, and clean water are becoming less abundant and accessible, limitless reserves of human creativity remain untapped. We can use this nonpolluting source of energy to transition to a new way of valuing the world. That's what we're equipped to do: adapt, improvise, and create. However, if we refuse to make exciting, adventurous changes now, our options will quickly narrow. For one thing, nature is starting to look like the empty tables of a discount store during a going-out-of-business sale.

In our current economic paradigm, profits and prices are often the *only* variables considered in a given decision or transaction; "If it makes monetary sense, let's go with it." But in the next era—now coming clearly into focus—ecological efficiency will be the dominant accounting tool, because resource realities have radically changed in our generation. We've never lived in a world so stripped of natural abundance, and the world's population is growing at the rate of another Turkey-size country every year. Standard operating procedures are no longer appropriate. So accountants and investors will not just ask, "How much oil can be pumped, how fast?" but "How much expensive *energy* does it take to pump, ship, and refine the oil?" Not just, "How cheaply can we manufacture and market our widget?" but "How brilliantly can we design the product so it uses the least amount of resources possible, fits nature like a glove, and precisely meets the needs of people?" In other words, how much value do our efforts and designs actually deliver? Consumers of the near future will demand nothing less.

We'll base our economy on things like nutrition per molecule of food, and the *quality* of work accomplished per unit of energy. We'll buy houses based on how well they satisfy our needs per square foot; and evaluate the efficiency of a car not just by miles per gallon, but by the number of *people-miles per gallon*. These new ways of living won't be thought of as sacrifices, they'll just become part of a new everyday ethic—the way we do it now. In all likelihood, future generations will look back at our high-consumption era—before the change—and ask, "What the hell were they thinking? How could they be so sloppy?" (They may even include us in a lumped-together era known as the Dark Ages.)

➤ Hitting the Nail on the Head

I believe *meeting needs precisely* should be the fundamental organizing principle in creating a new civilization, one mind, one commitment, and one policy at a time. A needs-meeting approach answers the question, "Exactly what *results* do we get from our efforts, designs, and inputs?" I propose that we pay greater attention to what minds, bodies, nature, and culture really need, and *supply* those needs to create a trim, zero-waste, zero-regret lifestyle.

Simple. You and I don't have to be rocket or even rock scientists; we just have to get deeper satisfaction from more meaningful, better-designed products as well as nonmaterial forms of real wealth. In the following chapters, I suggest various ways to get more value out of the energy we use, the houses we live in, and the food we eat. I'm not talking about "back to the basics," but rather "forward to greater inspiration and satisfaction," by mindfully meeting needs more fully. What's log-jamming our era is that we try to meet so many human needs with purchased commodities that are poorly designed, out of scale, and filled with dubious ingredients.

Imagine a healthy, satisfied Pacific Islander relaxing in a hammock that swings gently in front of a seaside hut made from palm fronds. He plays a wooden flute for his family and himself, and for dinner, he picks delicious tropical fruits and enjoys fresh sunfish roasted on an open fire. His family feels happy—lucky to be alive. They are meeting physical, emotional and psychological needs directly. Suddenly, like a tsunami, affluenza sweeps across the island. "A businessman arrives," writes Jerry Mander, "buys all the land, cuts down the trees and builds a factory. He hires the native to work in it for money so that someday the native can afford canned fruit and fish from the mainland, a nice cinderblock house near the beach with a view of the water, and weekends off to enjoy it."[1]

Suddenly, like most of us, the family tries to meet needs with products of lesser quality and that cost huge amounts of life energy to buy. I'm not suggesting that we should all live in thatched-roof huts, but simply that we should rely on efficiency (no waste), sufficiency (the right amount), and design (the right stuff) to meet needs directly. (In addition, we should vote that invasive, profiteering company off the island!)

➤ Who Needs Wants?

I used to think that wants were somehow superior to needs—that as we progress from basics like food, housing, affection, identity, and community to "loftier" goals like speedboats, second homes, or Dom Perignon champagne, we automatically become happier. In recent years it's become clearer to me that if happiness, balance, and meaning are primary goals, we stand a better chance of achieving them by squarely meeting needs than by obediently chasing wants. Like the Pacific Islander who now punches a time clock, we aren't meeting our needs *well*. For example, the diet of many Americans isn't based on what human bodies need to be healthy. The human body requires certain minerals, enzymes, and amino acids, and is equipped to digest certain foods; but many are in the habit of ignoring these anthropological parameters. Instead many eat from brightly colored packages that contain energy in the wrong places; the processing, packaging, and delivery of the food is rich in energy but often the food itself is not!

When we meet needs poorly, the result is discomfort and vulnerability. Really, how can we expect junk food that delivers obesity, anxiety, gum disease, osteoporosis, diabetes, depression, heart disease, cancer—and more—to make us happy? Unfortunately, we get dissatisfaction and dysfunction instead, which often compel us to acquire even more consumer goods to "fill ourselves up." Lacking energy, buoyancy, and self-confidence, we become vulnerable to the booming voices of the Market. We continue to consume more than we need partly because we're not at ease. Besides nutrition, we fail to satisfy other physical needs, such as water, sleep, sex, and housing. And we fail to meet psychological and spiritual needs, too, such as affection, connection, autonomy, and spirituality.

On the physical side, if a person lives in a house with five or six extra rooms that are never used yet have to be maintained, heated, cooled, and amortized, do the benefits of that large house outweigh the liabilities? By living in more space than he or she needs, isn't this person creating discomfort elsewhere, for example in biological habitats that are severely damaged to harvest building materials? Or in the creation of catastrophic weather patterns caused by global warming, which is in turn partly caused by the energy that house uses? Even if this person doesn't realize it, side effects cascade exponentially back into his or her own life, and into the lives of many others.

Is our learned desire for a trophy house really more valuable than the deep-seated human need for a home (and environment) that teems with life? Do we feel so secure in our inside world that we're willing to give up the outside, natural world for it? Is the air-conditioned, sometimes toxic indoor-universe really meeting our needs?

Donella Meadows cuts to the core of needs meeting in the book *Beyond the Limits*:

- People don't need enormous cars; they need respect. They don't need closetsful of clothes; they need to feel attractive and they need excitement and variety and beauty.

- People don't need electronic entertainment; they need something worthwhile to do with their lives . . . People need identity, community, challenge, acknowledgment, love, joy.

- To try to fill these needs with material things is to set up an un-
  quenchable appetite for false solutions to real and never-satisfied
  problems. The resulting psychological emptiness is one of the major
  forces behind the desire for material growth.[2]

To build on Meadows's statement, it's not money or things per se that
we need, but *value*. Not coal or oil per se, but energy to refrigerate our food
and clean our clothes. Renewable sources of energy in conjunction with appliances that use less energy can deliver these services even better, overall;
they deliver services with fewer side effects. It's not meat per se we need
but protein, which is also contained in other, less resource-intensive foods.
It's not prescription pills we need, but a healthy lifestyle that prevents illness. We don't need an endless stream of negativity on the evening news
but rather stories that show us by example how to live ethically. It's not just
facts we need to teach and learn in our schools, but an understanding of relationships and how whole systems fit together. Our waste-filled, often misguided lifestyle keeps generating deficient products and services that miss
their targets—sometimes as widely as if acupuncture were applied randomly, or baseballs were thrown by a broken pitching machine.

➤ Getting Full Value

Let's face it, with larger populations consuming more stuff faster and
faster, we often feel overwhelmed by a world littered with Jetson-esque
viaducts, broken gadgets, and packing peanuts. A good half of the resources,
time, and human energy spent in our economy results in frustration, illness
shame, or guilt rather than real value. In a way, waste and dissatisfaction
have become America's most lucrative products. When resources seem infinite, who needs precision? When schedules are tight, who has time to care?
But believe it or not, these bad habits are actually *welcome* news in our time
of great change, because they provide a bridge to a better quality of life. By
reducing the waste and carelessness that now litter our economy—with better design, greater efficiency, and less consumption—we can finance the
coming transition to a less destructive, more satisfying future.

Our economic strategy will change—from using resources *quickly* to
using resources *well*. By getting greater value from each molecule, each
electron, each drop of water, as well as each moment, we can create richer
lives without sacrifice. The new American lifestyle is not about what we
give up (remember, we only need to get rid of the dysfunction and excess)
but what we *get*.

➤ Wanted: Better Ways to Satisfy Needs

A central theme of this book is that when we become obsessed with *wants*, the root cause may be that we're off balance because of the dysfunctional ways we try to meet our needs. Our relationships aren't satisfying, our drinking water is contaminated, we aren't stimulated by our work, and so on. We're taught in school and in the media that basic needs are already achieved for most Americans; and that, in any case, meeting needs is not as worthwhile and "fun" as is satisfying wants. But I strongly disagree. Many billionaire CEOs hope we remain meekly dependent on deficient products, services, and experiences because, when we take charge of meeting some of our own needs (such as entertaining ourselves, maintaining our health, or changing our own oil), we don't consume as much. In a wasteful, design-challenged economy that often leaves us feeling empty, my priority is to

◆ The Excessive Material "Needs" of an ◆ Average American Lifetime

During its life, the average American baby will consume 3.6 million pounds of minerals, metals, and fuels! Now multiply that times 300 million . . . By using more efficient technology, reducing waste, and knowing when enough is enough in our personal lives, we can easily cut that mountain of materials in half.

572,052 pounds of coal	1.64 million pounds of stone, sand, and gravel	82,634 gallons of petroleum
69,789 pounds of cement	34,045 pounds of iron ore	25,244 pounds of phosphate rock
6,176 pounds of bauxite	1.692 Troy ounces of gold	22,388 pounds of clay
1,544 pounds of copper	31,266 pounds of salt	28,564 pounds of misc. minerals, metals
849 pounds of zinc	5.59 million cubic feet of natural gas	849 pounds of lead

Source: Mineral Information Institute, Golden, Colorado (www.mii.org), 2005

slow down, fully satisfy needs, and let the wants go find some other sucker. "For fast-acting relief," suggests Lily Tomlin, "try slowing down."

Mario Kamenetzky, formerly with the World Bank, wrote, "Human needs are ontological facts of life. Failure to satisfy them results in progressive human malfunctions, whereas unsatisfied wants lead to little worse than frustration."[3] Yet, in our world, the two categories often get mushed together like wads of Silly Putty. Wants become perceived "needs." For example, in a recent USA Today poll, 46 percent could not even imagine life without a personal computer (38 percent specified with "high-speed Internet"), and 41 percent felt the same way about their cell phone. But I'm guessing many could quite easily imagine life without leafy greens or organic grains rich in essential minerals.

A moment of truth—an "aha" moment—comes when we realize we've been duped by a value system based primarily on material objects and values. We realize that the way we live now is just something the marketers and inventors made up! In many cases, it's not based on biological or even psychological needs, but simply on the fact that someone has invented something (often accidentally) and wants to make a buck. In our way of life, we're instructed to select happiness from an endless display of goods and services—many of them defective or wasteful—but there's very little education about how to have "enough," the perfect amount. After being told three million times that Frosted Flakes contains more happiness than oatmeal does, we begin to believe it. But our bodies, psyches, and even bank accounts tell us differently.

Many are familiar with Abraham Maslow's hierarchy of needs. A pioneer of the Human Potential Movement, Maslow theorized that by meeting material needs (e.g., sleep, food, and water) and social needs (e.g., safety, security, and self-esteem), we ascend through moral needs (e.g., truth, justice and meaning) to the apex of the pyramid: self-actualization (presumably, only a few rungs from Heaven). This model is actually very useful, because it illustrates that humans can become truly satisfied by meeting anthropological needs.

However, Maslow's model has several shortcomings, in my opinion. First, being a hierarchy, it implies that we must rise above the muck of survival needs to become happy; that a low-income person struggling to put food on the table can't have a strong sense of justice, beauty, or self-esteem. Secondly, it doesn't evaluate how well a need is met. How clean are the air and water that meet our survival needs at the base of the pyramid? How resilient is the community in which we exchange affection, love, and acceptance? Precisely how are security needs met—with a $400 billion military budget, or a sense of trust in your neighbors?

As I began to research this book, a colleague asked if I'd seen the needs analysis work of Chilean economist Manfred Max-Neef. In the book *Real-life Economics,* edited by Max-Neef and Paul Ekins, I found a great "lens" for looking at value. Max-Neef's work is right in line with the scope of this book. Max-Neef proposes that in contrast to wants, which are infinite and essentially insatiable, basic needs are "finite, few, and classifiable." (What a relief—they are actually achievable!) "Needs are the same in all cultures and all historical periods," he writes. "Whether a person belongs to a consumerist or to an ascetic society, his/her fundamental human needs are the same . . . What changes, both over time and through cultures, is the *way* the needs are satisfied."[4]

Bingo. That's a major reason why we consume more than "enough": because of the excessive and shoddy ways we try to satisfy our needs. Our culture has been clobbered by advertising, peer pressure, defective economic policies, and the encoded emotions of fear, insecurity, and doubt. In addition, we're programmed to believe that natural ways of meeting needs are inferior, though a sizable chunk of our economy is beginning to question that programming. "Alternative" health and wellness practices—many of which have been around for thousands of years—are coming back into the mainstream. For example, many insurance companies now pay for chiropractics and acupuncture. Organic food—which we've eaten for 99.9999 . . . percent of our time as a species—is becoming normal or at least acceptable once again. People are beginning to actually understand what their bodies need, to feel healthy and content.

Commenting on the Max-Neef model, Terry Gips, president of the Alliance for Sustainability, says, "The good news ecologically is that it is possible to actually have more satisfaction with less stuff, because it's not the materials and energy that provide satisfaction, but the degree to which basic needs are met." Gips is a longtime advocate of sustainability who uses the Max-Neef matrix of needs in workshops and presentations to demonstrate how we often miss the mark, remaining dissatisfied. "It's a great tool for helping people find shared values," says Gips. "I used Max-Neef's ideas in a design workshop for a $2.7 million renovation of a Minneapolis church. Our discussion about the interrelationship of needs resulted in a space that people love to use for meetings, that's easier for custodians to clean, that has better lighting, and that has operable windows for greater comfort and participation."[5]

By choosing more appropriate satisfiers for each of Max-Neef's nine fundamental needs—subsistence, protection/security, affection, understanding, participation, leisure, creation, identity/meaning, and freedom—we can be happier with less consumption. One of the reasons why is that

· Fundamental Human Needs Matrix, · by Manfred Max-Neef

Fundamental Human Needs	Being (qualities)	Having (things)	Doing (actions)	Interacting (settings)
Subsistence	physical and mental health	food, shelter, work	feed, clothe, rest, work	living environment, social setting
Protection	care, adaptability, autonomy	social security, health systems, work	cooperate, plan, take care of, help	social environment, dwelling
Affection	respect, sense of humor, generosity, sensuality	friendships, family, relationships with nature	share, take care of, make love, express emotions	privacy, intimate spaces of togetherness
Understanding	critical capacity, curiosity, intuition	literature, teachers, policies, educational	analyze, study, meditate, investigate,	schools, families, universities, communities
Participation	receptiveness, dedication, sense of humor	responsibilities, duties, work, rights	cooperate, dissent, express opinions	associations, parties, churches, neighborhoods
Leisure	imagination, tranquility, spontaneity	games, parties, peace of mind	daydream, remember, relax, have fun	landscapes, intimate spaces, places to be alone
Creation	imagination, boldness, inventiveness, curiosity	abilities, skills, work, techniques	invent, build, design, work, compose, interpret	spaces for expression, workshops, audiences

Fundamental Human Needs	Being (qualities)	Having (things)	Doing (actions)	Interacting (settings)
Identity	sense of belonging, self-esteem, consistency	language, religions, work, customs, values, norms	get to know oneself, grow, commit oneself	places one belongs to, everyday settings
Freedom	autonomy, passion, self-esteem, open-mindedness	equal rights	dissent, choose, run risks, develop awareness	anywhere

choosing the most complete satisfier fulfills more than one need at a time. We also pay attention to the needs of other people and the environment, becoming something grander than an ego in the process.

For example, feeding a baby with formula meets nutritional needs fairly well (depending on the brand); but breast feeding, in addition to giving the baby better nutrition, also supplies a mutual need for bonding, affection, and building the infant's self-esteem. Similarly, a prescription drug may treat the symptoms of an ailment, but preventive health approaches are more likely to treat the *cause* of the illness (such as stress, or unhealthy diet). They meet the human needs for participation (e.g., in one's own health) and for understanding (e.g., how nature works). They also avoid bizarre side effects like my mother experienced: She took a drug to reduce cholesterol that also reduced her ability to use her hands effectively.

When needs remain unmet but we reach for wants anyway, we leave gaping holes in our lives. "Any fundamental need that is not adequately satisfied reveals a human poverty," writes Max-Neef. Some examples are: poverty of subsistence (due to insufficient income, food, shelter, etc.), of understanding (due to poor quality of education), and of participation (due to discrimination against women, children, and minorities). We face similar poverties throughout our economy. There are far too many side effects in the way we eat, sleep, form community, create housing, and get around. Basic needs remain unmet because of bad choices, design flaws, and inefficiencies. As a result, we feel physically and psychologically deficient, which we try to overcome by consuming *more* defective goods and services. When we relearn how to meet fundamental needs well, many of the wants will just wither away, because we'll feel more self-reliant, and more content.

➤ *Do* You Get What You Need?
Sex, Sleep, Food, and Water

Max-Neef considers the way a culture meets needs a defining aspect of that culture. This is a key concept for the themes in this book, because many of the ways we meet needs are flawed, superficial, and based strictly on that abstraction known as currency; on quantity rather than quality. Because individuals learn behavior culturally, our challenge is to reshape our culture to fit reality.

We are so accustomed to buying our lives that we forget we can meet many needs *naturally.* For example, frequent sex (once or twice a week) has been proven to deliver various physical benefits such as 30 percent higher levels of immunoglobulin A, which boosts the immune system. A large percentage of the advertising that bombards us capitalizes on the benefits and compulsions of sex. Although it's true that even a prostitute could supply some of the physical benefits, to satisfy basic needs for affection, trust, and emotional connection, only real intimacy will work. It is for this reason that men who have a significant bond with another person are half as likely to have a fatal heart attack. And studies have shown that the hugs that accompany a close relationship dramatically lower blood pressure and boost blood levels of stress-reducing oxytocin, especially in women. When researchers asked couples to sit close to one another and talk for ten minutes, then share a long hug, they measured slight positive changes in both blood pressure and oxytocin.[6]

What about sleep, another of Max-Neef's subsistence needs? It's clear that various substances in our familiar, hyperactive lifestyle often sabotage sleep, which we compensate for with sleeping pills. Our bodies become battlegrounds of conflicting biochemical responses. Contentedness is not really a possibility when we're exhausted from sleeplessness, but vulnerability and loss of self-esteem are.

Habits clash with biology when we eat large meals before going to bed. We need about three hours to digest dinner but sometimes, especially in European cultures that dine late, we are still digesting as we try to sleep. The average American consumes about two to three cups of coffee a day. But many also consume two or more caffeinated sodas and a little chocolate, too, resulting in sheep counting, mantra reciting, and compulsive snacking in the wee hours. And caffeine isn't the only stimulant that screws up our sleep; although alcohol relaxes us when we drink it, it later becomes a stimulant. Once again, moderation is the way to go. Beyond "enough" is the "too much" that keeps us awake. (The word "moderation" doesn't apply to tobacco, another substance that disrupts sleep, because its main appeal is that it's a legal addiction. As someone who was once briefly addicted, I say, Just don't go there!) We sometimes think a given problem is all in our head, but often it's in our endocrine system or stomach. If we are dehydrated, our body feels a sense of alarm—"something is wrong"—which can also disrupt sleep. (But the right time to drink water is in the morning and afternoon, not evening).

According to psychologist Richard Friedman, it's quite normal to wake up in the middle of the night, as many humans and animals do routinely. It's even physiologically normal to be awake for an hour or two. The problem comes when the "gears" begin to turn and we become increasingly conscious; thoughts begin to focus on what needs to be done tomorrow and what we did wrong yesterday. I keep a good magazine by the bed for when that happens, and I'm learning that after a half hour of article reading, I fall back to sleep without any negative consequences. If I get less sleep than usual, I make sure to exercise the next day and stay away from processed food. I don't feel sleep deprived, and I sleep fine the next night. It really helps to know that nature will provide the sleep we need.

In the United States, we eat slightly more than a ton of food a year (and it sometimes seems like a large portion of that is consumed on Thanksgiving Day). But how much of that food supplies nutrients our bodies and psyches can actually use? Does the American diet really meet our needs? The federal government's Food Guide Pyramid recommends a diet high in fruits, vegetables, whole grains, low-fat milk, lean meats, poultry, fish, beans, eggs, and nuts; and low in saturated fats, trans fats, cholesterol, salt, and added sugars. But to the average American, it's too boring to eat vegetables (because they typically aren't fresh) or to learn what exactly a trans fat is. So this average American simplifies—and companies like Kraft, ConAgra, and PepsiCo are delighted to help.

Says anthropologist Katharine Milton, "A wild monkey eats better than Americans do!" The monkey has a diet richer in essential vitamins and minerals, fatty acids, and dietary fiber than the more intelligent (ahem) *Homo sapiens americanus*. Milton followed monkeys through tropical rain forests with plastic bags, picking up the food they dropped from the trees. "They would bite off the tips of leaves and throw the rest away," says Milton, who analyzed the leaves and found that the tips were especially nutritious. If

Americans followed a similar strategy, would we eat the cardboard box a fast-food burger comes in, for the fiber, and throw away the fatty burger and white bread bun? Research now pouring in about excessive fat, sugar, and refined carbohydrates tends to suggest that. Even meat, an American institution, is coming under fire. In today's news, federal health officials have approved the spraying of bacteria-eating viruses onto meat and poultry products just before they are packaged. This approval is well intentioned, since meat infected with the listeria bacteria does infect an estimated 2,500 Americans every year, killing 500.[8]

Yet, a more systemic problem is the way meat is produced, with a potential for contamination on a much larger scale. Forced to eat grain and beans they aren't equipped to digest well, and housed in close quarters where disease spreads quickly, livestock are routinely injected with heavy doses of antibiotics. Mutant strains of bacteria may evolve resistance to the antibiotics, in effect making feedlots potential "bacteria factories." A case in point is the recent, widespread contamination of spinach with a strain of E. coli that grows in the stomachs of grain fed cows but not grass-fed cows. Apparently, some of the manure got into the irrigation water of farms in the region.

In terms of overall calories, the government's Center for Nutritional Policy recommends from 1,600 calories for sedentary women and older adults to 2,800 calories for teenage boys and active adults; but Americans wolf an average of 3,800 calories. This tally includes two-fifths more refined grains and a fourth more of both added fats and sugars than in 1985. We're literally consuming more than enough, eating as much for "fun" as we are for health. As with other matters concerning health and the environment, scientists can't seem to figure out *what humans should be eating.* We don't differentiate between good fats and bad, good carbs and bad, good sugars and bad. We act as if we're carnivores, hunting ground chuck and veal cutlets like the great cats of the Serengeti hunt gazelles and wildebeests. But anatomy may tell a different story.

"I think the evidence is pretty clear," says cardiologist William C. Roberts, from the beefy state of Texas. "Humans are not physiologically designed to eat meat. If you look at the various characteristics of carnivores versus herbivores, it doesn't take a genius to see where humans line up." (He points out that while a carnivore's intestinal tract is three times its body length, an herbivore's is twelve times its body length, and humans are closer to herbivores. Our digestion takes place without benefit of strong acids in the intestine, as carnivores have. Herbivores (and humans) chew their food before swallowing with grinding molars, whereas carnivores rip meat in chunks with incisors and swallow it whole. Herbivores and humans get vitamin C from their diets, but carnivores make it internally.

Although it's not likely that most humans will suddenly decide to become vegetarian, why not pay attention to the way human bodies actually work? Why can't we share a few great vegetarian recipes with each other and decide to eat one-third less meat, or even just a tenth less? Albert Einstein, himself a vegetarian, believed that, "Nothing will benefit human health and increase the chances for survival of life on Earth as much as the evolution to a vegetarian diet." And Thomas Jefferson, who lived to be eighty-three— pretty good for his day—ate meat "as a condiment to the vegetables which constitute my principal diet." When we reduce the space allocated to billions of grazing, chewing, squealing, tail-swishing livestock (about twenty billion of them!), we'll free space for other uses: open space or wilderness, which will make nature more resilient and humans healthier; the growing of cellulosic crops (maybe algae) for vehicle fuels; and a place for additional homes and communities, since world and U.S. populations continue to expand. With less meat in our diets, we'll also use much less energy per capita (since nitrogen fertilizer is made from fossil fuel), generate far fewer greenhouse gases, and conserve water for more critical uses, such as drinking, sanitation, and the irrigation of fruits and vegetables.

We're not meeting the need for water, either. Says physician and water expert Fereydoon Batmanghelidj, "People in industrialized countries aren't sick, they're thirsty!" He's documented a link between dehydration and inflammation; heartburn; back, joint, and stomach problems; digestive difficulties; blood pressure problems; diabetes; depression; stress; and being overweight. Professor Friedrich Manz of the Research Institute of Child Nutrition in Dortmund, Germany, reports that students should be drinking 20 percent more water, because dehydration also causes an inability to focus. What's the right amount to drink? Instead of counting glassfuls, Batmanghelidj counsels, "You can tell if you've had enough water, because your urine will be colorless."[9] A general rule of thumb is that 20 percent of the liquids we need come from food, and, in season, I can easily get that amount with just peaches and plums.

Why should it surprise us that our bodies require water? The human brain is 75 percent water; muscles, 75 percent; and even "bone-dry" bones are 22 percent water. Water is needed (in blood) to carry nutrients and oxygen to cells, and helps convert food into energy, remove waste, moisten oxygen for breathing, regulate body temperature, and—the grand finale— create life. But although the need for water is indisputable, the ability to continue to meet that need well is less certain. Water tables are falling throughout the world, reservoirs are filling up with silt, and our use of water is often very careless, especially when subsidies keep costs artificially low in agriculture or industry.

But water is far from free; in my hometown, its price has jumped from $1.85 per thousand gallons to $3.85 in just the last six years. My neighbors and I feel very fortunate to have purchased water rights for our community garden in 2001—accessed from an irrigation ditch with a solar-powered pump—because our half-acre shared garden and orchard uses as much as half a million gallons of water every growing season—more than a thousand dollars of value at potable water prices.

While each American drinks a daily four to ten glasses of water and other beverages, the amount of water our food "drinks" in the fields and processing plants is more like 2,000 gallons a day. About an equal amount is used in the United States by the power industry to cool natural gas turbines as well as nuclear cooling towers. (In the broiling summer of 2006, nuclear plants in both the United States and Europe were forced to shut down because cooling water from ponds and rivers wasn't cool enough to ensure safety.) So really, the best ways to conserve water are to pay attention to what we eat, and to use energy efficiently. It's also very important to use water-efficient fixtures in the home, and landscaping that minimizes water use. The 100 gallons a day that we each use in our homes can easily be cut by a third to a half by substituting efficient conveyances—in the form of well-designed fixtures, showerheads, toilets, and aerators—for resources. The need for water will only get stronger, since the global populations continue to expand, but the amount of fresh water remains exactly the same.

➤ Efficiency and Sufficiency

The consumption of resources for tangible needs, such as lights, heating, mobility, food, and water, can be delivered with a higher level of ingenuity and more mindfulness about what result we are trying to achieve. When we choose the right size, the right time, and the right place for both devices and actions, saving resources becomes automatic. However, the way we meet intangible needs, such as affection, creativity, identity, and freedom, isn't usually a question of engineering or design, but rather psychology and behavior. That makes them no less of a problem; if the intangible needs remain unmet, we cling to consumption and careless technologies as would-be pathways to satisfaction.

12

Energy Savings

Finessing the Carbon Conundrum

Our energy supply will become increasingly diverse, dispersed, and renewable. In time, centrally located, traditional thermal-power plants will come to be sentimentally admired, like Victorian steamships are for us.
—Amory Lovins

Suburbia, 2012—The microwave beeps nonstop as Eric and Margo Petrovich set the table for dinner. They're listening to a feature story on National Public Radio about the rising costs of energy, water, and food, a topic much in the news these days. The year 2012 has been a wakeup call for the fifty-something couple whose four-bedroom Colorado home is becoming less affordable every month. They've talked about moving to a smaller, more efficient house—closer to their jobs, stores, parks, and theaters— with good solar orientation and insulation. But they really hate to give up their big suburban backyard, and what would they do with all the antiques they refinished themselves?

"It's true that roughly half of the world's oil reserves are still in the ground," an expert explains on the radio, "but the fact is that it's more expensive to get these low-grade, remotely located supplies. More importantly, we need more oil than we can get, since world oil production has reached its peak and will soon begin to decline. *Global demand now exceeds supply, it's that simple*; we want more than we can have. As prices rise for food, fuel, medicine, and consumer products, we are finally seeing how dependent we are on fossil fuels in agriculture, transportation, food processing, and the chemical industry . . . That's why oil at a hundred and twenty dollars a barrel is having such a ripple effect on our daily lives . . ."

"Why didn't we see this coming?" Margo comments as they sit down.

"Why didn't we insist on more efficient vehicles and appliances back in the seventies? . . . New sources of energy and new ways to make chemicals from plants and waste?"

"Well, at least we're learning to use renewable energy," says Eric. "Did you know that wind energy now supplies electricity for seventy-five million of the world's households? That's about one-thirtieth of the electricity we need, and growing fast . . ."

They both want to feel secure and upbeat about the future, but instead they feel a little overwhelmed by the lifestyle changes that face them. Since 2006, the cost of gasoline has risen 300 percent, and the price of natural gas has increased sixfold as Canadian supplies became less dependable. Steadily expanding demand for large homes, hot tubs, computers, HDTVs, and an infinite fleet of must-have appliances has been matched by a persistent thirst for fuel. Record-setting weather extremes haven't helped, either. While there are now many models of hybrids and flexible fuel vehicles on the market, most of America's 230 million vehicles are still gas guzzlers, and it takes ten or fifteen years to replace that many vehicles. In 2012, Americans drive 25 trillion miles a year (the equivalent of a billion times around the earth), and some households are paying $200 or more a week just for gasoline. Eric and Margo's household, which accounts for 31,000 of those miles, is one of them.

The typical front lawn is not quite as shamrock-green as it used to be, as the price of water continues to rise, and Eric's and Margo's big backyard is becoming an expensive luxury. Last year they spent more than $700 to water, fertilize, and mow it, and they are now considering taking some of the lawn out and planting a few fruit trees in one corner of the yard, and a bed of strawberries in the other. Like the rest of us, they're feeling the pinch of rising food prices, and they're reading up on techniques like "biointensive" gardening that supplies cartloads of food from small, well-tended spaces. Says Eric, "I didn't realize there were so many hidden costs in things like packaging and processed food." With all the recent media exposure, he's learned that nitrogen fertilizer is made from natural gas, that conventional pesticides are made from oil, and that producing a single hamburger patty uses enough energy to drive 20 miles. The water expended to produce that burger could supply half a year's worth of hot showers.

"Instead of Wheaties or Heart Smart, we may as well call cereal Petro Flakes," jokes Eric, "because the grinding, milling, wetting, drying, and baking of a breakfast cereal requires about four calories of energy for every calorie of food energy it produces. A two-pound bag of breakfast cereal burns the energy of a half-gallon of gasoline to manufacture." As you can see, Eric is beginning to dimly understand how much energy is contained in standard, energy-hungry products such as aluminum, plastic, cement, computers, drinking water, and cars. For example, that the manufacture of an average desktop computer uses more than ten times its weight in fossil fuels and materials.

Even energy itself "costs" more energy the deeper and more remotely we drill and mine. The oil industry once produced about hundred barrels of oil for each barrel of oil spent to bring the oil to market, but in today's economy each barrel returns less than ten. Many people are reassured because of the abundance of coal, biomass, tar sands, and hydrogen, overlooking the fact that it takes a lot of energy to convert these materials into transportation fuel.

These days, Eric and Margo hear unfamiliar words like benzene, anhydrous ammonia, and polyvinyl chloride more than they really want to. These are all petrochemicals used to produce such familiar products as plastic, shirts, cleaners, adhesives, surgical gloves, safety glass, watchbands, building insulation, electrical insulation, packaging, lubrication, and pipes for plumbing. And every day the couple hears news stories about energy supply glitches that shut down factories, cause airline delays, or cause power outages in hospitals. "When a backup generator failed in a Saint Louis hospital," writes a *New York Times* reporter, "donor organs were lost, operations were terminated or completed under flashlights. Temperatures in the hospital hovered near a hundred degrees . . ."

The Colorado couple is learning that a scarcity of resources means more than rising prices. When there isn't enough energy to go around, choices need to be made about *who will get the energy*—commuters, farmers, food processors, residents of trophy homes, surgeons, snow plowers, or vacationers? Answer: whoever pays the highest price. They're also realizing how energy-hungry their own habits are. For example, many of their friends live across the city, and it costs 2 gallons of gas to go see them. Keeping up with the latest media gadgets requires "buying" all the energy that goes into the manufacture, distribution and packaging of each new toy. Every long-distance vacation they take is filled with energy, and so are the clothes, furniture, and appliances their current lifestyle seems to require.

➤ Peak Civilization

Earth scientists can't definitively explain where all the oil we've been consuming came from, but their best guess is that most was formed when the algae and plankton that flourished in warm, ancient seas settled in thick deposits on ocean floors, some of which later became dry land. We have a better handle on where it ended up: in the fuels whose emissions are toxic in any form; and in such products as crayons, ink, bubble gum, dishwashing liquids, deodorant, eyeglasses, tires, ammonia, plastic bags, allergy pills, asphalt, shirts, and heart valves. In today's market, it's just the opposite: three-fourths of our consumer goods are made from fossil fuels. In contrast, as recently as 1950, three-fourths of all the consumer goods we used were made from natural materials, such as wood, rubber, and cotton.

An eye-opening article on the Energy Bulletin Web site, called "The Long Fingers of Petroleum," pictures a Boston lawyer standing in his driveway, next to his Porsche 911 Turbo. As each petroleum-related aspect of his life is considered, we imagine a world without oil, and remove the item from the scene:

> John is wearing a nice suit and tie. Unfortunately, the suit is wool and polyester, the buttons are plastic as well as the zipper in the pants. Remove 25% of the material from his suit, all elastic and plastic stays, the buttons and the zipper. Why? Polyester, dacron, rayon, orlon—are all petroleum-based, human-made fibers. All plastic is petroleum based, as is elastic. Better get rid of the waistband on his under shorts too while we are at it. Abruptly, our friend John is rather chilly, as what is left of his suit, pants, shirt and undershorts have fallen around his ankles.[1]

John's glasses have polycarbonate lenses, and the frames are also plastic. He stands bewildered, as credit cards, shoe heels, watchband, driver's license, and the bills in his wallet (printed with petroleum-based ink) all disappear. Then he realizes that his car is useless, without gasoline; its transmission fluid, gear oil, brake fluid, grease, automotive paint, tires, steering wheel, and all the plastic-insulated wires likewise disappear. Now, naked, broke, partially blind, and extremely embarrassed, he turns to go inside to see what's left of his house!

John's predicament helps us realize what "peak oil" really means: that the emperor has no clothes. Along with peak oil, we may soon hear phrases like "peak grain production" and "peak water consumption," because we are reaching supply limits for these basic resources as well. A recent U.S. Department of Agriculture bulletin announced, "World grain supplies are expected to be much tighter in 2006/07, boosting global grain prices. Rising consumption is expected to outstrip production for the second straight year, which would push world grain ending stocks to their lowest levels in more than 25 years." Put simply, there are too many mouths to feed, and too many of those mouths are eating energy-intensive food (grain-fed meat, heavily packaged, processed, and transported). Grain-based ethanol will also be in the competition. Especially troubling is China's rising appetite for grain. As that country's standard of living continues to rise, their diet contains a larger percentage of grain-fed, energy-intensive livestock products such as pork, poultry, eggs, beef, and milk. The recent opening of a handful of drive-through McDonald's restaurants in China (among eight hundred mostly sit-down locations, total) is significant; the Chinese automobile market is expanding as fast as is its taste for Big Macs.

➤ The Carbon Conundrum

Says Harvard psychology professor Daniel Gilbert, "No one seems to care about the upcoming attack on the World Trade Center site. Why? Because it won't involve villains with box cutters. Instead, it will involve melting ice sheets that swell the oceans and turn that particular block of lower Manhattan into an aquarium." He argues that human reactions are often based on morals and emotions, not facts. "When people feel insulted or disgusted, they generally do something about it, such as whacking each other over the head, or voting . . . If climate change were caused by a brutal dictator or an evil empire, the war on warming would be this nation's top priority . . . Or if it were caused by gay sex, millions of protesters would be massing in the streets."[2]

No, it isn't a brutal dictator that causes global warming, it's Pop-Tarts, chilly movie theaters on hot days, and Hummers. In a frenzy of consumption, we've mined geologically massive quantities of carbon from below the ground and redistributed it above the ground. In the planet's atmosphere, it creates a translucent blanket that holds heat in (another example of putting something in the wrong place). It's that simple. The maddening, slow motion debate over the human role in global warming continues, but really, it doesn't matter whose "fault" it is. The Earth is heating up, in direct proportion to the blanket of carbon dioxide, methane, and other gases building up in the atmosphere—just as Nobel Prize–winning scientist Svante Arhenius predicted back in 1896. Without further "fiddling," we need to control the emissions that are in our power—literally—to control.

Anyone who's ever climbed into a sweltering car on a hot summer day has experienced the greenhouse effect that causes global warming. The rolled-up car windows are the greenhouse gases, and the broiling person— or panting, dehydrated dog—is the Earth. Those who insist this effect could never occur on a planetary scale need only view photographs of cloud-covered Venus, where the temperature today will be about 850 degrees Fahrenheit. Or else read a detailed Earth science textbook that relates the history of anaerobic bacteria. Many eons ago, these oxygen-hating microbes were the planet's headliner species, and when they began to run out of hydrogen—an essential element for building cellular structure—they improvised a way to tear apart water molecules to get it. They made use of the hydrogen but brainlessly dumped massive quantities of oxygen into the biosphere. Oops. Their minute but ubiquitous actions began to render the Earth's surface unfit for their own habitation, except in stinky (to us), oxygen-starved places like swamp slimes. Then evolution's greatest innovation, photosynthesis, made matters even worse for the anaerobes, since plants and photosynthesizing microbes take up carbon dioxide but "exhale" oxygen.

The lesson is this: When you mess with the bio-geological cycles of elements like carbon, nitrogen, and oxygen, Mother Nature comes unglued. So, to avoid further wrath, let's quickly absorb the carbon back out of the atmosphere by farming organically (which sequesters carbon dioxide in the soil and crops), by planting and maintaining billions of CO_2-utilizing trees, by reducing the planetary herd of livestock (now about fifteen to twenty billion methane-emitting animals), and by reducing the amount of greenhouse gases our technologies and activities emit. As I write this, more than three hundred U.S. cities have declared their intent to operate under the agreements of the Kyoto Protocol. Why can't individuals accept a similar challenge? What steps can the above-average American take to cut his or her resource use (and emissions) roughly in half, without reducing quality of life? Can YOU accept the challenge of cutting your resource use in half in the next ten years?

By generating energy at or close to the point of use, we can reduce the loss of energy in transmission lines, and also meet some of our own energy needs. Credit: Eric Wahl

✦ Ten Ways to Cut Individual Energy Consumption in Half ✦

- Tune up your house (see suggestions that follow).

- Downsize your house and car—and your expenses.

- Eat one-third less meat.

- Use carbohydrate fuel (food) rather than fossil fuels, by being more active.

- Live in a neighborhood that requires less driving.

- Use highly efficient public transportation.

- Reduce the amount of energy-intensive packaging you use.

- Replace part of your lawn with something you can eat.

- Buy durable, high-quality products and learn how to maintain them.

- Learn to enjoy forms of entertainment other than fuel-hungry, mind-numbing media.

Energy use in the United States is roughly divided into three sectors: industrial, residential/commercial, and transportation. The products, infrastructure, and services Americans consume add up to the highest per capita use of energy in the world. American consumers are directly responsible for half the energy and materials used in this country's economy, largely in the residential and transportation sectors. Designers, architects, engineers, and politicians *directly* affect much of the rest because the use of land, the design/operation of technology, and the implementation of policies are all major factors in how much energy we use.

Energy consumption per capita is calculated by dividing the total amount of energy consumed in a country by that country's population. We each have a share in the relative efficiency of the whole economy, and our informed participation in policy making can and must improve that overall efficiency (For example, we can vote for transportation choices like light rail and high speed rail that are more efficient than cars). An important reason why Europeans consume less energy per person than Americans is that EU populations are denser, their homes and yards are smaller, and public transportation is readily available, all of which result in greater efficiencies. The average car in the United States

---

· Per capita consumption by selected countries ·

(million BTU)

U.S. 340	Russia 203	Germany 173	Japan 176	China 35

One BTU is roughly the energy a wooden match has. So we Americans
annually burn the equivalent of 340 million matches, per capita!

Source: U.S. Energy Information Agency (2005)

---

travels 10 percent farther per year than a British car and 50 percent more
than a German car.[3] In addition, Europeans are more likely to value public amenities. In Denmark, for example, where bike and rail infrastructure is well used, 30 percent of all households don't even own a car.
West Europeans in general use public transit for 10 percent of all urban
trips—and Canadians for 7 percent—whereas, in the U.S., transit use is
only 2 percent.

Personal consumption is less of an obsession in Europe, where more
time is spent on energy-neutral activities such as lively conversation,
reading, gourmet cooking, civic celebrations, and direct participation in
sports. Europeans have a stronger environmental ethic; there's less food
waste and much higher recycling rates. Manufacturers are more conscious of designing regional systems that conserve resources. It simply
takes less energy and fewer materials to live a good life in many parts of
Europe.

Americans are at a disadvantage in several critical ways concerning
personal consumption. We've become accustomed to the luxury of extra-
large everything; convenience, comfort, and lack of responsibility are perceived necessities; we've lost many of our maintenance and craft skills; we
don't know how to entertain ourselves; and we've built a car-and-suburb
culture that can't just be quickly rearranged. (So much energy and effort
has been sunk into roads, energy grids, building materials, and construction
that it will take at least a generation to reshape it.) To symbolically comply
as individuals with the Kyoto Protocol and reduce personal consumption to
half our current levels, we'll have to try a bit harder than EU citizens, but
why not make it an "energy Olympics" that can spin off millions of jobs and
ultimately save trillions of dollars? Are we Americans so out of shape that
we can't compete?

◆ Prioritized, Street-Smart Remedies for Auto-Dependency

1. Stay out of your car. Live where you can meet more needs on foot and by shar-ing rides. The greenest vehicle of all is the one that doesn't get driven much. Even an SUV is far greener when it has multiple riders. When you do drive, combine er-rands. Shop on the Internet when it makes sense; telecommute or consider be-coming self-employed. Investigate home delivery of groceries from the whole foods store. Start a food co-op. Promote teleconferencing and high-speed rail. Challenge yourself to try car-free vacations!

2. Purchase a high-efficiency hybrid or a conventional high-performer like Toy-ota Corolla, Honda Civic, Saturn Ion, or Chevy Cobalt.

3. If buying a new car isn't in the budget, buy a used, highly efficient vehicle. Consider retrofitting your car to a natural gas-fueled or electricity-powered car. Visit the offices of your political representatives with a small group of friends and neighbors to advocate much higher fuel efficiency standards: 44 mpg for cars, 35 mpg for trucks.

4. Get back on the old (or new) bike: Cycling is the most efficient form of transportation yet invented. In Davis, California, 80 percent of the streets have bike lanes, and 20 to 25 percent of all local trips are by bike. Imagine a world designed for bicycles, with safe bike lanes, bikes with trailers, electric bikes, and folding bikes that are easy to take on a bus or train. In the past twenty years, Germany has tripled the length of its nationwide bikeways, and the Netherlands has doubled its network. All over the Netherlands, parking for bi-cycles far exceeds spaces for cars at railway stations as a result of customer demand.

5. Learn to love public transit. After a few years of taking a comfortable re-gional bus to work, I was hooked. No more hunting for a parking place; extra time for reading, sleeping, and conversing. Now I'm very excited about light rail coming to my town! When Boulder, Colorado, reorganized its transit system, substituting minibuses for the big old dinosaur buses, and introducing a city-wide Eco Pass that buys a year's travel for just $50, the share of trips made by transit increased from 1.6 percent to 4.6 percent.

6. Try a car-sharing program, if you live in one of the more than forty American cities that now has a car-sharing organization. These European-inspired, rent-by-the-hour businesses enable a household to eliminate one or all cars in the household fleet. This not only saves payment, maintenance, insurance, and other costs, but equally as important, teaches participants how to avoid making unnecessary trips, how to break the cycle of auto-dependent behavior.

7. Keep your vehicle well tuned and tires inflated. Regular oil changes, air-filter changes, and spark plug replacements improve fuel economy. Buy low-rolling-resistance (LRR) replacement tires. Minimize evaporation of fuel and keep your car cooler in the summer by parking in the shade.

8. Lose weight! A study at the University of Illinois found that Americans are pumping about a billion more gallons of gas annually today than four decades ago because extra body weight brings down fuel economy. About 1.7 million cars could be filled with gas for an entire year with that "extra" fuel.

Sources: Sierra Club Web site (wwwsierraclub.org); Worldwatch Institute, http://www.worldwatch .org/node/1480; "Getting There on Less" by Guy Dauncey, in *Yes! Magazine*, Summer 2004; Jon Hilkevitch, *Chicago Tribune*, October 25, 2006, Chicagotribune.com.

➤ The Currents and Currency of Energy

"I get about nine miles per potato," environmentalist Lester Brown told me recently. I knew exactly what he meant—that a potato's 300 calories fuels nine miles of bicycling (or three miles of walking, since bikes are three times as energy-efficient). Fossil fuels contain calories, too: Each barrel of oil contains the calorie equivalent of twenty-three thousand hours of human labor! No wonder our era has been the most productive—as well as wasteful—in human history; we've been coasting on solar energy stored as compressed fossil fuel, which it took nature up to one hundred million years to manufacture.

Now, forty thousand years after humans learned to domesticate livestock—which also store the solar energy contained in grass as meat and milk—two trends are emerging in our world: Inactive lifestyles are negatively affecting our health and vitality, and the supplies of carbon-rich energy that built our civilization are beginning to decline. These trends are two sides of the same carbonaceous coin, because clearly, we need to use our bodies more and fossil fuels less. (There's an energy crisis in our bodies, too.) We're evolving from a hydrocarbon economy, in which stored fuels are burned to release power, into a "carbohydrate economy," in which solar energy is used directly both by advanced technologies and our bodies. The high cost of energy will soon provide a renaissance of human-powered crafts and creativity—an enjoyable, productive way to spend calories!

Not since the Second World War, when we patriotically salvaged everything from bones to baling wire, have we had to focus so precisely on the real value of our resources, products, and processes. In recent decades, we've been far more preoccupied with quantity, speed, and size than with quality, appropriate scale, or resource efficiency. It's easy to see why: Variables such as quantity and speed that keep the assembly lines and semi trucks rolling often yield higher profits in a world engineered and legislated for excess. In an era of energy abundance, utilities routinely gave discounts for the consumption of electricity and fuels. The more a large customer consumed, the lower its cost per unit of energy. What has resulted is a society made of cheap energy.

In the emerging economy, calories stored in plant material will be supplemented by other renewable energy sources such as wind, solar, and geothermal power—flows that are already here. Energy guru Amory Lovins of the Rocky Mountain Institute calls the ingenious substitution of renewable energy for combustion "the undiscovery of fire," an anthropological tipping point that will help put the monster of global warming back in its cage. "The *good* news about global warming," says Lovins, "is that it's far cheaper to fix than to ignore." For four decades, Lovins has asserted that the best way to generate energy is with efficiency—what he calls "negawatts." He and his colleagues find hidden treasure in fatter pipes that have less friction so they deliver liquids more efficiently; lighter cars made of carbon fiber rather than steel, so they burn less fuel; and smaller, less expensive heating and cooling systems made possible by adding extra insulation to a building. The cheapest form of energy, he demonstrates, will always be information—in other words, great design and engineering that reduce the *need* for energy. If each device, method, or building is designed for peak efficiency, then renewable energy—what he calls the "soft path"—will be sufficient to meet human needs.

I believe this methodical way of thinking can be applied in many other aspects of our lives, from what we eat to what we buy and where we live. If we meet each need precisely—for example, by living in an energy-smart house, or eating food that gives us energy but not obesity, we won't be constantly craving "more." A very useful component of Lovin's soft-path strategy is to use the right amount and the right *kind* of energy for the job. He's famous for the analogy that using nuclear-generated electricity to heat a house is like "using a chainsaw to cut butter," because so much energy is wasted in the fission of atoms, transmission of electricity from the power plant, and reconversion of electricity back to heat. Certainly, the 10,000 degrees Fahrenheit of heat that a nuclear plant generates is overkill; why not use precisely what a given task requires? Passive solar energy, efficient windows, thick insulation, and a superefficient, backup natural gas–powered furnace meet the need for heat much more appropriately.

Similarly, since conventional lightbulbs (invented back in 1879) produce far more heat than light, they add to a building's air conditioning load and a utility bill's bottom line. A global switch to state-of-the-art lighting will trim the world's electricity bill by one-tenth, says the International Energy Agency (IEA). The energy for lighting releases about three-fourths as much carbon dioxide as the world's passenger vehicles—a great opportunity for immediate results. The IEA advocates stricter lighting standards in building codes to prohibit lighting such as the halogen uplighter (torchiere), which spotlights the ceiling rather than directly lighting a living room or lounge.[4] (Similarly, a person working late at the office often lights a tennis-court-size area with a whole bank of lights when he really needs to light just a desk-size area. And the light coming out of many large homes on a given night can be seen from the window seat of an airplane.

The compact fluorescent bulb (CFL), now available at a fraction of its original cost and offering a warm-toned light, is a great example of meeting lighting needs precisely. Replacing a 100-watt incandescent bulb with a 32-watt CFL can save $30 in energy costs over the life of the bulb, because CFLs use two-thirds less energy than incandescent bulbs to deliver the same amount of light, and last up to ten times longer. If every household replaces just *three* 60-watt incandescent light bulbs with CFLs, we will eliminate as much pollution as is generated by 3.5 million cars, according to the nonprofit group Environmental Defense.

Wal-Mart's commitment to sell at least one CFL to every one of its 100 million customers sprang from a back-of-the-envelope calculation: Its stores could save $6 million a year just by replacing the display lightbulbs for its ceiling fans with CFLs. Even if each American home bought just one compact fluorescent to replace a 60-watt incandescent, the energy saved would be enough to power all the homes in Delaware and Rhode Island.

Writes Charles Fishman in *Fast Company* magazine, "For two decades, CFLs lacked precisely what we expect from lightbulbs: strong, unwavering light; quiet; not to mention shapes that actually fit in the places we use bulbs. Now every one of those problems has been conquered. Since 1985, CFLs have changed as much as cell phones and portable music players."[5]

Even more appropriate than efficient bulbs for daytime lighting in houses and offices is natural daylight, which makes good use of our solar system's most efficient bulb, the Sun. To use the Sun most efficiently, invisible space-age window coatings, about 70 atoms thick, are precisely designed to let light in but filter out heat in the summer; and let light in but prevent heat from getting *out* in the winter. There's more to it than a sunny ambience: various studies have proven that well-designed natural daylight results in higher quality and reliability in factories, 6 to 16 percent higher labor productivity in offices, and 40 percent higher sales in stores with atriums and skylights.[6] Lovins summarizes, "If properly done, measures to protect global climate actually *reduce* costs, not raise them." He points to results already achieved by mega-companies such as DuPont, BP, and Wal-Mart, all financial beneficiaries of company-wide efficiency measures. While boosting production by 30 percent in the last decade, DuPont also cut energy use by 7 percent and reduced CO_2 emissions by 72 percent, saving $2 billion in energy costs so far. Oil giant BP cut its energy bills $650 million over ten years, and reduced CO_2 emissions 10 percent below the company's 1990 levels.

Wal-Mart's recent declaration of efficiency—that the corporation will reduce its carbon footprint by 20 percent in seven years—will create ripples throughout the U.S. economy. Methodically examining how they meet retailing needs, the company has come up with a long list of measures. They became the largest purchaser of organic cotton, eliminating huge volumes of pesticides (and the energy in them) that are used on the most widely sprayed agricultural product. They "right-sized" the boxes on toys, making them just large enough for the contents and saving $3.5 million in trucking costs; and they replaced standard oil-derived plastic wrap with corn-derived wrap on four kinds of produce, saving the equivalent of 800,000 gallons of gasoline.[7]

Green design and efficiency pay for themselves many times over. In fact, efficiency has boosted the entire U.S. economy in the last thirty years, reducing energy costs by $1 billion a day. The nation now uses 47 percent less energy per dollar of economic output than it did in the mid-1970s, says Amory Lovins. "These savings act like a huge universal tax cut that also reduces the federal deficit." What if each business, large and small, were to follow the lead of these mega-companies? What if city governments, churches, unions, and individuals, too, continue to focus on efficiency, basing decisions on how well a given action or device meets the need? With less waste and fewer social side effects dragging us down, our whole way of life will become less burdensome.[8]

Lovins makes a strong distinction between efficiency based on great design/engineering, and conservation, based on "doing without." When Jimmy Carter urged Americans to wear sweaters to stay warm in the 1970s, it felt to some like deprivation. But when Lovins suggests that our economy can save hundreds of billions of dollars every year with efficiency and better engineering, it sounds far sexier. The truth is, we'll need to use both approaches. Behavioral changes like wearing a sweater inside on the coldest days will seem like less of an imposition as energy costs continue to climb. At the same time, efficiency improvements that substitute ingenuity for resources without significant differences in behavior are a breath of fresh air. When you think about it, the two approaches to using less energy are variations on the same theme—mindfulness. The same tool that enables good use of resources, our brain, can design things more ingeniously and also figure out what daily actions to take. Every time we double up on errands to save gas and time, give a tool we've never used to a neighbor who needs it, or tune up the car to get better gas mileage, we rediscover what a good thing it is to have a brain.[9]

13

The Benefits of Right-Sizing

Better Than Better Homes and Gardens

I never had any other desire so strong, as that I might be master at last of a small house and a large garden, with very moderate conveniences joined to them . . .
    —Abraham Cowley

A wedding dress or tuxedo is a pleasure for an evening, but few of us want to live in a costume. So why are so many houses filled with gimmicks such as whirlpools, and multiple fireplaces, that don't fit the actual activities of their owners?
    —Shay Saloman

Since 1982, an area the equivalent of New York State has been developed—largely by businessmen who buy a chunk of farmland and build five hundred similar-looking houses on it.[1] The resources required by each home include 14,000 board feet of lumber (about an acre of trees) and 19 tons of cement. It's not just pesticides that make spring in America more silent than in our grandparents' days— it's also the smothering of habitats. Since Rachel Carson wrote *Silent Spring* in the 1960s, the size of an average American home more than doubled, as the average household income continued to climb (up fivefold, adjusted for inflation). How many trees will it take to build the 90,000-square-foot home designed for time-share industry billionaire David Siegel and his wife, Jacqueline? The next time you watch a pro football game, imagine a house about as big as the playing field. (Think how long it takes to return a punt from the end zone at full speed.)

When my ex-wife and I bought our first house, we wanted something smaller than we could afford. We didn't know at the time that the word "mortgage" comes from old French and means "death pledge," but we did sense that a big house was a heavy load to carry, and that it took a huge toll on the environment. It was 1973 when we bought a house for $17,000 in the foothills outside of Denver—a log cabin that had been added onto, but not by much. The total square footage was 1,100 square feet, and after ten effortless years of $114-a-month payments, we paid the cabin off. We grew to a family of four (plus a dog, a cat, and chickens who roosted in an old outhouse). We lived in that house and garden for twenty years, and by the time we left, the average size of a Denver-area house had swollen to more than 2,000 square feet. I now live in a 1,750-square-foot house, but I rent the 600-square-foot apartment in my basement. My 1,150 square feet is still plenty of space—especially for a divorced man or bachelor—with its kitchen, living room, bedroom, balcony, bathroom, and home office. (It also helps a lot that my neighborhood has a community building with a guest room, living room, dining room, and terrace.)

Despite much evidence to the contrary, I believe small houses will be in high demand in the next decade, not just because resource costs are destined to climb, but also because small houses are easier to customize, easier to maintain, and are often located in pre-boom neighborhoods that are closer to the things we need—groceries, banks, libraries, and restaurants. In fact, it occurs to me that we really should call small houses "regular," and the others "XL," because for most of our stay as humans, we've lived in shelters even smaller than 1950-size houses. Now that single people occupy one-fourth of American households—up from 10 percent in 1950—shouldn't

A 600-square-foot house over a garage at the Holiday neighborhood, and the front yard of David Wann's townhouse in Harmony Village, with strawberries instead of grass in the front yard. Courtesy of the author

we accelerate the remodeling and building of regular-size houses? There are distinct disadvantages to XL homes, as financial planner Ilyce Glink points out: "When you buy a bigger home to accommodate your stuff, you pay higher taxes, higher heating bills, bigger cooling bills, a bigger mortgage, plus whatever the upkeep costs are for the stuff itself."[2]

I also predict that within the next ten to twenty years, many of the Hummer homes that now dominate the American landscape will be partitioned and remodeled to accommodate multiple households, with the blessing of local zoning departments. (Already, many immigrants live three or more families to a house.) As coauthor Dan Chiras and I speculate in the book *Superbia! 31 Ways to Create Sustainable Neighborhoods*, their large, resource-hungry lawns may well become vegetable gardens, mini-orchards, and even fenceless neighborhood parks. In the meantime, many XL house owners are cashing out, regardless of a faltering housing market, and downsizing to elegant little cottages, townhouses, houseboats, bungalows, and lofts.

➤ A House for Good Reasons

The American home is the greatest single expression of our addiction to energy. A large percentage of the power plants, roads, factories, and discount palaces service a lifestyle for which the home and yard are the epicenter. The decision to live in a smaller, more efficient, more conveniently located home offers huge opportunities for *increasing* one's quality of life while reducing the consumption of resources. Says Shay Soloman, author of *Little House on a Small Planet*, "Live in less space but have more room to enjoy it. Does that sound like a contradiction? On the contrary, living small frees up your mind, your wallet, and your soul."[3] Admittedly, there are psychological roadblocks to overcome. The house is a perceived symbol of success in our world (ironically, it's also a refuge from a world so preoccupied with material success). But a person who lives in a smaller house than he or she can afford probably has a healthy level of self-respect, plenty of time, and may also have a desire to do more with his or her life than consume.

According to sociologist Paul Ray, at least a quarter of the U.S. population—the "cultural creative" sector—look at what's happening in suburbia, shake their head, and say, "I know I don't want that." Instead, they may choose to buy an existing house in the inner ring of the suburbs, built when 1,500 square feet was considered a good-size house. Or they may decide to build a new home that incorporates precisely the features they want, like hardwood floors and kitchen cabinets, lots of skylights, solar energy, efficient appliances, and built-in shelving. An amusing but very affordable example is the house that Jay Shafer built for himself in Occidental, California, where three really *is* a crowd. His house, one of the units he now markets as president of Tumbleweed Tiny House Company, is 70 square feet—smaller than some walk-in closets or tree houses built for the kids.[4]

But Shafer knows what he's doing. In California, one in four people are considering moving out of state to reduce their housing costs. For example, only 2.7 percent of San Francisco's teachers, 5.7 percent of its cops, and 4.2 percent of its nurses can afford to buy a home there.[5] "I like to say that a well-designed little house is just a big house with all the unnecessary parts cut out," he says. "When people have too much stuff in their lives and too much space that needs heating or cleaning, it becomes a liability." Shafer's tiny house, which includes a loft bed, dorm-size refrigerator, hot-plate desk, closets, and miniature sitting area, is no liability! Many of his houses are built with small front porches, and range from 70 square feet, like his home, to 700 square feet—what Shafer calls "palatial."[6]

I don't imagine most Americans would consider living in a Tumbleweed Tiny House unless it was a vacation cabana; after all, we imagine ourselves living in what we see on TV shows like *Extreme Makeover: Home Edition*, where, in one show, a tireless crew built a six-bedroom, seven-bath, seven-television house for a family of four. (Now, how will they ever pay the utilities and taxes?) But there's a definite niche market for small houses. Many Americans *might* consider moving into a 1,000-square-foot home, as large or larger than the average houses still being built in such places as England, Ireland, and Japan. And 1,500 square feet may be more realistic as a moderate, transitional benchmark. When well designed, a small gem of a house is far more valuable per square foot than a mansion is.

I recently toured a "not so big house" designed by Tina Govan, a colleague of author/architect Sarah Susanka. I was impressed by the "livability" that skylights, interior glass partitions, built-in shelving, and other features give the house. It felt like a sailboat, with everything in its proper place, and the beautifully kept landscape outside the house felt like an extension of the inside. You could see diagonally from one corner of the house to the other—a feature that conveys a feeling of spaciousness. As I walked through the 1,700-square-foot interior, I realized several things at once: that it's not really space that we want in a house, but a *feeling* of spaciousness. Furthermore, if we live in houses that really meet our needs, they will connect us with the world rather than cutting us off from it by being in scale with both the human body and the land where the house is located.

Sarah Susanka observes that when her clients seriously evaluate how they use their current home on a daily basis, they are usually quite comfortable with a new, custom-designed house that's one-third smaller. She recommends that they use money saved in construction to incorporate their favorite materials, shapes, and patterns, from tile counters and wainscoting to bamboo floors—these are what add charm and a feeling of truly being at home. Concludes Susanka in the best seller *The Not So Big House,* "It's time for a different kind of house that is more than just square footage; a house where each room is used every day. A house with a floor plan inspired by our informal lifestyle instead of the way our grandparents lived." (In 1901, we should remember, the average size of a family was 4.9 people; whereas, in 2006, the average household has shrunk to 2.6 people. Even so, our houses are larger on average now than then.) Susanka fervently believes that the typical American house has too many bathrooms and too large a living room to be comfortable and cozy. It is less like a nest than like a "massive storage container."[7]

Although I remain challenged when it comes to the *organization* of my stuff, I've definitely seen my enthusiasm for garage sales and home furnishing stores wane since moving to a house with less storage space. What a relief! I'm not likely to acquire house stuff unless it has a story behind it—for example, it was made or given to me by a friend, bought on a special vacation, or something like that. It's far easier to feel "full" in a small house, and if that feeling is synonymous with being satisfied, then small really *is* beautiful.

➤ Cutting Your Fuel Bill in Half (and Not with Scissors)

Typically, utility bills aren't popular pieces of mail, especially as the costs of electricity and heating fuel continue to climb. There's really only one way to look forward to opening one of these monthly greetings: Live in an efficient home—ideally a "regular-size" one—that doesn't pig out on BTUs and kilowatt hours. In the typical kitchen, a groaning dishwasher cycle is in progress to clean seven plates and four favorite mugs. And the old workhorse refrigerator—replaced by an ice-making thoroughbred—is banished to the garage, where storage for a six-pack of soda and a rump roast costs about $125 a year. Most winter nights, we forget to turn the furnace down at bedtime, and spend sweaty nights dreaming about fuel bills. As energy costs go up, these habits will change.

When my most recent utility bill came, I was curious to see how I'd done, and delighted that it had sunk to a new low: $28 for the very hot

· Intrinsic Values of Small Houses ·

- *Use Fewer Building Materials:* By living in a house with a human scale, we prevent the destruction of habitat, conserve resources, and teach ourselves how to live without kitchen gadgets and tabletop knickknacks.

- *Use fewer resources:* For example, the large size of a U.S. household, with its long pipes, wastes hundreds of gallons of water a year—just waiting for the hot water to arrive.

- *Require less time and money for payments and maintenance,* which can be spent on other things, like vacations, special people in your life, or continuing education. The average annual utility bill is $1,500 and climbing quickly—so just in fuel bills, the small house yields continuing dividends.

- *More likely to be found in places (like first-ring suburbs) that are near the things we need*—stores, schools, theaters, banks, and so on. So there may be considerable savings and a higher quality of life from reduced transportation. Some banks are now offering "location-efficient mortgages" for that reason. We're a better financial risk if we save on transportation costs.

- *Are often "homier,"* and more intimate. They make people feel larger, and less overwhelmed. We should take a cue from beaver dams, bird's nests, and bear dens, none of which are larger than is necessary.

- *Reduce the stress of constant maintenance and insecurity* about theft, deterioration, and isolation. The less flamboyant our houses are, the safer we are, statistically.

- *Can be fixed up just the way we want them,* since there is less space to decorate and furnish.

- *Enable us to focus on nonmaterial forms of wealth*, like taking care of family, and participating in civic activities. Small, comfortable houses encourage humility, lack of pretense, and creativity. They confer a sense of "doing the right thing."

month of July, for both gas and electricity. My latest improvements were to install a solar panel on my roof to heat water; add eight newly available, dimmable compact fluorescent bulbs to unconverted fixtures; and put up new window coverings to keep the summer heat at bay. The improvements had worked! I looked in the column of the bill that compared my use of "therms" with last year's month of July, and saw that the solar panel had cut my natural gas consumption in half. The only other gas I used was for the stove and oven—used minimally in a thermometer-popping month filled with temperatures in the high nineties. Another column indicated that I'm enrolled in Windsource, a voluntary program that entitles me to get a portion of my electricity from Colorado wind farms. At first I paid a premium for several shares of electricity to support the infant wind industry, but now a slight rebate has been given to Windsource customers because the wind industry is maturing and has actually become as cheap as coal-generated electricity.

It's exciting to be part of a sustainable industry that's growing so fast. The wind industry is one of the brightest prospects in the global transition to renewable energy. (We're lucky we've been perfecting it for a thousand years.) Overall, the cost of wind power has fallen by nearly 90 percent since the 1980s. Taller turbine height and longer rotor blades produce up to two hundred times as much power as turbines did just twenty years ago. Between 1995 and 2005, the wind industry expanded twelvefold, with especially strong growth in Europe: Germany leads the way, with 19,000 megawatts of installed wind power in 2006 (the equivalent of about 50 average-size coal or natural gas power plants). Germany gets 6 percent of its electricity from wind; Spain gets 8 percent; and Denmark, 20 percent. The United States has installed about twenty-five power plants' worth of wind power so far, and enough outstanding wind sites remain to provide at least twice the electricity the country now uses, according to the U.S. Department of Energy.[8] In just the last few years, wind has become a full 13 percent of Colorado's electrical capacity.

My efforts continue to lower my energy use and my utility bill. This year, I'll also install a thousand watts of photovoltaic solar energy, which qualify for federal tax incentives. The "juice" from the solar panels will further reduce my utility bill and be conveniently wired to my electric meter rather than specific DC-powered appliances. Fortunately, I live in a development that won awards for energy efficiency, so my house has great solar orientation, very efficient windows, and unusually thick layers of cellulose insulation that help with both heating and cooling. (Together, heating and cooling comprise 42 percent of a typical house's energy demand.) I live in a townhouse that's "insulated" on both sides by neighbors' houses, but since the walls are a double thickness, the only sounds I hear are the faint, occasional thumps of an enthusiastic Lohre kid.

So far, I've survived a five-year string of unusually hot summers without air-conditioning or evaporative cooling, by letting cool Colorado air in at night and closing windows and blinds to retain the coolness during the day. This summer has required a little extra effort, though. In semi-desperation and on a fixed budget, I jerry-rigged a cooling system: a fan placed in series behind a mail-order humidifier and a 2-gallon metal bowl full of ice (which I just refreeze at night). It works great, and only cost $39. As the humidity evaporates, it creates coolness in my second-story office as a swamp cooler would, which mixes with the coolness from the bowl of ice, as in an air conditioner. Voilà, a sophisticated, nineteenth-century technology, at my service! To cool the first floor, I use another fan to bring cool air up from the basement. So what if 85 percent of Americans now have air-conditioning and I don't? I'll bet they don't have the insulation my house does, or the willingness to appear a little foolish—and be a little more in tune with what the weather is like outside in the real world. (Maybe the right way to look at it is that I'm in the top 15 percent.) This do-it-yourself experiment proves an earlier point: It's not an air conditioner I need, just coolness.

I've developed a relationship with resources that's as much a sport as it is a chore. I think about the synergies among heat, sun, water, soil, the garden, and other resources that circulate through and around my house—and how I can get the most value from each of them. For example, when I take a shower, I catch the half-gallon of cold water that comes out before the hot water does and water houseplants with it. When I use the dishwasher (yes, I do have a dishwasher), I do it at night when I need the heat (in winter) or at least can tolerate it (in summer). Similarly, I use the oven when I'm cooking several things at once, on days that require more heat than solar energy can supply. I cover pots with lids because that makes the heat a third more efficient.

I compost kitchen scraps—largely the leaves, roots, and skins of organic vegetables and fruits from the garden—and later use finished compost to grow more vegetables, as well as bringing it inside for my houseplants. I've just come back to making "sun tea" rather than boiling or nuking it. Why not? It just takes a few more minutes for the sun to make a glass bottle of peppermint tea, which I put in the refrigerator for an afternoon break. One recent addition in my quest for resource-cutting opportunities involves my office printer. Not only do I turn it off until I'm ready to print something, eliminating the standby power consumption, but I've also learned how to make double-sided copies, even on my inexpensive printer, just by going into "properties" on the Print page and selecting "long-edge binding" in the "duplex/booklet" box. The only additional effort this takes is turning over the stack, feeding it back into the machine, and clicking on "proceed." That's so easy even I can do it.

These are the kinds of strategies that resulted in my $28 utility bill this month, but I have to admit they are extremely clumsy compared with my friend Dan Chiras's efforts—he hasn't paid an electrical bill since 1996. Solar energy passively heats his south-facing house, located at 7,500 feet in elevation; and photovoltaic panels provide the house's electricity. Dan's present, off-the-grid home was built after he learned an important lesson from a previous house: *For renewable energy to be feasible, efficiency comes first.* This lesson is important to remember as the world transitions away from easy-come, easy-go fossil fuel energy.

In 1987, Dan lived in a house that was heated by the sun but relied on electrical baseboard heating for backup when the sun didn't come out for several days in a row. His stove was also an electric range; other appliances were less efficient than they could be, and the total energy demand of the house made solar electricity economically impossible. Even with thorough conservation measures like caulking, a solar-electric system to power the whole house would have cost $50,000 to install. Writes Dan in *The Home-owner's Guide to Renewable Energy* (one of the more than twenty books Dr. Dan has written), "Using energy efficiently is like giving yourself a big fat raise. And the energy you save can be used by others; your savings have become their energy source." I love that idea—the more energy we save, the fewer power plants we'll need.

Dan's current house is heated by solar orientation, lots of thermal mass (tires and straw bales incorporated into the thick back walls), and superefficient windows, with an efficient woodstove as backup. He tells the story of a Denver family that used to hold season tickets to Denver Bronco games but couldn't afford them when the prices went up. So being die-hard fans, they decided to watch the games on TV instead. But their 1970s home was like an icebox in the winter; poorly insulated and full of leaks that allowed cold air in on winter days, it felt like millions of inefficient residences throughout North America. Says Dan, "To watch the games, the family had to bundle up in jackets and sweaters and don thermal socks or huddle under blankets. It wasn't a whole lot different than a December game outside at the stadium . . ." But thanks to an extensive utility-sponsored energy makeover, the house is now comfortable enough to watch the games without blankets or occasional clouds of breath. The same kinds of improvements that save more than a thousand dollars a year in their home will work in any home: Either by working with a contractor or doing it yourself, seal the leaks with caulk; install efficient, "low-E" windows if your current ones leak; add insulation; install a programmable thermostat; and upgrade appliances—especially the heating and cooling systems and refrigerator.[9]

➤ Priorities for Home Energy Savings

Any household in search of a smaller footprint and lower utility bill should consider having an energy efficiency consultant do an audit. Sometimes these experts are available though the local utility, and in most regions, a person can find them in the Yellow Pages or on the Web. With the escalating cost of energy comes a consolation benefit: the payback for investing in efficiency is much quicker, often competing favorably with returns from mutual funds.

Replacing a fifteen-year-old furnace with a high-efficiency model may cut heating fuel usage by 1,000 therms (as much as $1,000), since furnaces installed in the 1980s and early 1990s are only about 50 percent efficient compared with newer models that boast 96 percent efficiency now. By shopping for Energy Star appliances, a household can reduce payback time as well as CO_2 emissions. (In fact, if Americans bought only appliances with Energy Star ratings over the next fifteen years, says Worldwatch Institute, the reduction in greenhouse gases would be like taking 17 million cars off the road.) Upgrading a central air-conditioning system offers less dramatic cost savings, since electricity hasn't spiked as quickly as natural gas; but if a system is fifteen years old or else oversize, a new system can save hundreds of dollars a year because, on average, cooling consumes 11 percent of a household's energy.

Another high priority is the refrigerator, responsible for 7 percent of an average home's total energy usage. Such large efficiency improvements have been made in recent years that a refrigerator more than five years old should be scuttled as part of a household's efficiency plan. The payback from a new refrigerator will be slow but steady.[10]

Heating water is also a big chunk of a house's fuel bill. On-demand, inline units are still higher in cost than conventional tank units, but their payback in both energy and water savings can be substantial. After a year of experience with solar water heating (a technology in use for more than a century in the United States), I can recommend it for any household with a good southern exposure. There are and will be good rebates and tax credits available for solar, and the showers feel so much more luxurious! I saved a bit by scavenging the panel from a family in a nearby town, but the payback period will still exceed six years. For clothes washing, a front loader is worth the investment, saving energy, water, and wear-and-tear on clothes. These units are so well programmed, they are almost as entertaining to watch as a baby eating birthday cake. (Okay, not quite).

◆ Mindful Steps to Cut Household Energy Use in Half ◆

- Install a programmable thermostat for heating and cooling, and learn how to use it—it saves a lot of energy. Each degree below 68°F during colder weather saves 3–5 percent more heating energy, and keeping your thermostat at 78°F in warmer weather will also save you energy and money.

- Set the refrigerator thermostat at 37°–40°F. Clean the condenser coils twice a year to raise efficiency by up to 30 percent.

- Install curtains, awnings, and shutters to control heating and cooling, and plant a shade tree in your backyard to reduce AC costs. Shading an air conditioner can improve efficiency by 10 percent.

- Wash clothes in warm or cold water rather than hot, and rinse with cold water.

- Set up a clothesline. Clothespins aren't hard to figure out!

- Air-dry dishes rather than heat-drying them, especially in dry climates.

- Turn the water heater down to 120°F, and insulate the pipes that exit your tank.

- Install faucet aerators and low-flow showerheads that deliver a satisfying shower for thousands of gallons less annually.

- Bake in ceramic or glass pans that hold the heat better and require 25°F less heat, but use the pressure cooker, Crock-Pot, toaster oven, microwave, or stove before resorting to the oven.

- Unplug coffeemakers, microwaves, computer printers, and other appliances when not in use, to eliminate "phantom" power loads.

14

Trimming the Fat

Farewell to Fossil Food

The food industrialists have by now persuaded millions of consumers to prefer food that is already prepared. They will grow, deliver, and cook your food for you and (just like your mother) beg you to eat it. That they do not yet offer to insert it, prechewed, into our mouth is only because they have found no profitable way to do so.
  —Wendell Berry

Don't dig your grave with your own knife and fork.
  —English proverb

In addition to contributing to erosion, pollution, food poisoning, and the dead zone in the Gulf of Mexico, corn requires huge amounts of fossil fuel— it takes a half gallon of fossil fuel to produce a bushel of corn.
  —Michael Pollan

At home I serve the kind of food I know the story behind.
  —Michael Pollan

Seventeen percent of U.S. energy is spent to produce and distribute food; three-fourths of all the water used in this nation is for agriculture, and about a fourth of the country's land is devoted to growing food for both domestic consumption and export. By paying more attention to what we eat and how our food is grown, we can use fewer resources as well as increase the quality of our lives. The choices we make at the supermarket or farmers' market can literally change the world

If we bring a sense of connection and quality back into the food chain, we can improve our health, rebuild the world's soils, and regain a sense of control and participation in the market. Says Paul Hawken, a guru of the emerging new economy, "The cash register is the daily voting booth in democratic capitalism." When we buy groceries, we cast a vote for the kind of farming, processing, and packaging we support, as well as what we believe healthy humans should eat. The best chefs in the country prefer organically grown produce because it tastes better. When conventional crops get too much nitrogen fertilizer they take up extra water, diluting the taste. (Conventionally grown produce often looks like something on a magazine cover, but eyes can't taste and taste buds can't see.) Growing food organically means using organic fertilizers and natural pest control; rotating crops to avoid disease, build the soil, and minimize erosion; and using great, region-specific varieties to optimize the flavor. These techniques are of great interest to consumers who want a chain of quality from field to table.

Retailers are getting the message: Organic food has been growing by 20 percent annually since the mid-1990s, and when giants like Wal-Mart and Safeway expand their organic inventories, it's clear that organic is here to stay. In fact, except for a hundred-year dot-point in human history, we've always eaten organically! It's not a fad, and considering the far higher quality, it's also not really an extra expense—we get what we pay for with better health, more flavorful food, and a less polluted world. Besides, the supermarket costs of mainstream food don't reflect hidden costs ultimately paid by taxpayers, including billions of dollars in federal agricultural subsidies, water contamination, loss of bees, soil erosion, and so on. If you add environmental and social costs to a conventionally grown head of lettuce, for example, its price would be twice as high.

A hundred years ago, Americans spent 43 percent of their household budget on food, but now household spending for food has dropped to 13 percent. As the exploitation of soil, water, and fossil fuels expanded, farms became food factories, fast food became an institution, and the price of food came down. But if convenience food is cheaper over-the-counter, it's expensive in many other ways. Americans spend the least per capita for food of any country in the world, as a percentage of income, but we spend the most for health care. What's the connection? Many people don't realize that good food maintains health and makes us feel happy. That simple wisdom was culturally eroded when convenience food seduced the generation that is now our elders. But whole foods are making a comeback and, as the market expands, prices for organic food will come down. In any case, the percentage of total household spending for food may well go up voluntarily in the next few decades, as food's full value becomes more widely known. At the same time, unnecessary spending for things like media entertainment, clothing, and household knickknacks will go down.[1]

As both oil and water become more expensive, we'll return to information-rich, resource-efficient agriculture. There have been many innovations in recent times that will make small farming much more pleasant than it was in the past, and the market is quickly expanding to support the small, local, organic farmer. Although five million family farmers were lost between 1935 and 2000, and most of those remaining are fifty-five years old or older, a new generation of organic growers is emerging like a field of seedlings. For example, the number of farmers in the largest organic cooperative in the country, Organic Valley Family of Farms, doubled over the last three years. Its sales rose 17 percent to $245 million in 2005 and is expected to climb to $285 million in 2006. Cities like Bellingham, Washington, that value local food, have programs to train new farmers in organic growing.

➤ Kicking the Habit

The American food system as a whole is distressingly inefficient at each link of the chain. It needs greater consumer scrutiny, and not just in search of the cheapest price. Our individual share of food's impact includes huge amounts of oil, soil, land, and water to grow the crops; and more pools of resources to transport, process, preserve, and prepare the food. Just the farm and processing sectors of the chain cost roughly the equivalent of ten barrels of oil annually, for each of us. Fortunately, there are many ways that slight changes in lifestyle will help bring the food system out of crisis and back into balance.

Breaking the oil-dependency of industrial agriculture won't be easy, but we'll ultimately kick the habit because agribusiness is so inefficient and so unhealthy—from hazardous chemicals in water and human tissue through soil erosion and depletion. Most pesticides are petroleum based, and so is the nitrogen component of fertilizers—as well as the mining and processing of the other primary components, potassium and phosphorous. Chemical fertilizers alone comprise one-fifth of the energy used in agriculture. Although these industrial nutrients have helped feed (and also enable) a swelling world population, we are now seeing diminishing returns. It appears we've been coasting on natural fertility in the soil that nature built up over the eons. Like fossil fuels and "fossil water" (underground water stored in aquifers), soil was built up over the millennia by the incremental addition of organic material like prairie thatch, and the grinding down of rock. When we try to replace the nutrients that crops have removed with synthetic fertilizers that contain only some of these nutrients, we're mining the soil rather than building it.

Transportation of food comprises another 14 percent of the energy used in U.S. agriculture. Public enemy number one is shipping produce by airfreight. Not only is its energy cost per mile outlandish, but total miles traveled by an average morsel of food now averages about 2,000. Traditionally, we've shipped food long distances by ocean freighter or refrigerated semi truck, but our expectations for flawlessly fresh produce keep jumbo jets in the air, especially during North America's winter months—filled with New Zealand apples and kiwis. What's wrong with citrus fruit in the winter, that at least comes from the same country it's eaten in? (Even that has far more value when it's fresh, as Dr. Michael Colgan discovered when he tested oranges that had been picked the same day as the analysis; their vitamin C content was 180 mg. He then tested oranges from the same grower that had been in storage for a week at a local supermarket. They looked and tasted the same, but their vitamin C content had dropped to zero).[2]

As Joan Gussow observes in *The Organic Life*, "The water content of luxury foods (for example, 88 percent of a peach is water) means we're burning a lot of petroleum to ship cold water around. . . . Tomatoes are even more watery than peaches. Keeping all that water cool as it moves north from Florida or east from California is helping warm the planet."[3]

If you already have an efficient refrigerator, canvas shopping bags, and a grocery close enough to walk to, the next step in shopping green is to pay attention to "food miles," the distance the items travel to get to your table. Researchers at Iowa State University are investigating the feasibility of mandatory labels that indicate where the food was grown. They've also calculated the energy costs of various produce items. A pineapple shipped from Costa Rica consumes a third of a gallon of gasoline to get to an Iowa supermarket, while a pineapple from Hawaii consumes 2.8 gallons. The reason the Costa Rican fruit's food miles are less consumptive is that half its journey is by sea, but the Hawaiian pineapple can only get there by air.

Food mileage is also a factor when the fishing industry travels long distances to harvest marketable fish. For example, sardines and anchovies thrive in coastal areas and can be harvested with minimal energy expenditure; large predatory species such as swordfish however, require energy-intensive, high-tech fishing trips.

The best way to get good food mileage, of course, is to look for and buy food grown or caught in your own region. Sometimes that's not so simple; because of deals made on the phone and computer, a produce buyer in Colorado may arrange to buy lettuce from Maine even though local growers could supply it much fresher without jet lag. Markets also encourage a

· Ten Ways to Eat Greener ·

1. *Eat a variety of foods.* Eating a wide variety of foods is the best way to meet all your nutritional requirements. The huge number of choices in supermarkets does not reflect biological diversity. Three species—rice, corn, and wheat—supply nearly 60 percent of the calories and protein people derive from plants. Of 200 crops eaten by humans, only 30 account for 90 percent of the world's calorie intake.

2. *Buy locally produced food.* The average mouthful of food travels 2,000 miles from the farm to our plates. Locally grown food is fresher and closer to ripeness, has used less energy for transport and is less likely to have been treated with postharvest pesticides. Buying local products also supports regional farmers and preserves farmland. If you get your fruits and vegetables at a farmers' market or from a Community Supported Agriculture (CSA) farm, you can ask the farmer whether the food has been genetically engineered or treated with pesticides.

3. *Buy produce in season.* Out-of-season produce is costly because transport uses so much energy. It's also more likely to have been imported, often from a country with less stringent pesticide regulations than the United States. Instead, in winter, prepare seasonal crops, such as potatoes, onions, sweet potatoes, and beets. Put away or freeze spring and summer produce, such as berries or snap peas, from local producers. All these foods retain their nutritional content in storage; using them cuts energy costs.

4. *Buy organically produced food.* Besides whatever food you eat the most, buy the following produce grown organically, to minimize exposure to pesticides, especially for babies: peaches, apples, pears, winter squash, green beans, grapes, strawberries, raspberries, spinach, potatoes.

5. *Eat fresh, whole foods with adequate starch and fiber.* Whole foods—fruits, vegetables, grains, legumes (beans), nuts, and seeds—are the healthiest we can eat. The National Cancer Institute recommends we each "strive for five" servings of fresh fruits and vegetables a day to protect against cancer, heart disease, and common digestive ailments. Also, most fresh produce, legumes, and whole grains, with the exception of corn and soy, are still genetically natural.

6. *Eat fewer and smaller portions of animal products.* Meat and dairy products are major sources of fat in the U.S. diet, contributing to higher risk of heart disease, cancer, and diabetes. Animal products, including farmed fish, may contain hormones, antibiotics, and toxic chemicals, such as dioxin, DDT, and other pesticides, which concentrate in animal fat. Fish caught in contaminated waters may contain high levels of PCBs or mercury. Cattle, chickens, pigs, and sheep consume more than 70 percent of the grains produced in the United States.

7. *Choose minimally processed and packaged foods.* A typical highly processed "food product" may contain little natural food and be high in fat, salt, or sugar. It's likely to contain genetically engineered soy- and corn-based additives, such as corn syrup and soy lecithin, which are present in 60 percent of all processed foods.

8. *Prepare your own meals at home.* Cooking from scratch can involve a little more labor and time, but you can be sure you'll save money and resources, because you're not paying someone else to prepare, package, transport, and advertise your meals. Home cooking is healthier and more nutritious because you start with fresh ingredients. And it can be its own reward, providing a truly creative outlet and rejuvenating the family meal.

9. *Start a garden and compost pile.* Growing at least a little of your own food gives you control over the quality of what you eat. There's nothing like eating your dinner or a snack right in the garden, ingesting vitality from produce that's still alive. A compost pile means that nothing is ever wasted.

10. *Avoid these fatty foods.* Whole-milk dairy products (ice cream, cheese); processed meats such as bacon, sausage, liverwurst; and tropical oils, such as palm kernel and coconut oils. They contain saturated fat, which clogs arteries and increases levels of the *bad* cholesterol, LDL. Fast-food fries and baked goods like packaged cookies and cakes may contain both trans fats (partially hydrogenated oils) and saturated fats.

Sources: Children's Health Environmental Coalition, http://www.checnet.org/healthehouse/education/quicklist-detail.asp?Main_ID=238; Consumers Union, Environmental Working Group; Msn.com Health & Fitness; also, parts of these steps are adapted from: Joan Dye Gussow, professor emeritus of nutrition and education, Columbia University Teachers College, and Katherine L. Clancy, director of the Wallace Center for Agriculture & Environmental Policy, "Dietary Guidelines for Sustainability," *Journal of Nutrition Education* 18, no.1 (1986).

single-crop, soil-depleting mentality that's unhealthy for the farm as well as the consumer. Idaho produces a third of all U.S. potatoes, for example—mostly for French fries. By USDA calculations, if Idaho residents were to consume all potatoes grown in their state, they'd have to eat 63 pounds a day. Pass the ketchup, please![4]

➤ Trashing the Throwaway Economy

A full two-thirds of the energy spent on food is not for growing and transportation but processing, packaging, marketing, maintaining freshness in the store, and kitchen preparation. Consumers influence each of these sectors by the choices we make. Many people are consciously buying less-processed food to reduce their consumption of excess sugar, salt, and fat (which occur at much higher levels in canned, frozen, and packaged foods). This sends a message to the food processing industry to change their way of doing business. It also delivers greater health to the consumer. For example, the processing of fresh produce into frozen dinners like lasagne eliminates from one-tenth to nine-tenths of its mineral content but, when we insist on fresh fruits and vegetables, we vote with our dollars. Market-savvy retailers such as Whole Foods step in to meet our needs more precisely by providing a higher percentage of unprocessed, locally grown food than a typical supermarket.

Those on the lookout for resource-reducing opportunities will find a mother lode in packaging, and save money at the same time, since about 9 percent of a product's cost is in the packaging.[5] By buying in bulk, buying in larger packages, and shopping for products with little or no packaging, we can literally begin to unpackage the world. One person's small contribution can eliminate a lot of the country's wasted fuel, if the rest of us do it, too. For example, if every New York City resident used just one less grocery bag a year, it would save $250,000 in disposal costs and 28,000 barrels of oil.[6] And if each American did the same (how hard can that be?!) it would save close to a million barrels of oil, or at current prices, about $70 million a year.

What if the entire grocery industry—or the federal government—decided to enable those savings by making plastic bags so expensive that people would decide to bring their own cloth or nylon bags? That may sound far-fetched, but a similar strategy is already working great in Ireland, where a fifteen-cents-per-bag tax has led to a 95 percent reduction in what some Irish call the "national flag." Australia, Taiwan, Singapore, Great Britain, and San Francisco are following Ireland's lead, and Bangladesh has already completely banned polyethylene bags.[7]

Beverage containers are another example of how affluenza and weak policy create incredible amounts of waste. Americans consume the most packaged drinks of any country in the world, and after the beverages are guzzled (and only the belches and containers remain), we go through over 650 plastic, aluminum, and glass containers per person, annually. Less than half of these containers are recycled, a lost opportunity for the national economy. About 350 of our annual share of containers are aluminum cans—compared with only 14 containers per person in France.[8] Despite the fact that recycling an aluminum can save three-fourths of the energy it takes to make a new can, we throw away more than half of them—wasting the energy equivalent of powering a million homes![9]

Although curbside recycling programs in America have tripled in the last decade, many of the beverages we drink are away from home, and there are not enough recycling receptacles on streets and in stores. On the positive side, according to the National Recycling Coalition, in 2000, recycling resulted in an annual energy savings equal to the amount of energy used in six million homes, and by 2005, recycling was estimated to have saved the amount of energy used in nine million homes. We still have a lot of opportunity for improvement.

According to the Washington, D.C.-based nonprofit Container Recycling Institute (CRI), a full 3 *percent of the world's electricity* goes into manufacturing aluminum cans, but the U.S. market continues to treat them like dirt. CRI's research director Jenny Gitlitz comments, "The irony is that while Americans are trashing almost three quarters of a million tons of cans a year, the major aluminum companies are forging ahead with plans to build new aluminum smelters—and hydroelectric dams for power in environmentally sensitive areas including Brazil, Malaysia, and Iceland." Gitlitz explained that a dam being built for Alcoa's new smelter in Iceland will submerge 22 square miles of tundra, including habitat for reindeer and the pink-footed goose; up to sixty waterfalls; and what has been called the "Icelandic Grand Canyon."[10]

Americans spent about $10 billion for bottled water in 2005, and making the one-use bottles for that market requires more than 1.5 million barrels of oil annually, enough to fuel some 100,000 U.S. cars for a year.

The solutions are obvious, yet they sound foreign to convenience-addicted, market-bound Americans like us: Put a mandatory and very compelling bounty on containers to make sure they get recycled (we don't throw away quarters, do we?), or in the case of glass and PET plastic containers, make sure they're reused and recycled. Ten states have bottle bills that put a deposit on bottles, but apparently the bounty is still too low, because the percentage of bottles being returned is slipping, along with the recycling of plastic and aluminum containers. Why are we letting all this value get away? As recently as 1960, 95 percent of all packaged soft drinks and 53 percent of all packaged beer was sold in refillable glass bottles, which were returned for reuse twenty or more times. In our frenzied times, it seems we can't be bothered; our version of the free market doesn't seem to be able to value something as small as a container. I strongly believe that for the

common good (including industry), the U.S. government needs to intervene to recapture the wasted value, as many other governments already
have. Here again, Europe is leading the way: In more than thirty EU countries, packaging manufacturers must recycle ("take back") their products.
In Germany, where Take Back regulations debuted in 1991, packaging has
become lighter and the volume has decreased. The reuse of refillable glass
and plastic containers now exceeds 70 percent in that country.

When we think about a resource-intensive commodity such as packaging, we begin to realize how interconnected resources are with expectations. In a very real sense, packaging assumes that we will ship products
long distances and store them on shelves for potentially long periods of
time. After all, the main reasons for packaging are to protect the product
during shipment and reduce the chances it will be damaged or stolen before
being purchased. Plastic bottles make sense to a distributor because they
are lighter and cost less to ship. But they aren't as reusable as glass bottles,
and they contain substances (phthalates) that have been implicated in the
disruption of human endocrine systems. If consumers demand local products, the whole game changes.

A final aspect of our diet that's wasteful is what we literally throw out:
A typical household trashes 10 to 15 percent of the food purchased. If just
a fraction of that waste were avoided, we'd save hundreds of millions of
dollars in landfill costs alone, and avoid the unnecessary resource costs of
growing more.

➤ It's What's for Dinner

The diet-related choice with the greatest leverage for reducing resource use is to eat less meat. As compared with a low-meat diet, a 200-
pound-a-year meat diet (about the American average) consumes many
times as much land, energy, and water. When humans relied on hunting
for a large part of their diet, meat was a rich source of range-fed protein.
Grazing animals convert grass into food—something humans aren't able to
do—a very efficient use of solar energy. But in the current industrial way of
raising beef, for example, after beginning their lives on grassland, the
animals are shipped to dense feedlots and fattened up with grain and soy-
beans, which create the tender "marbled" beef we're used to. This is where
the inefficiencies begin to stack up. It takes 5 to 8 pounds of grain to produce a pound of beef and, as a result, 65 percent or more of the grain eaten
in the U.S. feeds livestock, not people. According to the nonprofit British

A very determined cow escapes from Mickey's Packing Plant in Great Falls, Montana. After a six-hour chase in which she dodged vehicles, ran in front of a train, swam the icy Missouri River, wooed TV and print media across the country, and took three tranquilizer darts, "Molly" won her place in the pasture. © Robin Loznak/*Great Falls Tribune*

organization Vegfam, a 10-acre farm can support sixty people growing soy-beans, twenty-four people growing wheat, ten people growing corn but only two people by producing cattle.[11]

In the classic *Diet for a Small Planet,* Frances Moore Lappé writes, "Imagine sitting down to an eight-ounce steak. Then imagine the room filled with forty-five to fifty people with empty bowls in front of them. For the 'feed cost' of your steak, each of their bowls could be filled with a full cup of cooked cereal grains." Jean Mayer, a Harvard nutritionist, estimates that if each American reduced the amount of meat he or she eats by just 10 percent, sixty million people could survive, eating the grain directly.[12]

In addition to the hidden energy costs in meat production, half the *water* consumed in the United States is used by the meat industry to grow feed. Much of that comes from groundwater that's being pumped faster than it can recharge. In the High Plains region where I live, state governments have ordered some ranchers to stop pumping from the Ogallala Aquifer, which experts project will be depleted within sixty years.

Where does all the energy in grain go that's not converted to meat? It gets "expelled" as the greenhouse gas methane, and excreted at the rate of some 87,000 pounds per second of manure, according to the organization People for the Ethical Treatment of Animals (PETA). This makes every U.S. household's share of manure twenty tons annually—whether we want it or not. Such volumes of manure could be great natural fertilizer if the livestock were all home, home on the range. However, in concentrated factory-farm conditions, the wastes become potent pollutants. For example, in 1995, twenty-five million gallons of hog waste spilled from an 8-acre lagoon into a river in North Carolina, killing ten million fish.

A very graphic example of how U.S. meat production is *unnatural* is the E. coli scare over contaminated spinach that hit the nation in 2006. In a *New York Times* guest editorial, food expert Nina Planck explains, "California's spinach industry is now the financial victim of an outbreak it probably did not cause." The contamination didn't occur on the farms, she maintains, but in the industrial feedlots, where beef and dairy cattle are fed grains that they aren't equipped to properly digest. "This particularly virulent strain, E. coli O157:H7, is not found in the intestinal tracts of cattle raised on their natural diet of grass, hay and other fibrous forage. It thrives in the unnaturally acidic stomachs of beef and dairy cattle fed on grain. It's the infected manure from these grain-fed cattle that contaminates groundwater and spreads the bacteria to crops like spinach growing on neighboring farms." The problem cascades onto our dinner plates, because human stomachs don't produce enough acidity to kill the bacteria.[13]

Yet despite production deficiencies like these, the world's appetite for meat continues to grow, at the rate of 2 percent each year. To keep up with demand, we now "take care of" fifteen to twenty billion livestock animals![14] Since the industrial revolution began, the world's farmland has expanded from 6 percent of the Earth's surface to nearly a third, and much of that land supports the short lives of cows, hogs, sheep, chickens, and other livestock. In developing countries, eating meat is seen as a sign of wealth and prosperity, but it's also a sign of affluenza. Especially carnivorous are China, which now consumes half the world's pork, and Brazil, the second largest consumer of beef after the United States.[15]

Partly as a result of the meteoric rise of fast food, meat has become more of an institution than it ever was. "Meat and potatoes" became "Burgers 'n' fries." Writes Eric Schlosser in the book *Fast Food Nation,* "Americans now spend more money on fast food than they do on higher education. They spend more on fast food than on movies, books, magazines, newspapers, videos and recorded music—combined."

➤ Monster Thickburger vs. the Mediterranean Diet

A few years ago, Hardee's unveiled its Monster Thickburger—two ⅓ pound slabs of Angus beef, four strips of bacon, three slices of cheese, and mayonnaise on a buttered sesame seed bun. All that for only 1,400 calories. With fries (520 calories) and soda (400 calories), the meal meets or exceeds the suggested caloric intake for Godzilla—or at least an American male. (For a rough calculation of how many calories to consume, multiply your weight times sixteen. Of course, this will vary with your level of activity.)

With two out of three Americans overweight, and heart attacks the major cause of death in the United States, Hardee's executives suspected they'd get calls from the "health nuts," and they were right. Michael Jacobson, director of Center for Science in the Public Interest, quickly pronounced the Monster Thickburger "food porn." Said Jacobson, "Hardee's seems not only oblivious to America's obesity epidemic, but also to the trend toward healthier fast food." Hardee's chief executive Andrew Puzder was unfazed, telling reporters, "I hope our competitors keep promoting those healthy products, and we will keep promoting our big, juicy delicious burgers." Said Jacobson, "A good rule of thumb is that if a burger needs a comma in its calorie count, it's virtually impossible to fit into a healthy diet." Puzder quickly distanced himself from customers he never would have had anyway, saying, "The Monster Thickburger is not a burger for tree-huggers."[16]

Some people can't imagine life without thick burgers, but a growing number of people can't imagine life *with* them. For them, the so-called Mediterranean diet is far more appealing. The man who first popularized the connection between heart disease and saturated fat, Professor Ancel Keys, also lived more than hundred years. His personal diet, based on complex carbohydrates, fruits, and vegetables, may have been one of the reasons. He conducted a decadelong research project in the 1960s that studied the diet, lifestyle, and incidence of coronary heart disease among thirteen thousand randomly selected middle-aged men from seven countries: the United States, Japan, Italy, Greece, the Netherlands, Finland, and Yugoslavia. A clear pattern emerged from the study's data: in the Mediterranean and Asian countries where vegetables, grains, fruits, beans, and fish were dietary mainstays, heart disease was rare. But in the United States and Finland, where red meat, cheese, and other foods high in saturated fat were eaten, heart disease was all too common.[17]

Many studies since then have corroborated Keys's findings, leading to strong support among health experts for the Mediterranean diet, a flavorful composite of the traditional foods of Spain, southern France, Italy, Greece, Crete, and parts of the Middle East. Common to the diets of these regions are high consumption of complex carbohydrates (not refined), foods high in fiber, fish, nuts, wide use of olive oil, and moderate consumption of red wine—making them low in saturated fat but high in cholesterol-reducing unsaturated fats. Says nutrition expert Andrew Weil, "Researchers from the University of Athens recently published a study showing that people who ate a Mediterranean-style diet had a 33 percent reduction in the risk of death from heart disease. Their cancer death rate was 24 percent lower than the death rate for those who ate more Western-style diets."[18]

In another study from the Netherlands, published in the September 2004 issue of the *Journal of the American Medical Association,* those who maintained a Mediterranean diet had a 23 percent lower death rate than those on their regular diets. Says Weil, "Those who followed the diet and also consumed moderate amounts of alcohol, got regular exercise, and didn't smoke, reduced their risk of death from any cause by 65 percent over the 10-year duration of the study."[19]

Dr. Dean Ornish agrees that diets similar to the Mediterranean diet have the right stuff, conferring anticancer, anti–heart disease, and antiaging properties. "I'd love to be able to tell people that bacon and eggs are health foods, but they're not," he says. "A diet rich in animal protein increases your risk of osteoporosis, kidney disease, heart disease, and the most common forms of cancer." Ornish also cites a study in the *American Journal of Medicine,* concluding that a meat-heavy diet can cause halitosis—not life threatening, but potentially hazardous to your *social* life. Since the human body gets rid of toxic substances partly through breathing, Ornish asserts that on a heavy meat diet (like the Atkins diet he loves to hate), "you may start to lose weight and attract people, but when they get too close, they might have a problem with the way you smell."[20]

For Ornish, the bottom line is the return to vitality he's seen in his own patients when they changed to diets lower in saturated fat and sugar and did moderate exercise. "We found that even among people with severe heart disease, 99 percent were able to stop or reverse the progression of their disease . . . People who couldn't walk across the street before the light changed without getting chest pains, they couldn't have sex, they couldn't take a shower, shave . . . within a few weeks were essentially pain-free."[21]

If meat is so heavily implicated in various diseases, and if it takes such a heavy toll on the environment, isn't it time to question whether we want to be eating it ten or fifteen times a week?

Morgan Spurlock, producer and star of the documentary *Super Size Me,* was on the Monster Thickburger (or actually Big Mac) diet for ninety straight meals, an adventure that had alarming side effects. In one of the documentary's most candid moments, he says, "I was starting to become impotent through this diet and couldn't perform. How many people who are taking the little blue pill, if they started to change what they are eating most of the time, could change the way their sex life is?"[22] (The Erectile Dysfunction Institute supports Spurlock's conclusion, reporting that up to 90 percent of all cases of impotence are physical, not psychological. "Viagra may get you through the night," says the GoVeg.com Web site, "but a vegetarian diet can get you through your life.")

"For me," says Spurlock, "the most horrifying thing of the whole project is the impact the fast food culture has on the schools, and parents have no idea. They give their kids three dollars and say, 'Okay, see you later. Go off to school and have a good lunch.' And the lunchrooms are filled with pizza and burgers and soda and candy and chips. It's like you're in the middle of the 7-11 having lunch . . . If anything comes out of this movie, I really hope it has an impact on the school lunch programs, because they need to change . . ." "Here's a question for you," says Spurlock. "Why doesn't the clown eat the food, in the advertisements? If it's that good for you, why isn't Ronald McDonald eating it?"[23]

15

Infinite Information

How to Channel the Flow

Information wants to be free.
  —Stewart Brand

People don't actually read newspapers. They step into them every morning like a hot bath.
  —Marshal McLuhan

Capital can do nothing without brains to direct it.
  —J. Ogden Armour

Whether we think of our brain as a file cabinet, hard drive, or . . . wastebasket, we know that one of its primary functions is to obtain and contain information. And we sense that what we *do* collectively with that information will determine the fate of our civilization (no pressure, though). Interdependent with the human body and the culture that feeds it "brain food," the brain is the crown jewel of our species, where we do our daydreaming, investing, designing, and understanding of quantum physics. The brain accounts for just 2 percent of body weight, yet it burns 20 percent of our calories. What's going on up there on the top floor? Well, we're solving puzzles—including one called "reducing consumption and increasing quality of life"—and that requires a lot of caloric fuel.

In the transition to a less consumptive yet culturally more abundant world, the brain is like an empty stage set, right before opening night. The new story—our new way of viewing the world—will be created on that stage as the play progresses, and a new, more ingenious lifestyle will unfold. By changing just one line of script—that the brain's highest use is to create limitless economic growth—we can ensure rave reviews in the history books of future generations. Let's face it, our descendants won't be especially impressed with the size of our GDP or the fast pace of our life, but they will be *ecstatic* (we hope!) that we cared enough to stop tearing things apart for cheap burgers and infinite varieties of soap and underwear. That we learned how to use relevant information to cut waste, create an aesthetically rich way of life, and balance the biological budget so the future could be abundant, too.

Information can be like a 911 call that gets an immediate response. For example, Toxics Release Inventory (TRI) data, mandated by federal law, first came out in 1990, listing the dirtiest companies by volume of waste. This data informs citizens precisely what is coming out of the smokestacks in their towns and empowers them to hold companies and local governments accountable for toxic chemicals. The TRI regulations are not about permissible limits or penalties, just information. Within a few years of the data's release, emissions dropped 40 percent. One chemical company that found itself on the Top Ten Polluters list reduced its emissions by 90 percent, just to "get off that damn list."

Another example of the leveraging power of listed information involved philanthropic contributions. CNN owner Ted Turner suggested in an interview with *New York Times* columnist Maureen Dowd that someone create a ranking of philanthropic gifts to stimulate competition among the superrich. The online magazine *Slate* responded with an annual list, and contributions soared as America's wealthiest donors tried to climb *higher* on the list. Turner followed up as well, pledging a whopping $1 billion to bail out the United Nations in 1999.

➤ What Are Brains For?

Many religiously devout humans believe the brain's highest purpose is to serve God, whereas scientifically inclined people often believe its purpose is to understand how life works and ensure its continuity. In my opinion, these two mind-sets are simply different ways of saying the same thing. Both acknowledge that there's a right way to live; that when we distract our awesome brainpower with material wealth alone, we neglect loftier, more spiritual values. In the quest to refocus our collective mind and help heal the wounds our way of life has created, we'll need to make use of every available brain. In the world of computer technology, many individual computers are linked together to create a "supercomputer"; that's also the most powerful form of *human* intelligence.

As I began to research and write this chapter, several questions came up:

- How can we differentiate between *quality* information and money-chatter that has little nutritional value?

- What do we need to know to help our culture and economy mature?

- How can information substitute for resource use, and reduce consumption?

- How can we use the best and purest information to create and design products, art, services, tools, and technologies of great value—with a much wider purpose than profit alone?

Our first priority is to exorcise an obsolete worldview from our shell-shocked brains so we can actively *seek* information we can use—along with a more responsible, compassionate ethic. In the current worldview, success means being "smart" enough to exploit the planet's resources and collect stacks of paper money. The new worldview, already taking shape, is more mature: substituting brilliant design, curiosity, and creativity for resources and stuff. Einstein, no slouch in the brain department himself, had much to say about people who underutilize the equipment: "He who joyfully marches in the rank and file has already earned my contempt. He has been given a large brain by mistake, since for him the spinal cord would suffice."

I believe it is critical that we each accept responsibility for the information that comes into our own heads, and also for what we do with it. If we absorb junk information by mistake, it can be quickly discarded, as in a game of gin rummy. But if it's important or even critical information, we can't just ignore it! For example, choosing to ignore and do nothing with information about climate change is like clipping the wires on a smoke alarm and going back to sleep while the house burns down.

With luck and/or by the grace of God, we may be less ignorant than we appear. We'll soon know if that's true, since the biggest IQ test we've ever taken is happening *right now*. We need designs, policies and an unwavering ethic that quickly respond to challenges like climate change, population, economy, and shortfalls of water and oil, biodiversity, and human rights. We can handle these challenges, but there's a glitch: Vested interest sources of information (what I call weapons of mass *distraction*) have tainted media, politics, scientific research, and educational institutions with pop information of questionable value. For example, TV and newspapers bend their content to the will of their sponsors and advertisers, compliantly using canned video news releases and corporate press releases rather than doing their own investigative reporting. Schools and universities accept funds from corporate and philanthropic donors, with strings attached: The funds must be used for specified (profitable) research and curricula.

Some educational institutions actually ban textbooks that encourage holistic ways of thinking (see "Toxic Information Cleanup," page 221). The Internet, potentially a bright light in the dissemination of knowledge, is currently a jungle of flashing, popping commercials, teeming with viruses and cultural excess—a bit like the tail-finned cars of the 1950s.

Because both the story and mission of our culture are obsolete, information is flowing—often flooding—in the wrong direction, carrying some of our best minds with it. When the dominant story is, "must have more money," brain surgeons opt to become plastic surgeons, and brilliant Pulitzer Prize–winning journalists go into advertising. Our most powerful device for telling the story of a cleaner, greener lifestyle and ethic may be the high art of filmmaking; but for the most part, movie producers follow the money, too, reprising existing scripts and formula plotlines that depict a seductively affluent lifestyle—unavailable to most, and impossible to maintain over the long haul.

Then there are the ads, the sorry signature of our generation! As in the thought-provoking movie *Minority Report,* advertisements are in our faces no matter where we go: in school hallways and buses, doctor's offices, hospitals, supermarket floors, elevators, ATMs . . . Ads now decorate fruit, T-shirts, garbage cans, bus stop benches, restroom walls, bald heads, eggs, golf balls, mountaintops, and just about everything and everyone else. And guess who's paying for it all? You and me, to the tune of $600 or more per capita annually, payable at the cash register (With lower levels of consumption, we'll each subsidize less advertising.) The truth is, even our own mothers could be walking commercials: Undercover con artists are now paid to socialize with us as if they want to be our friends, sneaking consumer tips into casual conversations. Drug companies have also learned the value of personal persuasion, in the shape of sex appeal. They often hire cheerleaders right out of college to push prescription drugs to doctors, a job that dispenses salaries as high as six figures. The companies "don't even ask what their majors are," notes a cheerleading coach at the University of Kentucky. "Exaggerated motions, exaggerated smiles, exaggerated enthusiasm can get people to do what they want." Even if the drugs don't work.[1]

American brains are trying, heroically, to process and make sense of all this information, but the question is, how much of it is even *useful*? For example, a child who's adept at surfing TV channels or the Web may well encounter sharks. Recent studies have shown that the average age of first Internet exposure to pornography is 11, that four out of five children in the 12–17 age group have had multiple exposure to hard-core porn, and that one-fourth of *all* search engine requests are also for porn.[2] Clearly, we have some work to do—not only tuning up the Web, but also tuning up our lives to include more rewarding activities. A few key policies can make us less vulnerable. For example, requiring that sex browsers pay for each Web page they visit—and then collecting part of that income as tax—would dramatically reduce underage visits to the virtual red-light districts.

Still, despite the troubling liabilities of wide-open access, many people (including me) regard the Internet as the greatest communications innovation since the printing press. Between 1988 and 2006, Internet usage in the United States exploded from 60,000 to 207 million users—a stunning revolution in information access. I believe the genius of the Internet is that it gives us greater control, overall, of what goes in and comes out of our brain. Suddenly, freedom of expression is a much greater possibility. A whole new world of blogging, researching, and sharing knowledge has opened up with tools like Wikipedia (created entirely by volunteers who contribute, update, and revise articles in a collaborative process), YouTube, MySpace, and many, many others. The Internet is not centralized and authoritative but rather interactive, participatory, and democratic. On the right brain–inspired Internet, we follow our curiosity to find out *why* carbon dioxide heats up the planet, or what exactly the president said or didn't say in his latest speech. We can join the ranks of dissenters or supporters on politically active sites like MoveOn.org (see chapter 17 for more about this organization). With the right keywords, the Internet unlocks the context as well as the facts, offering choice, precision, and self-determined learning.

➤ Moldy Couch Potatoes or Spuds with Gusto?

What about TV? Certainly, with cable, satellite, Netflix, TiVo, and all the other available options, the tube now offers more *choice* than it used to, but the medium is still passive, hypnotic, and overconsumed. As musician Jerry Garcia phrased it, tongue in cheek, "Constantly choosing the lesser of two evils is still choosing evil." Who could deny that TV is a primary shaper of our current, high-consumption lifestyle? Says Jerry Mander, a senior fellow at Public Media Center, "It's become the main thing people do. It's replaced community life, family life, and culture. It has replaced the environment. In fact, it has *become* the environment that people interact with every day."[3] By the time the average American child has finished sixth grade, he or she will have witnessed 100,000 acts of televised violence, including 8,000 murders, and by the time that same student has completed high school, he or she will have absorbed 350,000 TV commercials that visually define the American lifestyle: working, driving, and spending (and sometimes mowing the lawn).[4] Every year, our young, impressionable friend veges out for 1,500 hours in front of the tube compared with 900 hours spent at school. What was once an American malady has now infected the world: A 2004 French survey representing 2.5 *billion people* in seventy-two countries documented an average of 3.5 of TV hours watched every day.

In an ad produced by the Canadian nonprofit Adbusters, we view-the-viewer from behind, sitting in a dark room, staring at the tube. "Your living room is the factory," says the voiceover; "the product being manufactured is you." In countless other rooms all over the country, other voices advertise *Survivor* or one of its primetime spin-offs. "They live, you watch!" exclaims a narrator in a taunting tone of voice. The implication, of course, is that ordinary viewers like you and me just aren't up to the task of *living*; we're barely hardy enough to be observers, slumping on the couch while video gladiators grapple for a million bucks in prize money. It appears we've been voted off the island of life without ever really giving ourselves a shot!

"We live, you watch," say the photogenic contestants. "We're too dazed and confused to live, anyway," respond the viewers, crunching handfuls of Cheetos.

You may have noticed that news sound bites have become shorter—from half a minute in the 1950s to eight seconds now, on average—eliminating opportunities to explain the context and the process of an event. And as sound bites shrink, advertising expands. The annual "clutter" report of the Association of National Advertisers verifies that the standard network hour now contains up to twenty-one minutes of advertising in addition to all the product-placement ads embedded *in* the programs. "The more television people watch, the more they think all American households should have tennis courts, private planes, convertibles, car telephones, maids and swimming pools . . ." observes Harvard scholar Juliet Schor. Unfortunately, what we see is what we crave, even if we know it's only an illusion. We think of television as entertainment but it's also recruitment into the army of consumers. That's why freethinker Dawn Griffin hasn't owned a TV for twenty-five years—she wants to retain control of her own mind. When she goes into a house (or airport lounge, waiting room, convenience store, gym . . .) where a TV is on, she feels irritated about how it dominates the room. "I get sucked into a trancelike state, and it's hard to have a conversation, write or think, because I'm distracted by all the mind chatter."

Susse Wright, another TV-free survivor, came to the United States from Denmark, where her parents didn't own a TV set. She hates TV news because it's "dumbed down." She says, "When I read the newspaper, I can scan for the stories I want to read. But with TV, you don't have any choice. You sit in front of this flickering, noisy box, wasting time." Is there life outside the box? Ask Susse when she's kayaking, bird watching, or cross-country skiing. "In real life," adds Dawn, "If someone is telling you a story, you have to create the related images in your own mind. You smell the flowers or feel the breeze, and you live the experience. With TV, you only experience chopped-up visual images." In a spoof news article in *The Onion* newspaper, a coal miner trapped 340 feet underground has only one major regret—that he can't see the coverage of his plight, "which, he assumes, is captivating the nation."

Of course, nothing captivated the nation like two events that worked so perfectly on television: the gruesome Kennedy assassination and the gruesome events of 9/11. Predictably, by about 9/21, America and the world were informed of countless ways to REALLY cripple the country: Here's how easy it would be to contaminate California's water supply, here's how to blow up a nuclear plant, here's the genetic blueprint of the Spanish flu virus that killed twenty-five million in 1918. Is that a good use of information, or just another fear-filled ploy to keep us watching? Local news reporters have increasingly been instructed to tease us with what lies ahead, after "the break." The break consists of fun-loving, seemingly satisfied actors who not only hawk their client's product but also attitudes, values, and situations in which every problem is happily solved by buying a product. When we return, at last, to the program, everything is mindlessly, laugh-trackingly silly. We assume that everything must be okay after all.

Is TV all bad? Of course not, but like any potential addiction, its use should remain moderate. I like to watch a serial program or two a week, and I try to catch *60 Minutes, Frontline,* and *Nova* when good shows are scheduled. (If I miss them, I can watch them now on Web archives.) One of my all-time favorite TV experiences was the late-1970s BBC series *Life on Earth,* which tracks the evolution of species from single-celled cyanophytes and primitive jellyfish through "The Compulsive Communicator," the final program. (Let's hope that's not an omen.) I loved seeing the various life strategies and how they interrelate—so much that a few years ago, I checked out all thirteen hourlong programs from the library and watched the whole series again, over the weekend. Our fellow species are so playfully, colorfully, miraculously inventive!

➤ That Same Old Story

At a movie recently, the audio levels of the previews were getting obnoxiously loud. I usually bring earplugs just in case, but I didn't have them with me this time, and Kleenex plugs (Susan tells me I look like Eeyore) didn't seem to be helping much, either. I got up to make a complaint, marching past what seemed like hundreds of theaters, to the now-idle ticket taker.

"I'd like to speak with the manager, please," I requested. "The sound level in theater 14 is REALLY LOUD." He got on his intercom and called the manager. While waiting, I explained to the ticket taker that the sound seemed to be 100 decibels or more—it was making my head buzz. "We do get some complaints," he acknowledged. I was determined not to seem like an "irate" customer but just a reasonable, good-natured guy, basing my argument on science.

The manager listened to my complaint and told me that the levels were preset; there wasn't much she could do. I held my ground, politely insisting that they were louder than usual, that I came to this movie theater often, and that maybe she could check them again? I almost wished the loosely stuffed Kleenex plugs were still dangling from my ears as proof that I was completely serious. But I did seem to be getting through to the human being in her, and before I left, she promised to turn the levels down just a bit. I walked back and took my seat, feeling a little heroic, like I'd made the world a tiny bit safer. I kicked back in the seat and enjoyed the movie, even though the sound still seemed loud throughout . . .

After the movie, I followed up, asking—still politely—if she'd turned the sound down or not. She had indeed turned it down, but then had gotten another complaint that it was too *soft*, and turned it back up. Realizing the absurdity of the situation—that the other complainer's hearing was probably already blown out—I blurted, "How much do movie companies pay you to maintain dangerous levels, especially for the previews? How many people do you think gradually lose their hearing at movies, these days? Why doesn't anybody care about protecting our hearing?" My elevated sense of consumer outrage did yield two free tickets to any upcoming show, but that didn't reduce my righteous indignation very much.

Before going to bed, I harnessed Google's awesome exploratory powers to find out how noisy movies actually are. I chuckled to myself when I came across a reference to typical audio levels for movie previews—right around 100 decibels, exactly as I had guessed. (I do have a master's degree in environmental science, you know.) "It's not your imagination," Desmond Ryan of the *Philadelphia Inquirer* wrote, as if addressing me personally. "The decibel level in movie theatres is rising." On another Web site, the *Wall Street Journal* reported that *Batman and Robin* peaked at 112 decibels in one monitored theater, while *Contact* measured 107 decibels at another—volumes equal to those produced by a jackhammer that never stops. And a U.S. EPA Web site added the kicker: exposure to sound above

84 decibels for an hour is dangerous. "Too late," I said to myself, shaking my head—though I was still able to hear geese honking in a pond nearby. At last count, more than thirty million Americans have some kind of hearing loss from all causes—and clinical research suggests that daily noise may play a significant role in everything from sleep disorders and stress responses to high blood pressure and heart disease.

Nevertheless, there's something very powerful, very transforming, about watching a great movie in the company of hundreds of other people, even if you have to wear a jacket in the summertime or push Kleenex into your ears to protect your hearing. Together, we react to the same stories and images and learn something new about life, and about each other. We may as well be a clan of hunter-gatherers sitting around a campfire, telling stories. Says Don Norman, author of *Things That Make Us Smart,* "Stories are important cognitive events because they encapsulate information, knowledge, context, and emotion in one compact package." I firmly believe that well-made documentary films can change the course of history. They remind us that information can be fascinating, useful, stimulating, and sometimes refreshingly conspiratorial. For example, from *Roger and Me* through *Bowling for Columbine, Fahrenheit 9/11*, and *Sicko,* Michael Moore's films make us think about the politics of human behavior. The PBS program *Affluenza,* produced by John de Graaf (before we collaborated on a book with the same title), made me stand up at the end and comment to friends, "That's the best TV I've seen in years." *Enron: The Smartest Guys in the Room,* was also an eye-opener.

In recent years, as evidence that our culture is changing, some beautifully poignant documentaries about nature have done very well in mainstream theaters, giving audiences a collective sense that humans are only *one* heroic species among millions. *Winged Migration* is an epic filmmaking effort that required a crew of 450 people, including 17 pilots and 14 cinematographers, to follow flocks of migrating birds across all seven continents in planes, gliders, helicopters, and hot air balloons. The audience applauded enthusiastically at the end, as they did at the conclusion of *March of the Penguins,* a brilliant, Academy Award–winning film about the talents, trials, and tribulations of emperor penguins (and we thought our lifestyle was challenging!). In films like *Microcosmos, The Wild Chimpanzees,* and *The Wild Parrots of Paragraph Hill,* we come to know the daily delights and discomforts of penguins, storks, chimps, beetles, parrots, and other animals, and we realize at a deeper level that the world's other species are trying to live joyful lives, too. In the absence of widely understood ecological knowledge about the valuable role each species plays, probably only empathy will motivate us to preserve the habitats where so many animals and plants are struggling. We need to imagine them with the faces of our dogs and cats. As scientist and author Donella Meadows asked so poignantly before she died, "Since the Earth is finite, and we will have to stop expanding sometime, should we do it before or after nature's diversity is gone?"

➤ Toxic Information Cleanup

A friend of mine, Dan Chiras, answered the phone not long ago and found out that the Texas Board of Education had blacklisted a textbook he wrote, *Environmental Science: Creating a Sustainable Future,* because it was thought to be "out of line with both Christian and free enterprise principles." Dan decided to contest the decision, and the Trial Lawyers for Public Justice brought a lawsuit against the board on his behalf. David Bradley, one of the board members named in the suit, was "disappointed" with the way the environmental science textbook portrayed the American economy and the free-enterprise system. He also didn't like negative implications about the petrochemical industry and offshore drilling, predominant industries in the Texas economy. "Maybe those people out there in Berkeley like it, but not here in Texas," he said. Chiras had written that air quality was unhealthy in a large number of American cities, using data generated by the U.S. Environmental Protection Agency. The board suggested that the author tone down statements such as this, which he refused to do despite the loss of the largest textbook market in the country after California.[5]

Bradley also cited sections in the book that showed panoramic views of housing developments and detailed the environmental impacts of them. "I'm in real estate," Bradley said. "I see a picture like that and I see $350,000 homes; I see mortgage bankers; I see carpenters; I see jobs. I see a tax base."[6]

It's what he *doesn't* see that hurts us. He doesn't see asthma victims of air pollution trying to get to the emergency wing at the hospital, or fish flipping on a riverbank, poisoned by chemical runoff from toxic lawns. His mental dictionary doesn't yet acknowledge the term "global warming," so he doesn't worry about how much energy those homes use. And he doesn't think about the acre of forest that was cut down to build each house, or how woefully inefficient most residents' much-driven cars are. He doesn't think about the fact that beneath the economic bottom line the far more tangible ecological bottom line is rapidly being dismantled.

We need to draw the line; to make sure we get information without contamination. As a starting point, let's make a clear distinction between *political* freedom of speech and *commercial* freedom of speech. As citizens in a democracy that requires our informed participation, we have a right and obligation to retain control of our own brain. The problem with bought information is that it takes too much time, energy, and focus to find the signal amid the noise, distracting us from looking at value in a wider sense. The most dangerous aspect of junk information may be that it lowers our ability to trust. Since advertisers are expected to make false claims to make money, how can we trust them, or anyone else who's just in it for the money? In the case of soaps, snack foods, cars, and all the rest, if a product is excellent, shouldn't word of mouth sell it? *Consumer Reports* and Ralph Nader were pioneers in supplying information we can use. Other innovators like Amazon and Netflix provide customer-rating systems that help others evaluate the value of a product. It may sound radical in our hyped-up world to consider banning advertising, but it's quite possible—and quite necessary—to find a higher purpose for our brain than soaking up mind-numbing jingles, posters, and fake testimonials. We have more important work, and play, to do.

Why not regulate all advertising the way we've regulated the cigarette and alcohol industries? Why not tax advertising in general, over a certain monetary limit? Companies will either cut back on advertising to save money, or the taxes they pay will help purchase open space or build new centers for performing arts. A similar strategy is used in some state lottery laws. For example, Colorado's GOCO regulations allot a certain percentage of lottery revenues for recreational uses of land.

In the case of TV, why not reclaim public oversight of the airwaves, charging broadcasters higher fees to use them? This is an especially hot button for me right now, after a company called Lake Cedar Group forced my hometown to accept the installation of a 9-million-watt "supertower" to broadcast HDTV, despite potential health effects and the availability of more remote, safer sites. How did they do it? By running TV ads in the Denver Metro area over and over that chastised "a small group of people" for obstructing the public's *right* to have HDTV. Just before a Congressional recess, a bill that overrides local control of land was tucked into a whole package of bills, quickly pushed through Congress, and rubber-stamped by the president. A bit of research on the Web revealed that at least one of the senators who introduced the bill, Ken Salazar, had received a $20,000 campaign contribution from Lake Cedar Group's legal firm. Is TV more important than local land use rights and the well-being of people?[7]

➤ Telling a New Story: Information We Can Use

I believe we need to use a martial arts approach to redirect the awesome power of the media. They are already scrambling for market share—newspapers are taking shelter on the web and companies like Sony are selling devices that enable TVs to access the Internet; network TV producers are scrambling to become as innovative as cable TV producers, who are hiring YouTube freelancers to teach them what the younger generation wants. Book publishers are tracking the reasons why we're reading less literature (a 2004 study by the National Endowment for the Arts documents an overall decline of 10 percent in the last twenty years). Now's the time to vote with our credit cards and the clicks of our computer mouse, showing those that gather such data that we want information we can *use?*

We are at a turning point with our infinite supplies of information, similar to a child who's learned to speak. Having mastered the technology of talking, the child must now figure out *what she or he wants to say.* To reduce consumption, we need to tell an ingenious story about the incredible value of nature, social connection, cultural richness, and human creativity. The new story is also about substituting information for resource use. In *Earth in Mind,* educator David Orr advocates transforming knowledge into products, cities, and systems that fit nature like a hand fits a glove: "Ecological design requires the ability to comprehend patterns that connect, which means getting beyond the boxes we call disciplines to see things in their ecological context."[8]

The term "value added," as used in the business world, refers to taking raw materials and shaping them into products. Yet, as many indigenous populations as well as enlightened economists know full well, it's also critically important to *retain* value. One great example is the decision New York City made in the 1990s. Required by U.S. EPA to provide safer drinking water for its nine million residents, city engineers and scientists were at a crossroads: either build a huge water treatment plant or preserve the natural purification assets of the upstate watershed, where the water comes from. They wisely chose nature over expensive, high-maintenance technology, saving more than $5 billion just for construction.

As naturalist Edward Abbey once said, "We must learn to think not only logically, but biologically." Movies, documentaries, journalism, literature, the Internet, and TV can help shift our thoughts; and nature can serve as a model. Mature ecosystems use nutrients much more efficiently and are more diverse, cooperative, and weblike than immature, wasteful systems, whose species haven't yet coevolved resource conserving designs and approaches. Similarly, a more mature version of our economy will accommodate diversity and local strengths, focusing on *preserving* nature rather than dismantling it; and tapping into its renewable flows and cycles, like wind, sun, decomposition, water and air purification, natural pest control, pollination, and so on. This is what futurist Lester Brown calls the "eco-economy," which relies on information and innovation to restore ecological systems like wetlands, produce biofuels and bioplastics, recycle and compost materials that are specifically designed to break down, and in general, substitute efficiency for waste. The new story is not just about economic growth—which often generates fear and insecurity—but human growth and natural regeneration, which generates joy.

The American public is hungry for a sense of mission, and the media can give it shape. By tuning out junk media and tuning in stimulating, coherent media, we can emerge from this gooey pupa we are currently trapped in to become a nature-friendly, butterfly culture.

For example, by acting quickly to prevent the worst effects of global warming, we can save huge amounts of money and prevent unimaginable misery, too. A recent British study estimated that the annual cost of climate change to Britons will eventually exceed hundreds of billions of dollars, and that it will be far less expensive and inconvenient to limit greenhouse gases than deal with the impacts later. Stalled, or faulty, information prevents political consensus and action. In the documentary and book *An Inconvenient Truth,* Al Gore points out that there were more than six hundred articles about global warming in the popular press from 1991 to 2005, 53 percent of which presented global warming as unproven. However, in 928 peer-reviewed articles in scientific journals, scientists were unanimous in their certainty that human activities are a primary cause. The discrepancy comes from a perceived need to present both sides of an issue in newspapers, magazines, and other media—especially if one side brings money. In many cases, the experts who dispute that humans cause global warming received funds from the fossil fuel industry, a primary sponsor of the media.

A recent issue of *Yes! Magazine* (a perfect example of butterfly media), Co-op America's Alisa Gravitz gives us information we can use: a very achievable Ten-Step program for reducing greenhouse gases that contribute to climate change. The steps, to be achieved by 2054, include:

- Double vehicle efficiency

- Reduce vehicle miles traveled

- Increase appliance and building efficiency to reduce energy use in buildings by 25 percent

- Eliminate tropical deforestation and increase replanting

- Increase organic agriculture to stop soil erosion

- Increase wind power seventy-five-fold over current capacity; increase solar power a thousand-fold over current capacity

- Double the efficiency of coal-fired power plants with no net increase in coal-generated electricity (for each new plant, take an old one out of service)

- Increase natural gas-fired generating capacity fourfold to replace coal plants as a temporary measure

- Develop fuels from biological waste (not crops)

- Capture and sequester CO_2 at existing coal plants

- Develop super-efficient plug-in hybrid vehicles and electric vehicles powered by renewable energy.[9]

Says Gravitz, "Just doing seven of the ten steps perfectly would at least keep emissions at current levels, rather than doubling by mid-century, as is projected."

In our everyday lives, we can substitute information for consumption by purchasing products that use fewer materials in their packaging, that are recyclable and durable, and that provide the service precisely—with no wasted energy or materials. In fact, the new story is largely about events that happen right in our daily lives: the way we prepare meals, stay warm, travel to a concert, design new clothing and new buildings, and treat each other. It's about cooperating to use information wisely rather than wasting it. It's about creating a country-scale suggestion box that chooses which technologies will deliver the most value, overall. We can even vote in our own backyards, by planting "biointensive" gardens that use profound knowledge and skill to optimize every square foot of garden space. By allowing useful information into our brain, we can support new policies and new technologies that result in more pedestrian-friendly communities, and information-rich innovations like "living machines." The living machine is an alternative way to treat wastewater—which we all are responsible for. It mimics the natural intelligence of a wetland, treating human or industrial wastes with snails, fish, flowers, cattails, and other living things.

Similarly, a whole new universe of natural solutions is waiting for us if we study the way other species meet their needs—without any monetary system at all! Says biologist Janine Benyus, "Life shows us there's plenty to go around." Benyus reports on innovations in the fascinating world of "biomimicry" (see her book of the same title). By studying how the lotus leaf stays clean without detergents (a bumpy surface that doesn't enable dirt to accumulate), engineers have invented bio-inspired, bumpy-layered paints. By seeing how peacocks and Morphos butterflies create pigment without dyes (they use transparent layers to refract light), we learn how to make our world more colorful, naturally. Although our primitive technologies use a philosophy of "heat, beat, and treat," which leaves piles of waste behind, the abalone shell self-assembles layer by layer, without any waste—selecting minerals from the palette in seawater. In the same way that the cocklebur inspired Velcro technology, we can learn how nature lubricates, communicates, recycles materials, purifies water, weaves silk, muffles sound, reduces friction, repels microbes, and heals itself. "From A to Z—amoeba to zebra—nature has already compiled the information we need," asserts Benyus.[10]

If we are smart enough to redirect the flow of information, we can learn to create a benign economy that doesn't require so much money; that creates wealth—*real* wealth—the way a bee creates honey. Without harming the flower.

16

Historical Dividends

New Rules for an Old Game

Capitalism is the astounding belief that the most wicked of men will do the most wicked of things for the greatest good of everyone.
　　—John Maynard Keynes

Laws and institutions must go hand in hand with the progress of the human mind. As new discoveries are made, new truths discovered and manners and opinions change, institutions must advance also to keep pace with the times.
　　—Thomas Jefferson

When money is plenty this is a man's world. When money is scarce it is a woman's world. When all else seems to have failed, the woman's instinct comes in.
　　—Ladies Home Journal, 1932

According to "reporters" at the satirical newspaper *The Onion,* nearly nine out of ten Americans are "tired of having a country." *Onion* reporters write, "Among the 86 percent of poll respondents who were in favor of discontinuing the nation, the most frequently cited reasons were a lack of significant results from the current democratic process (36 percent), dissatisfaction with customer service (28 percent), and exhaustion (22 percent). Many said they believe that having a country is 'counter to the best interests of Americans,' and that 'the time and effort citizens spend on the country could be better spent elsewhere.' Eight percent said they just didn't care. Wilmington, DE, accountant Karie Ashworth said, 'I don't want to get bogged down in the country anymore,' and Olympia, WA, student Helen Berg, expressing frustration with the country's voting process, said, 'I was gonna vote, but it rained. It wasn't for the president anyway, so what difference does it make?'"[1]

Satire so often touches the raw nerve of reality. It seems we've all but forgotten that as citizens, we each carry a piece of the truth; that in effect each of us has been granted responsibility for the well being of all the others. Like many other civilizations that precede us, we Americans too often assume that "someone else" is responsible for maintaining the values we hold in common, such as taking care of the environment, providing the general conditions for health, and ensuring equal opportunity for everyone. Historian Edward Gibbons offers an instructive, distant mirror to view another culture that took democracy for granted: "In the end, more than the Athenians wanted freedom, they wanted security. When the freedom they wished for was freedom from responsibility, then Athens ceased to be." While it's difficult to imagine American culture *ceasing to be,* it's not hard to imagine a country in which wealth and power are concentrated into fewer and fewer hands, armed by an unchallenged assumption of continuous growth. The only medicines strong enough to counter this epidemic of concentrated wealth and carelessness are democracy and community—the distributed power of the people.

Democracy is an incredibly rich asset that needs to be maintained and pampered, like a racehorse. In the book *The Healing of America,* Marianne Williamson speaks eloquently of the incredible value of the Constitution, with its all-inclusive invitation to take part in decision-making. She imagines the way it must have felt in the room where the Declaration of Independence was being signed: "The air must have crackled. Their hearts must have known . . ." Yet she questions whether, only seven or eight generations later, we've trivialized the intensity and *intention* of their passion: "The founding fathers were talking about the liberation of the individual soul, not just the right to be rich," she writes. "The statement that our "Creator . . . created all men equal and endowed them with 'certain inalienable rights,' is not just an early American public relations slogan. It is a bright light shot like a laser through thousands of years of history. It is a principle for which millions of people have fought and died. These words are a radical, revolutionary *force.*"[2]

Wrote Thomas Paine in 1776, "We have it in our power to begin the world over again." Paine's powerful pamphlet *Common Sense* was read by at least one in every five colonists, inspiring them to rip off the yoke of the Crown, and by extension, discard a whole way of life—authoritarian feudalism itself. An individual should not be subservient to any other human or human system, Paine and his compatriots believed, though they did de-fer to the will and omniscience of God. One of them, Virginia politician and revolutionary Patrick Henry, passionately told the Virginia House of Burgesses in March 1775: "There is no longer any room for hope. If we wish to be free, then we must fight . . . ! Give me liberty, or give me death!"

Another very influential event happened in 1776: the publication of Scottish economist Adam Smith's *The Wealth of Nations,* in which he proposed an economy based on the concept of a free market and a bright new doctrine called capitalism. The whole package seemed to fit together; the newly liberated individual was given something very compelling to *do* with his freedom: accumulate as much material wealth as possible. It must have seemed like a perfect marriage when divinely endowed Freedom and potentially limitless Fortune were wed. But there were skeletons in the closet, and it's high time to reveal them. Adam Smith, by most accounts a decent enough fellow, may as well have written, "Hey, I've got an idea—humans are weak and greedy, and nature is an infinite storehouse of resources, so let's harness our new technologies and have at it." Smith's proposal—that humans could make rational decisions resulting in collective prosperity—is not a bad idea, but in our time, the assumptions it was based on have become obsolete. Here are the most obvious perceptual blunders of a doctrine that currently rules our world:

1. Humans aren't just greedy, rational, and competitive (though there is some of that); we're also altruistic, empathetic, and cooperative.

2. Nature isn't just a storehouse of resources to make into plastic grocery bags and cell phones, it's a fragile, interdependent web of life that provides air, water, food, and shelter for us and for all the world's species. But as long as nature is perceived as a mechanical, infinite vending machine, the market doesn't perceive a need to maintain or preserve it.

3. Just because a technology is *possible* does not mean it is *desirable.* Technology can be either useful or destructive, depending on its scale and purpose. The logic of the market doesn't make qualitative evaluations very well so, empowered by democratic principles, citizens must help choose whether a given technology is socially and environmentally acceptable.

Adam Smith's free-market theories hitched a ride on the rationalist theories of scientists like Isaac Newton and René Descartes, who perceived the natural world as a mechanism, like a clock, an engine, or a waterwheel. In the Age of Enlightenment (the seventeenth and eighteenth centuries),

Western civilization was emerging from superstition and a fear of the dark forest. The shadows of natural catastrophes like the plague still hung over the world. Newton, Descartes, and other "enlightened" scientists proposed that humans could rise *above* nature. Only humans have souls, feelings, or self-awareness, they believed, setting a course for disaster. Adam Smith's capitalism was an adjunct to the new science, since a vigorous economy fueled by self-interest and technology would not only tame the dark forces of nature but also transform them into glittering assets in accountants' ledgers.

It's critical to understand and acknowledge this arranged marriage of personal freedom and capitalism because this will help us stop the spread of affluenza. Although the original goal of personal liberty was to create a "New Order of the Ages," nothing less, that motto ended up on the back of the dollar bill—*novus ordo seclorum*. Is it freedom or money we revere?

In Descartes's time, private property was just being "invented." Individual rights and privileges were being seen in a radically new light. For example, until about the time Columbus sailed to America, the Western culture didn't include individual chairs. Although royalty perched on plush, upholstered thrones, the common folk sat on wooden benches or stools, or squatted together on cushions on the floor. It was unusual to see a person walking outside city walls or on a country lane by himself, according to historian Georges Duby. "In the medieval era, solitary wandering was a symptom of insanity."[3]

In those days, most people ate from a common bowl and shared a tablecloth to wipe grease and gravy off hands and mouths. But by the 1700s, individual bowls were in wide use; along with the recently invented forks that separated humans from the "beasts" they were eating. Private rooms began to appear and manners were developed, to further distinguish "man" from beast. The pronoun "I" began to be seen more frequently in popular literature. Self-portraits became popular in art, and both personal and wall mirrors became common, literally reflecting a new interest in the self. René Descartes led the charge, proclaiming, "I think, therefore I am." (The critical question is, What was he thinking?)

I'm not suggesting that we should ever again share the tablecloth as a common napkin—certainly not with that sniffling, drooling bloke sitting between us! My point is that a new way of looking at the world emerged from a period that was far less comfortable, far less civilized, than our current era. Individual freedoms regarding consumption and possessions were seen as *human rights* issues. Life began to be more about "me" and what I own, and less about "we," and what we share. In a grand reordering of political and economic reality, the free market became an organizing principle of social change. Freed from the chains of feudalism, the crude-

Feudalism and Communism bit the dust; is Capitalism next? Many of the ideas that shaped our economy were products of a vastly different era. Credit: Susan Benton

ness of communal living and the cruelties of nature, the capitalist was encouraged—soon, all but required—to wage battle in the market. In our day, the individual still aspires and expects to be king of his own world. He's individually wired for direct audio, visual, and text messaging with the world. His customized car license plate reads "mybaby," and his golf clubs are monogrammed, just like Tiger's.

The point is, Adam Smith and his cohorts erroneously wrote greed and personal grandeur into the rules we still live by. Smith's assertion that "moral sentiments" would counter-balance a free market powered by self-interest was a product of different times. Back then, most people lived in close-knit towns and ran village-scale enterprises. People knew each other by name, and there was accountability and conscience-by-community. If the butcher sold spoiled meat, he would not only get a bad reputation in the town but townspeople wouldn't let their son marry his daughter. With constraints like these securely in place, competition was encoded as a primary motivator for creating wealth. Humans, like the rest of nature, were assumed to be naturally competitive—"red in tooth and claw," as the poet Tennyson later phrased it. But nature is not as competitive as Enlightenment scientists imagined. The overriding theme of nature is really more about mutual benefit and survival of those that *fit*. The world's species cooperate, barter, and negotiate to achieve ecological balance in tangible ways, such as building fertile soil for all life forms, stabilizing climate, purifying water, and operating with a zero-waste strategy.

Since the science of ecology (the patterns and relationships among living things) hadn't matured in Smith's time, the idea that species share a water hole by visiting it at different, mutually agreeable hours may not have occurred to Enlightenment scientists. The fact that chimpanzees, pelicans, coyotes, and many other species hunt cooperatively didn't impress them, either. And cooperation among humans at harvest time, in times of scarcity, in extended families, in social movements, and in noncompetitive forms of recreation was apparently not sufficient evidence to override philosophers' certainty that competition was the undisputed way of the world. They had their theory and they made the economic world fit it.

Biologist Elisabet Sahtouris argues that when taken to an extreme, competition starves the loser, which eventually also starves the winner. "Global economics is a hierarchical system where one level survives at the expense of another level," she says. "But this top-down approach is never seen in healthy biological systems. What species is in charge of a rainforest? What part is in charge of your body? Imagine the brain deciding not to allocate resources to certain organs, but keeping them to itself. You can't have some organs exploiting the others. You would die."[4]

➤ "Burn Baby, Burn"

Wouldn't it be interesting to watch Adam Smith's reaction to the obsessively competitive, immoral behavior of a modern company like Enron? In 2000–2001, Enron employees stretched the free market far beyond its intended limits, intentionally creating a phony energy crisis in California. Some utility customers died because of their behavior. In the documentary *The Smartest Guys in the Room,* we hear the actual taped voices of Enron employees requesting that plant managers "get a little creative" in shutting down plants for "repairs." At one point, the company had made arrangements to flip the switch on three-fourths of California's power supply, while the price of electricity soared 900 percent. In another tape leaked to the media, an Enron energy trader hears news that a forest fire has shut down a major transmission line into California. "Burn, baby, burn," he sings.

Sociologist Alfie Kohn gives the example of a sudden fire in an auditorium that creates mass panic. By acting competitively, panicked audiences have often smothered each other in a mad rush for the exit; but by acting cooperatively and forming fast-moving lines, everyone gets out alive. In Kohn's view, competition is both fueled by, and creates, anxiety and a sense of inadequacy. Since we're compelled to prove ourselves by beating others, we'll inevitably feel humiliated when they beat us.[5] How can we wish each other well when the rules of the game are "Show no mercy"?

Contemporary science is proving that cooperation, compassion and trust are hardwired into our genes and psyche, and we can successfully wire them into our economy as well. Scientists have mapped the biochemistry of trust (which makes cooperation possible), observing that the chemical compound oxytocin is produced naturally in the brain by such stimuli as breastfeeding, sex, and various other forms of social bonding.[6] Using MRI technology, scientists also observe that when participants in an experiment cooperate, the circuitry that feeds the brain's "pleasure centers" becomes highly active. The same sections of the brain that rejoice over chocolate, pictures of pretty faces, and windfalls of money also get very excited about cooperation. We cooperate because it feels good, and it feels good because it provides a better shot at mutual survival—whether or not there are record profits.[7]

What would Smith, David Ricardo, and their colleagues have said about the findings of an MIT-conducted computer analysis sponsored by the prestigious Club of Rome, an international group of business people, governmental leaders, and scientists? In the 1970s, the research team used a computer model (World3) to ask, "What will happen if population and economic growth continue at current rates? What can be done to ensure a human economy that fits within the physical limits of the Earth?" Their report, updated in 2004, included warning signs for any civilization living beyond its means, and alarmingly, ours shows evidence of all of them:

- Resource stocks fall, and wastes and pollution accumulate.

- Capital, resources, and labor are diverted to activities compensating for the loss of services formerly provided without cost by nature (e.g., water purification, flood control, pest control, and pollination).

- Scarcer, more distant, deeper, or more dilute resources are exploited.

- There is growing chaos in natural systems, with "natural" disasters more frequent and more severe because of less resilience in the environmental system.

- Growing demands for capital, resources, and labor are used by the military or industry to gain access to and defend resources that are increasingly concentrated in fewer, more remote, or increasingly hostile regions.

- Investment in human resources (education, health care, shelter) is postponed to meet immediate consumption, investment, or security needs, or to pay debts.

- There is declining respect for the instruments of collective government as they are used increasingly by the elites to preserve or increase their share of a declining resource base.

Adapted from Limits to Growth: The 30-Year Update (*176–77*).

And what would these pioneers of capitalism say about the fact that all major natural systems (such as fisheries, grasslands, forests, and farmland) are in decline, all over the planet; about species that are disappearing at the fastest rate since the demise of the dinosaur, *sixty-seven million* years ago? Would they insist that the free market is running as smoothly as an expensive gold watch, or would they finally admit that we are running out of time? I think they might say, "Well, we have *another* idea—one that's more moderate, easier on the environment, and more inherently democratic." They were smart people; they'd recognize that times have radically changed. In the clear words of Marianne Williamson, "The chaos of our times is a reflection of a profound reorientation of the human mind. This explosion is coming from the deepest levels of the psyche: it is not orderly, and no amount of tight, repressive force can contain it. We can no more stop its energy than a parent can stop the explosion of hormones in an adolescent child."[8]

Nor would we *want* to obstruct the momentous, positive aspects of this planetary shift, as visionary Paul Hawken reminds us: "A shared understanding is arising spontaneously from different economic sectors, cultures, regions and cohorts. And it is growing and spreading throughout this country and worldwide. No one started this worldview, no one is in charge of it; no orthodoxy can restrain it. It is the fastest growing and most powerful movement in the world today, unrecognizable to the American media because it is not centralized, based on power, or led by charismatic white male vertebrates. Its strength is increasing in direct proportion to the breakdown of environmental, social, and political systems."[9]

➤ Steady-State Capitalism: Something for Everyone

Based on the shaky foundations of insecurity and greed, America's current version of capitalism was flawed right from the start. But we don't have to throw capitalism out the window of history; it just needs to be adapted so it maximizes more than a single variable. We need a bigger mission than money; a wider purpose than material wealth. For example, former New York attorney Robert Hinkley has drafted twenty-eight words—a "do-no-harm" clause—that he believes could and should be inserted into all corporate charters. This clause would take away CEOs' chronic excuse for antisocial, antienvironment behavior: that they are just "serving their shareholders." Corporations could continue to make healthy profits, "but not at the expense of the environment, human rights, the public health or safety, the communities in which the corporation operates, or the dignity of its employees." What a great idea—that we tune up an existing institution so it serves everyone better![10]

Similar adaptations can be made throughout the dusty hallways of capitalism, as envisioned by people like Paul Hawken, Herman Daly, and David Korten—contemporary counterparts of Thomas Paine and Adam Smith. With greater public awareness and participation, the free market can be more responsive to the needs of both humans and environment and still provide sufficient jobs and returns on-investment. Far from being a dream, this resurgence in democracy is happening right in front of the eyes of the world's billionaires. In fact, one of the world's richest men, Warren Buffet, recently pledged to give away the bulk of his fortune, stating, "Society is responsible for a very significant percentage of what I've earned." As author Jonathan Rowe observes, "What would oil be worth without highways on which to burn it? What would an expensive mansion be worth in a city on any continent with no police protection, sewer service or zoning laws?" This acknowledgment of public values is indicative of the nonpartisan transition capitalism is undergoing.[11]

Albert Einstein once remarked, "A hundred times every day I remind myself that my inner and outer life depend upon the labors of other men, living and dead." Though we tend to think of our achievements as *personal* victories, even the most brilliant entrepreneurs ride on the shoulders of those who paved the way. For example, without significant government support a half-century ago for the emerging technology of computers, eBay, Microsoft, and Google billionaires might be selling hot dogs. At a far more modest level, without the awesome library system that my county implemented decades ago, this book would have been far less fertile. I checked out more than 250 books from my local library to help in my research. I just sit at my desk and request books online. A few days later, I receive e-mails when they magically arrive from other libraries in the region. Then I walk eight blocks—to get both books and exercise. A service like this enriches my life incredibly, helping make my moderate lifestyle very rewarding. Jefferson County also has an open space acquisition program that enriches many lives. By virtue of a mill levy years ago that remains in place, a small percentage of each resident's sales tax has purchased some of the region's finest land, holding it in trust for people now alive as well as all future residents and visitors. (Otherwise, much of that land might have been sprawling, 35-acre "ranchettes.") Public values like these are available to everyone—rich and poor. They give us choices, and they accomplish things we couldn't accomplish on our own.

➤ The Great Work Ahead

I can still hear the echo of John Kennedy's voice, urging Americans to "Ask what you can do for your country." The idea that the government (which is *us*) is the guardian of public values has been overlooked in recent decades, as politicians from both major parties promised voters they would "get government off our backs." Yet, where did these politicians think the funds were coming from to build public schools, highways, and water treatment plants? Without government involvement, who would have regulatory authority—and planning expertise—to protect the environment? Who would build and maintain the public transit systems that Americans are gratefully rediscovering? Who will perform the pure research on aspects of renewable energy that may or may not yield huge profits, but needs to be done? Who will maintain the nation's bridges, dams, landfills, hazardous waste sites, navigable waterways and energy transmission lines?

Have we become like the fictitious Americans in the *Onion* article above, preferring not to have a country? On the contrary, there are many inspiring examples of resurgent democracy. One of them is the progressive, Web-based, nonprofit MoveOn.org. Very effectively using a technology that's available to anyone, MoveOn.org educates and involves more than twenty million Americans on political issues that might otherwise be neglected. The organization has organized many "house parties" to stir the pot of participatory democracy. One such initiative—to identify the political priorities of its members—was attended by a cumulative one hundred thousand people. Among the top ten issues (see list on page 238), a few were significantly "hot": health care for all and energy independence through clean, renewable sources. Although identified by liberal-leaning

Americans, these all-important issues can be addressed in ways that will appeal to and reward all Americans, regardless of political convictions.

For example, health care is an issue of universal relevance and, with nearly one in six Americans now uninsured, the issue has reached a boiling point. Health benefits are emerging as a burden that many corporations can't or won't carry. Since the year 2000, health insurance premiums have risen 75 percent, and employees are paying an ever-larger slice of the coverage. In fact, the average U.S. employee paid $3,500 annually for health-care premiums in 2005, not including out-of-pocket costs for prescriptions and co-pays.[12] A national health-care system (as most of the world's industrialized nations already have) would make business more competitive, and would also increase the real wealth of Americans, since many cling to jobs they can't stand, strictly because of the health benefits. National health care would increase employee flexibility to work part-time, for example, or try self-employment. It would also reduce the fear that we won't have enough money or security in retirement years—insecurity that often results in high-income, high-consumption lifestyles.

What about the issue of energy independence and clean energy? Any nation that wants to be less reliant on unpredictable, politically volatile fossil fuel should meet more of its needs with efficiency and renewable energy sources. In many European and Asian countries, the strategy of "tax shifting" encourages economies to move toward this intelligent, inevitable strategy. Consumers pay more for environmentally damaging activities but *less* for income taxes, so market mechanisms reward socially desirable outcomes. What's not to like? Sweden was an early adopter (2001) of tax shifting, decreasing traditionally steep income taxes while increasing vehicle and fuel taxes. Germany's "green" taxes decrease the amount that employees and employers pay into pension systems. Spain, Italy, Norway, the United Kingdom, and France are among many other nations that tax pollution and resource uses like coal burning, gasoline, garbage, toxic waste, and car-choked highways. Just as the United States successfully used taxes to reduce the use of CFCs, we can join the world community in fighting human-caused climate change with taxes. And just as we banned smoking in many public places, we can now agree to ban excessive CO_2 emissions, for the benefit of all. (Many energy-related companies are wary of the legal precedents that were set when tobacco companies were sued for billions of dollars, for misleading the public about health effects. Global warming lawsuits have already begun.)

In the book, *The Great Work,* Thomas Berry reflects on the grand accomplishments of civilizations throughout history. For example, "the Great Work of the classical Greek world with its understanding of the western

• Top Priorities Identified by Americans at • MoveOn.org House Parties

(in thousands of votes)

Health care for all	65,091
Sustainable energy independence	61,030
Restored constitutional rights	35,675
Guaranteed accurate elections	35,133
Diplomacy over militarism	28,912
High quality education for all	27,874
Solutions to global warming	26,306
A guaranteed living wage	25,527
Publicly funded elections	21,096
A balanced federal budget	20,945

mind; the Great Work of Rome in gathering the peoples of the Mediterranean world and of Western Europe into an ordered relationship with one another . . . The symbols of the Great Work in the medieval period, the cathedrals rising so graciously into the heavens from the region of the old Frankish empire . . ." He then ruminates on the work that lies ahead, which is so much more significant: "The task of moving modern industrial civilization from its present devastating influence on the Earth to a more benign mode of presence is not a role that we have chosen . . . We were chosen by some power beyond ourselves. The nobility of our lives, however, depends upon the manner in which we come to understand and fulfill our assigned role . . ."[13]

Says futurist Duane Elgin, optimistically, "We are the leaders that we have been waiting for. We are the social innovators and entrepreneurs that we have been seeking." In this pregnant moment in history, individual actions can collectively disarm an economic militia whose marching orders are to "seek profits regardless of social and environmental impacts." But we are out of the habit of being citizens! We need to make political action more engaging, and more fun. I recently gave a talk in support of the Earth Charter, a global vision that recognizes the interconnections among economics, environment, ethics, and spirituality. Rather than dwelling on the enormity of the challenges, the participants at that conference celebrated the power and energy of human cooperation. A troupe of kids danced in celebration, there were reports about positive actions to reduce energy consumption, and there was a palpable sense of hope in this Buddhist-sponsored gathering. I showed slides of my Costa Rican rain forest experience (described in the chapter "The Currency of Nature") and I felt a sense of community, or communion, with the audience. I realized that we are wasting our time if we expel hope from our everyday lives, because without it, we can't win.

Last month, my neighborhood opened its community house doors to the public for a showing of Gore's film, *An Inconvenient Truth*. People brought homemade cookies and pies, and we shared both hot cider and a sense of certainty about our need and ability to take action. (We routinely invite political representatives to make presentations here, too, making sure other neighborhoods feel welcome to join us.)

➤ Don't Mess with the Mothers and the Others

As effective as Internet advocacy is, I think we need to be in the streets celebrating Earth Days, Buy Nothing Days, and Take Back Your Time Days. We need demonstrative, nonviolent, empowering *action*. I've always suspected that when women become a global political force, their innate capacity for empathy and holistic thinking will shift the course of history. (The same currents that bring their voices to the forum also indicate other shifts in the culture.) For example, in Colombia, the wives and girlfriends of gang members staged a "crossed legs strike" to convince the men that "violence is not sexy." Until gang members turn their guns over to city authorities, they aren't getting any, it's that simple. Advocates for more moderate consumption can learn something from their actions. In Colombia, men join gangs for status, power, and the attentions of attractive women. In the United States, monetary wealth plays a similar role. But when the rewards are cut off, these actions become less compelling. Isn't this the underlying intent of the bumper-sticker battle against monster SUVs? In effect, quip-loving protesters are using gas-guzzlers as a symbol: The size and sticker price of a car doesn't automatically win our respect—another basic human need—and neither does a person's net wealth. Money isn't an essential criterion for knowing who a person really is. So much of our behavior seems to come down to misguided mental patterns and runaway hormones! If what we learn becomes as *sexy* in our culture as what we earn, overconsumption will start to decline, and real wealth will be waiting to take its place, as it always is. Here's a good slogan for those who wear their convictions on their bumpers: "Spend less money; pay more attention."

Nobel Peace Prize–recipient Wangari Maathai knows as much as anyone on the planet about paying attention, and about meeting needs directly. In her Nobel Prize acceptance speech she explained, "In 1977, when we started the Green Belt Movement, I was partly responding to needs identified by rural women, namely lack of firewood, clean drinking water, balanced diets, shelter and income.[14]

"My response was to begin planting trees with them, to help meet the basic needs of rural women, heal the land and break the cycle of poverty. Trees stop soil erosion, providing water conservation and increased rainfall. Trees provide fuel, material for building and fencing, fruits, fodder, shade and beauty. As household managers in rural and urban areas of the developing world, women are the first to encounter the effects of ecological stress. It forces them to walk farther to get wood for cooking and heating, to search for clean water and to find new sources of food as old ones disappear."[15]

Maathai's idea evolved into a powerful force: the Green Belt Movement that has spread throughout Africa and, now, the world. Thousands of

To "save Salt Spring Island from the ravages of industrial logging and inappropriate development," a nonprofit group in British Columbia, Save Salt Spring Society, published the successful Nude Charity Calendar. Credit: Howard Fry

groups consisting largely of women, have already planted thirty million trees on farm, school, and church lands across Kenya. The women are paid a small amount for each seedling they grow and nurture, giving them an income as well as improving their environment—which is also a form of income. Though Maathai was initially beaten and jailed for challenging state policies, she was ultimately elected to Parliament to serve as the assistant secretary for Environment, Wildlife, and Natural Resources. Recently she has launched a *billion tree* planting initiative through the United Nations, to help counter climate change.

When we realize how far women and minorities have come politically, we see a larger, more hopeful picture of how fast America is changing. Only ninety years ago, on the "Night of Terror" (November 15, 1917) the warden of a Virginia prison ordered his guards to teach a lesson to the suffragists who had *dared* picket the White House. "They beat Lucy Burn, chained her hands to the cell bars above her head and left her hanging for the night, bleeding and gasping for air. They hurled Dora Lewis into a dark cell, smashed her head against an iron bed and knocked her out cold. Her cellmate, Alice Cosu, thought Lewis was dead and suffered a heart attack. Additional affidavits describe the guards grabbing, dragging, beating, choking, slamming, pinching, twisting and kicking the women." President Woodrow Wilson allegedly tried to have one of the women, Alice Paul, declared insane and permanently institutionalized, but a psychiatrist refused, declaring her strong, sane, and courageous By the time the 1920 election arrived, women had won the right to vote.[16]

As I write this, Nancy Pelosi is Speaker of the House—third in line for the presidency—Condoleezza Rice is Secretary of State; Hillary Clinton is running for president, and eighty-seven women hold Congressional seats. Drew Gilpin Farst is Harvard University's first female president in the school's 373-year history. The United States may be like a hulking, ocean liner, but we're starting to turn this ship around! Clearly, democracy can work, if we take ownership of it.

17

Cultural Prosperity

The Earth as a Sacred Garden

The plain fact is that the planet does not need more successful people. But it does desperately need more peacemakers, healers, restorers, storytellers, and lovers of every kind. It needs people who live well in their places. It needs people of moral courage willing to join the fight to make the world habitable and humane. And these qualities have little to do with success as we have defined it.
　—David Orr

Where there is no vision, the people perish.
　—The Bible, Proverbs 29:18

I'm not sure if my involvement in causes, benefits, marches, and demonstrations has made a huge difference, but I know one thing: that involvement has connected me with the good people: people with the live hearts, the live eyes, the live heads.
　—Pete Seeger

You never change something by fighting the existing reality. To change something, build a new model that makes the existing model obsolete.
　—Buckminster Fuller

With public sentiment nothing can fail; without it nothing can succeed. He who molds public sentiment goes deeper than he who enacts statutes.
　—Abraham Lincoln

As the dominant values of a culture change, so do many individual values; and conversely, when enough individuals express the need to change priorities, cultural habits shift in things as mundane as what we eat, the way we dress, and the way we use energy. Cultural change occurs in churches, workplaces, cafés and cyber salons, associations, and discussion groups; in the media, where actors, columnists, and newscasters imprint behavior; in stores, where what we buy often expresses who we are; in the chambers of city councils, state legislatures, and U.S. Congress. But most importantly, cultural changes occur in our minds, and this is where the tide is turning.

We're seeing only the tip of a huge iceberg of social change; the rest is still in our heads. We've been lost in thought (and in media "thoughts") for about a generation, and now we're reaching a tipping point. Said historian and cultural interpreter Joseph Campbell, "We are at this moment participating in one of the very greatest leaps of the human spirit." Environmentalist Lester Brown believes we're shifting to an age of ecological enlightenment, a shift comparable to the agricultural and industrial revolutions that shaped the course of human history. Futurist Marianne Williamson's interpretation is conceptual: "We are exiting a Material Age, which has lasted for thousands of years, and entering an Ideational Age; shifting our focus from extrinsic to intrinsic value."[1] And Marilyn Ferguson, a veteran agent of change, is poetic about the shift that is well underway: "Sometimes a people moves en masse because scouts and travelers carry tales of a distant land that is fruitful and temperate."[2]

These are exciting and challenging times, to put it mildly! Not only must we shift to a less materialistic age; we must do it quickly, before the Earth becomes a poached egg, and before we run out of cheap oil to fuel the transition. Fortunately, global communications have blossomed in our lifetime, enabling culture to change almost overnight if the right messages, stories, and evidence of consensus are conveyed. It feels like we are a crowd of people milling around in a park (the Earth), waiting for direction. We pace back and forth, ruminating over huge questions like these: How can we create a civilization that precisely and elegantly meets the needs of people and nature, letting nothing go to waste? How can the world's economies get *better* without having to get *bigger*? How can we learn to consider scarce resources as sacred? Given that humans now dominate the planet, how can we create a joyful, moderate lifestyle that ritualistically treats the Earth as a Sacred Garden?

➤ Culture-Shifts and What They Teach Us

In a thorough study of twenty-two civilizations throughout history, historian Arnold Toynbee concluded that the most successful among them made graceful transitions (soft landings) from materially dominated values to spiritual, aesthetic, and artistic values—what he called the path of "progressive simplification." Essentially, they learned how to meet the most needs with the least amount of resources and effort—developing an ethic that supported and ritualized this approach. They implemented policies that valued cultural traditions; they took care of nature with terraces that minimized erosion from hillside farms; and they minimized conflict with other cultures. Throughout its long, illustrious history, China has been a civilization with a moderate, culturally rich way of life, though its current cultural aspirations, like those of the United States, are unrealistic (see "Beyond the China Syndrome," page 250). Other modern examples of cultures based on moderation and meeting needs precisely are Costa Rica, Denmark, Kerala (in India), Cuba, and Switzerland—enclaves of cultural pride, relative peacefulness, and social satisfaction.

In fact, nonmaterial pursuits often characterized civilizations before the seventeenth century. For example, the salvation of pharaohs' souls preoccupied the Egyptians; art, philosophy, and fitness kept the Greeks busy; and the quest for eternal salvation and renunciation of worldly pleasures was a dominant feature of the Middle Ages and the Crusades in Europe.[3]

Then technology burst onto the scene, exponentially increasing human access to resources. The American moment in history is perhaps the highest peak in the mountain range of the industrial revolution. On the strength of inspired political foundations, can-do infrastructure, technical ingenuity, an influx of energetic and often destitute immigrants, and a stockpile of virgin resources, the United States led the world into an era of unprecedented material abundance. Although America's mainstream lifestyle currently centers on economic growth and consumption, the shift to a knowledge-based economy rich in efficiency, spirituality, storytelling, cooperation, and biologically inspired design is already well under way.

A culture shift like this—from an emphasis on material wealth to an abundance of time, relationships, and experiences—has already occurred in cultures such as Japan in the eighteenth century. Land was in short supply, forest resources were being depleted, and minerals such as gold, silver, and copper were suddenly scarce as well. Japan went from being resource-rich to resource-poor, but its culture adapted by developing a national ethic that centered on moderation and efficiency. An attachment to the material things in life was seen as demeaning, while the advancement of crafts and human knowledge were seen as lofty goals.

In this "culture of contraction," an emphasis on quality became ingrained in a culture that eventually produced world-class solar cells and Toyota Priuses. Japanese shoguns established strict policies for reforesting.

Training and education in aesthetics and ritualistic arts fluorished, resulting in such disciplines as fencing, martial arts, the tea ceremony, flower arranging, literature, art, and skillful use of the abacus. The three largest cities in Japan had 1,500 bookstores among them, and most people had access to basic education, health care, and the necessities of life, further enriching a culture that required very few resources per "unit of happiness."[4] Referring to this Tokugawa period of Japanese history, Jared Diamond concludes in *Collapse: How Societies Choose to Fail or Succeed,* "Future deindustrial societies could achieve just as much. That goal is within reach, and it's hard to think of a better gift we can offer the future."[5]

➤ Alternative Definitions of Success

The adventurous, vision-driven European Union has its sights set on something more valuable than monetary wealth, as Jeremy Rifkin documents in *The European Dream: How Europe's Vision of the Future Is Quietly Eclipsing the American Dream.* Whereas the American culture is hypnotized by economic growth, Europeans value a more moderate quality of life that doesn't bankrupt *non*monetary forms of wealth. Europeans are fond of saying they "work to live" as opposed to "living to work," and their paid vacation time tends to back that statement up: They average six weeks a year of vacation, compared to two weeks a year in the United States. Europeans have more physicians per capita, a higher voter turnout, greater equality of income, lower rates of infant mortality and homicide, and a *much* lower per capita rate of imprisonment: EU member states average 87 prisoners per 100,000 people, compared with the U.S. average of an astounding 685 prisoners per 100,000 people, which comprises one-fourth of the world's prison population. Social critic John de Graaf refers to current U.S. taxation policies as "you're on your ownership." A thirty-year trend of income tax rollbacks has decreased quality of life overall in America, he reports, reducing levels of trust, family cohesion, literacy, happiness, and preschool education in measurable ways.[6]

In contrast, Western European countries invested in their *social* contracts. "Their provision of more public goods, like healthcare, education, transportation, and common space, reduced the need (or desire) of individuals to maximize their own incomes," says de Graaf. The familiar economic yardstick, Gross Domestic Product, lumps "bads" together with an ever-increasing pile of goods and services, but an alternative to the GDP, the Genuine Progress Indicator, tells a different story. The GPI, which measures twenty-four quality-of-life indices, shows a fairly consistent decline in well being in the United States since a peak in 1973. Similar indices for Europe show consistent improvement in most areas of life.[7]

Rifkin, who divides his time between the United States and the EU, writes from the perspective of a perplexed American, in *The European Dream*. He regretfully concludes, "Europe is busy preparing for a new era while America is desperately trying to hold on to the old one." The American lifestyle is largely based on exclusivity, he observes, a cultural habit that not only neglects the social dimension of life but can also be environmentally destructive. In contrast, Europeans seek freedom and security in *inclusivity* and access to social networks. "The more communities one has access to, the more options and choices one has for living a full and meaningful life," says Rifkin. In a more public European lifestyle, it's more likely that a person will value such shared amenities as open space, libraries, and museums.[8]

Another aspect of American culture that puzzles many Europeans is America's religious fervor. "The very notion that God has made Americans a chosen people often elicits chuckles of disbelief among the more secular Europeans," says Rifkin. In America, 48 percent believe the country is under special protection from God, and close to half attend church every week. More than a third of Americans believe that everything the Bible says is literally true, and two-thirds believe, literally, in the devil. However, although more than 80 percent of Americans say that God is "very" important to them, less than 20 percent of Europeans express such devotion. In the Netherlands, the United Kingdom, Germany, Sweden, and Denmark, less than 10 percent attend church even once a month, and surprisingly, even in the Catholic strongholds of Italy and Poland, only a third of the population says religion is very important to them.[9]

I often wonder if unwavering religious convictions help Americans sleep a little too soundly. Are we in effect passing the buck to a God that *may* not even be there, at least in a super-human form? Instead of taking responsibility for the care of the Earth, an apparent majority of devout Americans can justify juggling the challenges of environmental protection and human rights by saying, "It's in God's hands." Yet it seems to me that God is probably very busy creating and maintaining gazillions of other worlds. If it took Him or Her six days to create *our* world, let's see, what's six times a gazillion gazillion? I think we'd better assume responsibility ourselves. In fact, an increasing number of very devout Americans agree that, in effect, the Biblical phrase about "having dominion over the Earth" may mean, "Take care of things whenever I'm away."

Fortunately, religious groups like the National Association of Evangelicals are using noncontroversial terms like "creation care" to express an urgent need for action on challenges like global warming. A recent manifesto from the thirty-million-member group calls on government to "encourage fuel efficiency, reduce pollution, encourage sustainable use of natural resources, and provide for the proper care of wildlife and their natural habitats." Yes!

It strikes me that as a young, energetic country, we've had a great kick-off party but now it's time to clean up and get back to work. We've been quite certain that our lifestyle is the best in the world, but now we're hearing that the world may not always agree. For example, according to a Pew Global Attitudes Projects survey, 79 percent of Americans believe that "It's good that American ideas and customs are spreading around the world." However, less than 40 percent of Europeans agree.[10] Pew's 2005 global survey asked people in sixteen countries as well as the United States what words or phrases they associate with the American people. Fully 70 percent of Americans described our society as "greedy," though the world at large was a bit less critical. However, 49 percent of Americans surveyed saw themselves as violent, and majorities in thirteen of the sixteen countries agreed with that one.[11]

➣ Creating a New Culture

Times have changed since America's dominant cultural traits took shape. We need a different ethic—not based on archaic deities or on the needs of world trade, but a cross-section of values like efficiency, humility, compassion, preservation, and restoration. We need a Mission to Planet Earth. Sociologists Paul Ray and Sherry Ruth Anderson, coauthors of *The Cultural Creatives,* see such an ethic taking shape. They document that more than a fifth of all Americans, and more than a third of all Europeans, are advocates for significant cultural changes. Many social movements, including environmental, civil rights, gay rights, and peace activists, took root in this population sector. Says Paul Ray, "If you hunger for a deep change in your life that moves you in the direction of less stress, more health, lower consumption, more spirituality, more respect for the earth and the diversity within and among species, you are not alone."

Their book begins with the words, "Imagine a country the size of France suddenly sprouting in the middle of the United States. It is immensely rich in culture, with new ways of life, values, and world views . . ." The traits of the fifty million or so cultural creatives in the United States cut across the currents of long-held assumptions about the free market, the mission of science, and the role of the individual in society. Cultural creatives sense that humans are a "future-creating species," and that a society's image of its future is a self-fulfilling prophecy.[12] "They pay attention to what's going on in the world as a whole, and they have very good BS detectors," comments Paul Ray.[13] They believe that by aligning their actions with their values, a much more enjoyable and sustainable future will take shape. Because their worldview is grounded in moderation and richness of experience, this population sector offers great potential for instigating a new American lifestyle that provides twice the current level of satisfaction for half the resources.

· Lifestyles of the Cultural Creatives ·

What They Do:

- They are readers, not TV watchers. They buy more books and magazines, listen to more radio, and watch less television than other Americans. They are more likely to be involved in the arts, are more likely to write books and articles, and to go to meetings and workshops about books they have read.

- They like to talk about food, experiment with new kinds of food, cook food with friends, eat out a lot, do gourmet and ethnic cooking, try natural foods and health foods.

- They go on vacations that are exotic, adventuresome, educational, experiential, authentic, altruistic and/or spiritual. They don't do package tours, fancy resorts, or cruises, and don't like taking the kids to Disneyland.

- They volunteer for one or more good causes.

What They Like:

- They desire systems views of the "whole process" in whatever they are reading, from cereal boxes to product descriptions to magazine articles. They want to know where a product came from, how it was made, who made it, and what will happen to it when they are done with it.

- They want access to nature, walking and biking paths, ecological preservation, historic preservation, and to live in master planned communities that show a way to re-create community.

- They care intensely about both psychological and spiritual development.

What They Buy:

- They are careful, well-informed shoppers who do not buy on impulse, and read up on a purchase first. They are practically the only consumers who regularly read the labels as they're supposed to.

- They invented the term "authenticity" as consumers understand it, leading the rebellion against things that are "plastic," fake, imitation, poorly made, throwaway, clichéd in style, and high fashion.

- They want safety and fuel economy in a midpriced car. These are the early buyers of hybrid cars. They buy fewer *new* houses than most people of their income level; instead they buy resale houses and fix them up the way they want.

- They are consumers of experiences rather than things, in search of intense, enlightening moments.

What They Believe:

- They dislike the emphasis in modern culture on success and "making it," on luxury and affluence.

- They love nature and are deeply concerned about its destruction.

- They place great importance on developing and maintaining relationships.

- They care about holistic health: body/mind/spirit are a single entity.

- They believe women should have more equality in the home and at work, and should be business and political leaders.

- They are concerned about actions and impacts of big corporations.

The heart and soul of a culture are its values, and how it meets them. Core values—expressed in words like diversity, moderation, responsibility, respect, durability, equality, quality, trust, prevention, care, and regeneration—translate directly into tangible goals like "clean energy," "great neighborhoods," and "wellness." In turn, these goals can drive specific policies and actions like "expand the use of public transit," or "reduce the consumption of cigarettes, gasoline, and saturated fats."

It's not only possible but extremely important for the different factions of American society to agree on *which direction we're going*! Do we want the greatest good for the greatest number of people or are we willing to passively default to a latter-day form of feudalism, in which a small minority holds the wealth and power? Do we want a world in which species are on the rebound, or one in which habitats are being swallowed up by poorly planned development and computer-controlled machinery? Do we want clean energy, provided with ingenious design, or dirty energy we literally pay for with our blood? Do we want a world we hurry through stressfully and fearfully, or a world worth slowing down for? As I've said throughout the book, there's only one basic change we need to make to begin the shift to a new era: Define and value wealth in wider, deeper, more holistic terms than money.

When a sufficient number of individuals take pleasure in the elegance of a need well met, it will become obvious that efficiency is not about "cutting back" but "cutting waste." There may be a prolonged debate concerning the best route to renewable supplies of energy, but surely we can agree that the sooner we switch to clean power, the stronger and healthier our culture will be. It will be a larger challenge to agree that consumption should be reduced, since spending and consuming is so deeply embedded in our current lifestyle. But when we ask ourselves if we're meeting our real needs with a given product, we start to understand that it's not the stuff we want, but the values the stuff is trying to satisfy. We buy a sporty car to attract a partner so we won't feel lonely. We eat a quart of ice cream in one sitting, but the real hunger is for something worthwhile to be doing.

➤ Beyond the China Syndrome

For this book, I interviewed Lester Brown, an eminent environmental analyst whose work (with Worldwatch Institute and Earth Policy Institute) I've followed for almost thirty years. He's authored or coauthored more than fifty books that have been translated into forty languages. *The Washington Post* called him "one of the world's most influential thinkers" and the U.S. Library of Congress requested his personal papers, noting that his writings "have strongly affected thinking about problems of world population and resources." He routinely addresses the Parliament of the European Union and meets with party leaders in China.

We sit together in a hotel lobby and I ask him why we seem unable to take action on major challenges like climate change and species extinction. "We're monitoring false signals," he says. "The price of a gallon of gas, for example, includes the cost of production but not the expenses of treating respiratory illnesses from polluted air; or the repair bill from acid rain damage to lakes, forests, crops, and buildings; or the costs of rising global temperatures, melting glaciers, hurricanes, and relocation of environmental refugees." His words put the problem in a nutshell: As currently structured, the world's economies are consuming not just products but the living systems they come from.

He explains his recent research on the startling economic growth of China. "They've now overtaken us in the consumption of the most necessary resources," he says. "They are the world's largest consumer of all the basic commodities—grain, meat, oil, coal, and steel—except for oil, and they are closing that gap quickly. In fact, if their economy continues to grow at 8 percent per year, in 2031 income per capita in China would be same as in the United States today. They would have a fleet of 1.1 billion cars—well beyond the current world fleet of 795 million. Their paper consumption would be double the world's current production—there go the world's forests," he says. "China also imports vast quantities of grain, soybeans, iron ore, aluminum, copper, platinum, potash, and the cotton needed for its world-dominating textile industry. Its voracious appetite for materials is driving up not only commodity prices but ocean shipping rates as well."

Two monumental Chinese landmarks are now visible from space—the Great Wall of China and the Great *Mall* of China. Covering an area more than 5 million square feet, the "Golden Resources Mall" is twice the size of our huge Mall of America in Minnesota, a popular vacation destination for devout consumers. A recent news story offers clear evidence that affluenza has now infected one of the world's oldest cultures: A Chinese father was under considerable consumer pressure from his daughter; becoming so desperate to silence her whining, he spent 5,000 yuan ($625) on ten school bags and twenty Barbie dolls. According to the Xinhua news agency story, the father's shopping sprees ended up frightening his daughter, who stopped making gift demands. But the wasted money angered his wife, who threatened to divorce him. Partly as a result of its one-child policy of past decades, China is filled with pampered kids known as "little emperors." Who knows what kind of pent-up consumer demand lurks in these ranks?

Certainly, China's "progress," like America's, puts the rest of the world at risk. China is now by far the world's biggest driver of rain forest destruction, says a recent Greenpeace report. Nearly one-half of the tropical hardwood logs shipped from the world's threatened rain forests are headed for China. And the footprints from those rain forests lead through China right to America's doorstep; as fast as China manufactures products made from wood, American consumers buy them. Wal-Mart, which in 2006 generated about 2 percent of the U.S. GDP, now imports $19 billion a year of Chinese products, selling them at prices we can't refuse.[14]

Feeling a bit overwhelmed by Brown's comments, I ask him for a bit of good news. I'm sure he gets that question a lot, and he quickly replies, "With each wind farm, rooftop solar panel, paper-recycling facility, bicycle path, and reforestation program, we move closer to an economy that can sustain economic progress," he says. "Change can happen very quickly. For example, the Berlin Wall coming down was essentially a bloodless political revolution; there were no articles in political science journals in the 1980s that said, 'Hey, keep an eye on Eastern Europe, big change is coming there.' But one morning people woke up and realized the great communist experiment was over.

"Or what if we'd been sitting together ten years ago and I'd said, 'I think that the tobacco industry is going to cave'? It was the most powerful lobby in Washington. It controlled congressional committee chairs. But there was a steady flow of articles on smoking and health over a period of a few decades, along with persistent denial. The industry just lost its credibility. Another example is World War Two. If you did a poll on December 6, 1941, that asked, 'Do you think we should get involved in the war?' probably eighty-five percent would have said, 'Nothing doing—we're not going to make that mistake again,' and then twenty-four hours later, everything changed.'"

He gives me a long list of reasons to be hopeful: "Iceland is experimenting with what it might mean to be a 'hydrogen economy,' where energy would be generated with fuel cells and by direct combustion of hydrogen, that produces water vapor as a by-product. Denmark, Germany, and Spain are world leaders in wind-generated electricity, with Denmark now meeting eighteen percent of its electrical needs from wind. Ontario, Canada, is emerging as a leader in phasing out coal; the province plans to replace its five coal-fired power plants with natural gas-fired turbines, wind farms, and gains in efficiency. The resulting reduction in CO_2 emissions in Ontario will be equivalent to taking four million cars off the road."

Israel leads the world in the efficient use of water, he explains; the United States is expert at stabilizing soil, reducing soil erosion by 40 percent in less than two decades. Japan is a world leader in the production of solar cells; and, in the Netherlands, 40 percent of all trips are on bicycles, demonstrating that, with good planning and design, bikes can be a viable alternative to cars. Brown recalls a stay in the Dutch college town of Utrecht, where he gave a presentation. "From my hotel room, I looked down on streets that were mostly one-way—intentionally inconvenient for cars—and I did a vehicle count. For each car, I counted about nineteen bicycles. From there, I flew directly to Seoul, Korea. Again, I was in a hotel in a horrible downtown area of Korea, and there was a thoroughfare in front of the hotel. I was there two or three days before I saw a single bicycle. Korea has been so driven on creating a modern economy, they think what they have just built is the future, but it's not.

"If the United States over the next decade were to shift its whole automobile fleet to highly efficient gas-electric hybrid engines with efficiencies comparable to today's Toyota Prius, the country could easily cut gasoline use in half," he said. "The potential for cutting coal use and carbon emissions by developing wind resources to generate electricity also has enormous potential. By 2020, half of Europe's four hundred million people are projected to get their residential electricity from wind."

➤ We Are Trained for This!

Do Americans have the guts to become a joyful, moderate culture? Of course we do. Although the United States currently consumes a fourth of the world's oil and even larger percentages of resources like paper and aluminum, we still have the memory of frugality from Depression and World War II days. After being reluctantly drawn into the war, the entire U.S. economy adapted its cultural concept. In this stunningly swift conversion of American industry, automobile factories converted to tank and armored car factories, a merry-go-round factory made gun-mounts, and a corset manufacturer made grenade belts. Strategic goods like tires, gasoline, fuel oil, and sugar were rationed beginning in 1942, and incredibly, the production and sale of cars and trucks for private use was banned, along with driving just for pleasure. Highway construction stopped. Americans salvaged tin cans, bottles, bits of rubber, and waste paper. About twenty million Americans produced two-fifths of the nation's vegetable produce in their Victory Gardens. Both on the war front and home front, there was an elevated feeling of camaraderie. Women marched into the factories by the millions to build aircraft and operate large cranes. A poster released by the Office of War Information stated simply, "Do with less so they'll have enough," and we did, temporarily.[15]

Now, the time for a permanent culture shift has come, powered by renewable energy sources, the elimination of waste, and a reawakened population of citizens. I believe the best measure of a civilization is how well it can absorb disruption and keep going; the same might be said of individuals. One poignant example is Victor Frankl, a physician and psychiatrist imprisoned during World War II in Auschwitz. In *Love and Survival*, Dean Ornish writes, "Frankl wondered why some people survived and others did not. Some who were relatively young and healthy seemed to

· How to Support the Transition to a · Moderate, Sustainable Society

These initiatives and others like them can counteract the formidable trends discussed in this book, and create a world less reliant on finite resources, less focused on money.

- Reduce U.S. energy consumption per capita by half—to levels equivalent to Italian and German energy consumption. Changes in lifestyle will help: Eat less meat (since it "costs" so much energy to produce); live in pedestrian-friendly neighborhoods; consume fewer things but better things, since consumer goods are filled with "hidden" energy.

- Implement high-leverage policy changes already proven in EU countries, such as Extended Producer Responsibility ("Take-Back Laws"), which requires manufacturers to recycle/refurbish products at the end of their lives; and Tax Shift policies, which place economic burden on undesirable outcomes such as energy consumption, pollution, and inefficient technology. For example, Sweden's tax shift lowered income taxes but increased energy taxes. Revitalize deposit systems for containers and incentives for reusable packaging.

- Invest in "socially responsible" companies and mutual funds that enable you to make a good return while aligning your portfolio with your personal values. Participate in shareholder advocacy and community investment opportunities. For more information, see www.socialinvest.org.

- Support more useful ways of measuring wealth and well-being than GDP, which includes the "bads" with the goods and services and thus shows only how much money was spent, not how well it was spent. For example, the Genuine Progress Indicator, a tool devised by the group Redefining Progress, shows how we're really doing. At the personal scale, consider self-evaluation measurements that report "real wealth" such as creativity, connection, and care-taking.

- Support and subsidize alternative transportation that's less energy intensive, for example, revitalize the train industry for both passenger and freight use. Optimize train performance with high speed and Maglev design. Continue to build bike trails, separate from roads, which enable access to shopping, commuting, and travel within a metro area. Support the United States' becoming a world leader in automobile efficiency.

- Support scientific research to make the transition from petrochemistry to "phytochemistry" (based on plants). In the manufacture of plastics, fertilizers, fabrics, and medicines, for instance, transition from a hydrocarbon economy to a carbohydrate economy. Algae may be a key material of the future.

- Support a diversity of solutions in energy, transportation, manufacturing, and other industries so that regional strengths are optimized. For example, support wind-generated electricity in those regions with the best wind potentials. Generate renewable energy at the community and rooftop scale; recycle water and solid wastes at the local level, too.

- Support sustainable agriculture that maintains the health of the soil and prevents erosion with techniques such as cover crops, crop rotation, and composting to increase the organic content of the soil, which increases its water retention and nutrient value per unit of food.

- Begin the inevitable transition to a national wastewater strategy that doesn't waste the nutrients that are now flushed down the drains of homes and small industries. At a minimum, cities should separate wastewater containing toxic materials from wastewater containing sewage and biological waste. At best, they should optimize the use of both neighborhood scale "living machines" that purify water in a greenhouse setting, and computer-controlled compost toilets that convert wastes into fertilizer.

- Support the construction of mixed-use neighborhoods that reduce consumption and increase satisfaction. Support the gradual transformation of suburbia to a mosaic of villages and communities in a metropolitan setting.

- Support social change that reduces the linkage between security and the need for higher incomes. For example, support a national health-care system that uncouples health care from employment. Support workplace legislation to create more part-time jobs that have prorated benefits.

- Support the creation at the regional scale of wildlife corridors, integrated private land conservancy strategies, and open space strategies at the local and county level.

- Support increased U.S. participation in the United Nations, to ensure an equal voice in developing nations as well as global consensus on environmental issues.

give up and often died soon thereafter; others who were old, frail, and quite sick were able to survive and function despite overwhelming odds. He noticed that their survival was much less a factor of age or infirmity than their ability to find a sense of meaning in the midst of this horrible experience. Some people wanted to live to bear witness; others for love—to help a parent or spouse or child who was there with them . . ."[16]

If humans like Frankl are capable of enduring such nightmares, why do so many Americans refuse to even acknowledge the challenges we face? From the top of the hill, gazing at a commanding view, they ask, "Why should we be expected to give up our 300-horsepower cars, our homes that are large enough to shelter two hundred people, and personal diets that a hundred could survive on?" I think the most persuasive argument is that in each case, moderation *feels better* than excess, when all values are considered. Not only can we feel better about ourselves but we'll get daily dividends from a natural world on the rebound: cleaner air, happier nonhuman Earth mates, and a stable, dependable climate. Think about it—would you rather have an expensive SUV or a world that takes care of our kids? A Mc-Mansion, or a home in a much larger sense—that resonates with birdcalls, beaver dams, and iridescent dragonflies? A diet of refined powders and tasteless produce or a society whose citizens are full of vitality, hope, and purpose?

I believe that as individuals and as a culture, we long for a slower, saner world—less transfixed by money and stuff. As visionary Paul Hawken notes, our lives are often played out by the rhythm of capital, whizzing around the planet at the speed of a trillion dollars a day. But other rhythms are more comfortable, more compelling. "What makes life worthy and allows civilizations to endure are all the things that have "bad" payback under commercial rules: infrastructure, universities, temples, poetry, choirs, literature, language, museums, terraced fields, long marriages, line dancing, and art," says Hawken. "Commerce moves faster and requires the governance of politics, art, culture, and nature, to slow it down; to make it pay attention to people and place. In between culture and business is governance—faster than culture, slower than commerce. At the heart, the slowest chronology is earth, nature, the web of life. As ephemeral as it may seem, it is the slowest clock ticking, always there, responding to long, ancient evolutionary cycles that are beyond civilization."[17]

By slowing down to the speed of life, a new American lifestyle—which reveres the Earth as a Sacred Garden—can save the pieces, allowing nature and culture to regenerate on their own terms. The high-consumption lifestyle we lead *will* change dramatically in the years to come, whether we choose it or are chosen by it. The problem isn't just one of high incomes and ego-trips—those are the least of our problems. Because of resource shortages, a reduced capacity of the environment to clean up after us, an epidemic of debt and possible foreclosure by foreign lenders, a longing for meaning and purpose, and a deep-seated instinct for ecological stability, we'll invent a more culturally abundant lifestyle, as many civilizations have before us.

The secret of success at the national and global scale is not really a secret; it's in plain sight, and it's called moderation. We'll get more value from less stuff and better stuff, by tapping into riches like quality products, brilliant design and redesign of cities and towns, cultural and aesthetic greatness, curiosity and fascination about how nature really works, cooperation with coworkers and neighbors, and generosity, just because it feels right. Like former addicts who walk victoriously away from the cliff, we'll choose to experience and embrace life rather than try to dominate it. Although the pace and density of our world are often confusing, we are very certain about some things. For example, we know we want more meaning in our lives; we know we want to use logic that's based on reality (what I call biologic) rather than obsolete rules and policies. We've always loved the idea of rising to the occasion, of being heroes in the last minutes of a game. We've practiced heroism for many thousands of years in our myths and scriptures. We're ready, in these most critical times, to continue the transition —individually and culturally—from the "love of consumption" to the "love of life."

Notes

Chapter 1. Taking Stock

1. Anthony C. Woodbury, "What Is an Endangered Language?" Linguistic Society of America, http://lsadc.org/info/ling-faqs-endanger.cfm.

2. Steven Greenhouse and David Leonhardt, "Real Wages Fail to Match a Rise in Productivity" August 28, 2006, *New York Times*, http://www.nytimes.com/2006/08/28/business/28wages.html?th&emc=th.

3. Robert J. Samuelson, "The Next Economy," *Washington Post*, December 29, 2004, http://www.washingtonpost.com/wp-dyn/articles/A32610-2004Dec28.html, A19.

4. "Consumer Resistance to Marketing Reaches All-Time High; Marketing Productivity Plummets, According to Yankelovich Study," Yankelovich press release, April 15, 2004, http://www.yankelovich.com/.

5. "From War Zones to Shopping Malls: New Study Reveals Deadly Link Between Consumer Demand and Third World Resource Wars," Worldwatch Press release about Michael Renner book, *The "Anatomy of Resource Wars,"* October 17, 2002, http://www.worldwatch.org.

6. Paul Salopek, "The Pay Zone," *Chicago Tribune*, July 29, 2006, http://www.chicagotribune.com/.

7. Lester R. Brown, *Plan B* Book Byte 2006–6, May 5, 2006, http://www.earthpolicy.org/Books/Seg/PB2ch02_ss2.htm.

8. Dave Tilford, "Why Consumption Matters," Sierra Club, 2000, http://www.sierraclub.org/sustainable_consumption/tilford.asp.

9. Associated Press, "Much Toxic Computer Waste Lands in Third World," February 25, 2002, http://www.enn.com/today.html?id=10032.

10. Alan Thein Durning and John C. Ryan, *Stuff: The Secret Lives of Everyday Things*, Northwest Environment Watch Report #4, Seattle, WA, 1997, 20–25.

11. "Americans and Biodiversity: New Poll Shows Growing Awareness, Strong Support for Biodiversity," March 2002 Poll conducted by Belden, Russenello, & Stewart for the Biodiversity Project. http://www.biodiversityproject.org/newsletters/news0102.htm #Americans.

12. Global Footprint Network Web site, http://www.footprintnetwork.org/gfn_sub.php?content=national_footprints.

Chapter 2. Evolutionary Income

1. Darrin M. McMahon, "Happiness: A History" (New York, Atlantic Monthly Press 2006), 419.

2. Cara Buckley, "A Man Down, a Train Arriving, and a Stranger Makes a Choice," *New York Times,* January 3, 2007, http://www.nytimes.com/2007/01/03/nyregion/03life .html?th&emc=th.

3. "Rising from Ruin: Two Towns Rebuild After Katrina" Posted: Thursday, November 3 at 10:12 pm CT by Sean Federico-O'Murchu http://risingfromruin.msnbc.com/ 2005/11/for_soldiers_mo.html#comments.

4. Richard Ryan, in foreword to *The High Price of Materialism*.

5. Tim Kasser, *The High Price of Materialism* (Cambridge, MA: MIT Press, 2002).

6. Thich Nhat Hanh, "Calming the Fearful Mind," in *Calming the Fearful Mind* (Berkeley, CA: Parallax Press, 2005), 17.

7. Richard Layard, lecture delivered at Brookings Institution, Washington DC, February 9, 2005, http://www.brookings.edu/comm/events/20050209happiness.htm.

8. Ibid.

9. John Geirland, "Go with the Flow," *Wired* magazine interview with Mihaly Csikszentmihalyi, September 1996 Issue 4.09, http://www.wired.com/wired/archive/4.09/czik .html.

10. Claudia Wallis, Elizabeth Coady, et al., "The New Science of Happiness," *Time*, January 17, 2005.

11. Adam Phillips, *Going Sane* (New York; NY, HarperCollins 2005), 153, 158.

12. Darrin M. McMahon, *Happiness: A History* (New York: Atlantic Monthly Press, 2006), 64–65.

13. Daniel H. Pink, *A Whole New Mind: Moving From the Informational Age to the Conceptual Age* (New York: Riverhead Books, 2005).

14. Ibid.

15. Ibid.

16. Pamela Chang, "10 Most Hopeful Trends," *Yes! Magazine*, March, 2006, http:// www.yesmagazine.org/article.asp?ID=1402.

Chapter 3. Personal Growth

1. Allison Arthur, "Islanders Pay Homage to Reddick," the Vashon Beachcomber Feb. 7, 2006, http://www.vashonbeachcomber.com/portals-code/list.cgi?paper=90&cat= 23&id=&more.

2. Jonathan Daniel, interview with author, January 11, 2006. The people have been fictionalized to avoid violating confidentiality.

3. Ibid.

4. Bode Miller, interview, *60 Minutes,* July 16, 2006, http://www.cbsnews.com/ sections/60minutes/main3415.shtml.

Chapter 4. Mindful Money

1. This passage is adapted from a *Denver Post* column.

2. Bureau of Labor Statistics, http://www.bls.gov/cex/csxann04.pdf.

3. Jim Merkel, *Radical Simplicity* (Gabriola Island, BC, Canada: New Society Publishers, 2003), 181.

4. Ibid.

5. Sandy Clark, e-mail communication with author, May 5, 2006.

6. Shlomo Reifman, "The Cost of Living Extremely Well Index," *Forbes*, October 9, 2006, http://www.forbes.com/

Chapter 5. The Bonds of Social Capital

1. Shankar Vedantam, "Social Isolation Growing in U.S., Study Says," *Washington Post,* June 23, 2006, A3.

2. Robert Putnam, *Bowling Alone. The Collapse and Revival of American Community* (NY: Simon & Schuster, 2001).

3. The Social Capital Community Benchmark Survey, Saguaro Seminar Report, http://www.siliconvalleygives.org/communitysurvey/index.html.

4. Malcolm Gladwell, *The Tipping Point* (Boston: Little, Brown & Company, 2000), 56–58.

5. Martin Buber, *I and Thou,* trans. Ronald Gregor Smith (New York: Charles Scribner's Sons, 1958), 26.

6. Dean Ornish, in *Imagine* by Williamson. "Health," in *Imagine: What America Could Be in the 21st Century,* by Marianne Williamson (Emmaus, PA: Daybreak, 2000), 50.

7. Ibid.

8. Dean Ornish, *Love & Survival: The Scientific Basis for the Healing Power of Intimacy* (New York: HarperCollins, 1998), 35.

9. Ibid.

10. Ibid.

11. Daniel Goleman, *Social Intelligence: The New Science of Social Relationships* (New York: Bantam Books, 2006), 227.

12. Ornish.

13. Goleman, 9.

Chapter 6. Time Affluence

1. Jonathan Rowe, "Wasted Work, Wasted Time," in *Take Back Your Time: Fighting Overwork and Time Poverty in America*, ed. John de Graaf (San Francisco: Berrett-Koehler Publishers, 2003), 58–65.

2. Ibid.

3. Henry David Thoreau, "Life Without Principle," in *Civil Disobedience, Solitude and Life Without Principle* (Amherst, NY, Prometheus Books, 1998), 13.

4. Rowe, 58–65.

5. David Wann, "Haste Makes Waste," in *Take Back Your Time*, ed. de Graaf, 58–65.

6. Robert Bernstein, "The Speed Trap," in *Take Back Your Time*, ed. de Graaf, 103.

7. Beringer Founders' Estate "Living 5 to 9," http://www.living5to9.com/5to9/page/time_truths.jsp.

8. Vicki Robin, "The Time Cost of Stuff," *Take Back Your Time,* ed. de Graaf, 135–36.

9. Ibid.

10. Survey commissioned by Beringer Founders' Estate wines and conducted by Harris Interactive.

11. Poll commissioned by the Center for a New American Dream and conducted in August 2003 by Widmeyer Research & Polling of Washington DC. This information is based on a nationally representative telephone study.

12. John de Graaf, interview with author, December 12, 2006.

13. Ibid.

14. Benjamin Hunicutt, "When We Had the Time," in *Take Back Your Time,* ed. de Graaf, 118–19.

15. Carol Ostram, "Jobs to Share," in *Take Back Your Time,* ed. de Graaf, 146–53.

16. Ibid.

17. Lore Rosenthal, interview with author, January 15, 2007.

18. John de Graaf, interview with author, December 12, 2006.

19. Wendell Berry, *The Unsettling of America* (San Francisco, Sierra Club Book's, 3rd Edition, 1996).

Chapter 7. The Stocks of Wellness

1. Dean Ornish, in "Health," *Imagine,* ed. Williamson, 46, and Dean Ornish, interview, in *Healing and Mind* by Bill Moyers (New York: Bantam Doubleday Dell Publishing, 1993), 99.

2. Jim Merkel, conversation with author, August 2005.

3. Dean Ornish, in "Health," in *Imagine,* Williamson.

4. James Jill, conversation with author, September 2006.

5. Marco Visscher, "You Do What You Eat," *Ode* magazine, no. 26, September 2005, http://www.odemagazine.com/article.php?aID=4143.

6. Ibid.

7. Marco Visscher, "Unhappy Meal," *Ode* magazine, no. 4, May 2004, http://www.odemagazine.com/article.php?aID=3685.

8. Ibid.

9. Brian McBrindle, "Pediatric Cardiologist Warns of Childhood Obesity Epidemic, *Toronto Sun*, April 27, 2006, http://torontosun.com/News/OtherNews/2006/04/27/1553084-sun.html.

10. N. R. Kleinfeld, "Bad Blood: Living at an Epicenter of Diabetes, Defiance and Despair, *New York Times,* January 10, 2006, http://www.nytimes.com/2006/01/10/nyregion/nyregionspecial5/10diabetes.html?th&emc=th.

11. Marc Santora, "Bad Blood: East Meets West, Adding Pounds and Peril," *New York Times,* January 12, 2006, http://www.nytimes.com/2006/01/12/nyregion/nyregionspecial5/12diabetes.html.

12. N. R. Kleinfeld, "Bad Blood: Diabetes and Its Awful Toll Quietly Emerge as a Crisis," *New York Times,* January 9, 2006, http://www.nytimes.com/2006/01/09/nyregion/nyregionspecial5/09diabetes.html.

13. Daniel Lorber, in conversation with author, February 10, 2007.

14. Marian Burros, "Producers Agree to Send Healthier Foods to Schools," *New York Times*, October 7, 2006, http://www.nytimes.com/2006/10/07/education/07snack.html?th&emc=th.

15. MSNBC Staff and Reuters, "Midnight Munchies Linked to Sleeping Pills, Ambien Users Report Short-Term Memory Loss, Uncontrollable Binge Eating," MSNBC, March 15, 2006, http://www.msnbc.msn.com/id/11835999/.

16. Stephanie Saul, "Some Sleeping Pill Users Range Far Beyond Bed," *New York Times*, March 8, 2006, http://www.nytimes.com/2006/03/08/business/08ambien.html.

17. Ibid.

18. *Frontline*, PBS, interview took place on January 9, 2004, http://www.pbs.org/wgbh/pages/frontline/shows/dict/interviews/willett.html.

19. Robert Bazell, "Diabetes Pill Works—But Is It Worth the Cost? MSNBC, September 26, 2006, http://www.msnbc.msn.com/id/15001746/wid/11915773?GT1=8506.

20. Ibid.

21. Richard Corliss, Michael D. Lemonick, et al., "How to Live to be 100," *Time*, August 30, 2004, 34–42.

22. Dan Buettner, "The Secrets of Long Life," *National Geographic*, November 2005.

23. "15 Ways to Live Longer," Forbes.com, April 28, 2006, http://www.forbes.com/2006/04/28/cx_vg_0501featslide2_print.html.

Chapter 8. The Currency of Nature

1. Richard Louv, *Last Child in the Woods: Saving Our Children from Nature-Deficit Disorder* (New York: Algonquin Books of Chapel Hill, 2005), 45.

2. Robert Greenway, "The Wilderness Effect and Ecopsychology," in *Ecopsychology: Restoring the Earth, Healing the Mind* (San Francisco: Sierra Club Books, 1995), 128–29.

3. Richard Louv, "A Dialogue on Getting Kids Outside," *San Diego Union-Tribune*, September 26, 2006, http://www.signonsandiego.com/news/metro/louv/20060926-9999-lz1e26louv.html.

4. Louv, *Last Child in the Woods*, 48.

Chapter 9. Precious Work and Play

1. Associated Press, "PlayStation 3 Customers Attacked: Robberies, Beatings, Shootings Reported in the Waiting Lines, November 17, 2006, http://www.msnbc.msn.com/id/15764297/.

2. Christopher Maag, "Surfing in Cleveland, Before Brown Water Freezes," *New York Times*, December 10, 2006, http://www.nytimes.com/2006/12/10/us/10surf.html&OQ.

3. Diane Ackerman, *Deep Play* (New York: Random House, 1999).

4. Ibid.

5. Phil Lohre, conversation with author, December 22, 2007.

6. "Mob Football," Wikipedia, http://en.wikipedia.org/wiki/Mob_Football. Various contributors to Wikipedia (uncited).

7. Mihaly Csikszentmihalyi, *Flow: The Psychology of Optimal Experience* (New York: HarperPerennial, 1991).

8. U.S. Bureau of Labor Statistics, http://www.bls.gov/cex/csxann04.pdf.

9. John de Graaf, Take Back Your Time Web site, www.timeday.org.

10. Sam Roberts, "Fatter, Taller, and Thirstier Americans," *New York Times*, Dec. 15, 2006, A27, http://www.nytimes.com/2006/12/15/us/15census.html?ei=5088&en=0854d746f02031e3&ex=1323838800&partner=rssnyt&emc=rss&pagewanted=print.

11. Studs Terkel, *Working* (New York: Random House, 1974), xxiv.

12. Bob Black, "Why Work?" *Yes! Magazine*, Summer 2001, http://www.yesmagazine.org/article.asp?ID=406.

13. Goleman.

14. Ibid.

15. Reuters, "Stay-at-Home Mom Would Be a High-Paying Job," May 3, 2006, http://cc.msn.com/cache.aspx?q=4964969232412&lang=en-US&mkt=en-US&FORM=CVRE.

16. "Are We Happy Yet?" Pew Research Center, February 13, 2006, http://pewresearch.org/social/pack.php?PackID=1.

17. Associated Press, "NYC's Oldest Bartender Still Going Strong at 90," August 22, 2006, http://msnbc.msn.com/id/14462796/?GT1=8404.

18. Edward Deci, http://www.oncourseworkshop.com/Motivation004.htm.

19. Lance Secretan, "The Spirit of Work," in *Imagine,* ed. Williamson, 123–33.

20. Csikszentmihalyi.

Chapter 10. The Real Wealth of Neighborhoods

1. Blanche Evans, "Neighborhood More Important Than the House, Survey Finds," *Realty Times*, October 24, 2006, http://realtytimes.com/rtpages/20051012_homepages.htm.

2. Jay Walljasper, "America's 10 Most Enlightened Towns," *Utne Reader,* May/June 1997, 43.

3. Joel Kotkin keynote address, 2006 California American Planning Association Conference, Orange County, CA, October 23, 2006.

4. Dan Chiras and David Wann, *Superbia! 31 Ways to Create Sustainable Neighborhoods* (Gabriola Island, BC, Canada: New Society Publishers, 2003), 144.

5. "Designing a Great Neighborhood: Lessons from the Holiday Neighborhood," a TV program produced by David Wann for the Sustainable Futures Society. March 2005.

Chapter 11. Higher Returns on Investment

1. Jerry Mander, *Four Arguments for the Elimination of Television* (New York: William Morrow, 1978), 118.

2. Donella H. Meadows, Dennis Meadows, and Jorgen Randers, *Beyond the Limits* (Post Mills, VT: Chelsea Green, 1992), 216.

3. Mario Kamenetzky, in "Human Needs and Aspirations," in *Real-life Economics: Understanding Wealth Creation* (London: Routledge Publishing, 1992), 181.

4. Manfred Max-Neef. *Real Life Economics,* Manfred Max-Neef and Paul Ekins, editors.

5. Conversation with author, Terry Gips, June 2006.

6. Sarah Mahoney, "How Love Keeps Us Healthy," *Prevention,* http://health.msn .com/womenshealth/articlepage.aspx?cp-documentid=100123218.

7. University of California–Berkeley, "Monkey Diet Is Richer in Vitamins and Minerals than Human Diet, UC Berkeley Anthropologist Discovers," news release, May 18, 1999.

8. "Rethinking Your Drinking," *Ode* magazine, November 24, 2005, http://www .odemagazine.com/news.php?nID=646&a=true.

Chapter 12. Energy Savings

1. "Oilman, The Long Fingers of Petroleum," Energy Bulletin, March 16, 2005, http://www.energybulletin.net/.

2. Daniel Gilbert, "If Only Gay Sex Caused Global Warming," *Los Angeles Times,* July 2, 2006, http://www.latimes.com/news/printedition/opinion/la-op-gilbert?jul02,1, 7788831.story.

3. Worldwatch Institute, http://www.worldwatch.org/node/1480.

4. Http://www.iea.org/.

5. Charles Fishman, "How Many Lightbulbs Does It Take to Change the World?" *Fast Company* magazine, no. 108, September 2006, 74.

6. Amory B. Lovins, "More Profit with Less Carbon," *Scientific American*, September 2005, 74–82.

7. Jerry Adler, "Going Green: With Windmills, Low-Energy Homes, New Forms of Recycling and Fuel-Efficient Cars, Americans Are Taking Conservation into Their Own Hands." *Newsweek*, July 17, 2006, http://www.msnbc.msn.com/id/13768213/site/ newsweek/.

8. Lovins.

9. Ibid.

Chapter 13. The Benefits of Right-Sizing

1. Graphic, "This New House," *Mother Jones,* March/April 2005, 26.

2. M. P. Dunleavy, "The Hidden Costs of Too Much Stuff," MSN Money Central, http://moneycentral.msn.com/content/SavingandDebt/P43217.asp?special=0403life.

3. Http://www.littlehouseonasmallplanet.com/.

4. Jordan Rosenfeld, "No Place Like Home," *Metroactive* magazine, December 7, 2005, http://www.metroactive.com/bohemian/12.07.05/creative-0549.html.

5. Nathan Fox, "This New House," *Mother Jones,* March/April 2005, 26.

6. Rosenfeld.

7. Christopher Soloman, "For Many Homeowners, Less Is So Much More," MSN Real Estate, http://realestate.msn.com/loans/Article.aspx?cp-documentid=353659&GT1 =7929.

8. Joseph Florence, "Global Wind Power Expands in 2006," Eco-Economy Indicator (e-mail bulletin), June 28, 2006.

9. Dan Chiras, *The Homeowner's Guide to Renewable Energy* (Gabrio La Island, Canada: New Society Publishers, 2006).

10. Mark Clayton, "As TVs Grow, So Do Electric Bills," *Christian Science Monitor,* June 16, 2005, http://www.csmonitor.com/2005/0616/p13s02-stct.html.

Chapter 14. Trimming the Fat

1. U.S. Bureau of Labor Statistics, http://www.bls.gov/opub/uscs/reflections.pdf.

2. Http://www.eataboutit.com/ez-gicolgan.htm.

3. Joan Gussow, *This Organic Life: Confessions of a Suburban Homesteader* (White River Junction, VT: Chelsea Green Publishing, 2002).

4. Decoder Department, *Sierra* magazine, May/June 2006, 34–35.

5. Kenneth Berger, "The Role of Packaging in Society and the Environment," University of Florida IFAS Extension, May 10, 2005, http://edis.ifas.ufl.edu/AE20.

6. Http://www.epa.gov/boston/communities/shopbags.html.

7. Worldwatch Institute, http://www.worldwatch.org/node/1499.

8. Worldwatch Institute, http://www.worldwatch.org/node/1479.

9. "The Aluminum Can's Dirty Little Secret" Container Recycling Institute, http://www.container-recycling.org/aluminum/dirty.htm.

10. "More Aluminum Cans Trashed Last Year Than Recycled," http://www.mindfully.org/Sustainability/2003/Aluminum-Cans-RecycledSep03.htm; Jenny Gitlitz, conversation with author, August 14, 2006.

11. Jim Motavalli, "The Case Against Meat," emagazine.com, http://www.emagazine.com/view/?142; January/February, 2002.

12. Ibid.

13. Nina Planck, "Leafy Green Sewage," *New York Times,* September 21, 2006,

14. Worldwatch Institute, "This Little Piggy Went to the Global Market," 2006, http://www.worldwatch.org/node/1480.

15. Ibid.

16. "Hardee's Serves Up 1,420-calorie Burger," MSNBC, November 16, 2004, http://www.msnbc.msn.com/id/6498304/?GT1=5809.

17. Andrew Weil, Question and Answer department, DrWeil.com, October 8, 2004, http://www.drweil.com/u/QA/QA342569/

18. Ibid.

19. Ibid.

20. Dean Ornish, *Love and Survival: The Scientific Basis for the Healing Power of Intimacy* (New York: HarperCollins, 1998), 35.

21. Ibid.

22. Jeff Otto, http://filmforce.ign.com/articles/511/511370p1.html.

23. Ibid.

Chapter 15. Infinite Information

1. Stephanie Saul, "Gimme an Rx! Cheerleaders Pep Up Drug Sales," *New York Times*, November 28, 2005, http://prorev.com/healthdrugs.htm.

2. Family Safe Media, http://www.familysafemedia.com/pornography_statistics.html.

3. "Unplug Your Brain," Jerry Mander, *YES! Magazine,* September 2001, http://www.yesmagazine.org/article.asp?ID=460.

4. Jeanne Sather, "TV: How Much Is Too Much?" http://encarta.msn.com/encnet/departments/elementary/default.aspx?article=toomuchtv&GT1=8138.

5. Alicia Gooden, "Textbook Lawsuit 'Silly,' Board Member Says," (Galveston, Texas) *Daily News,* November 2, 2003, http://www.galvnews.com/story.lasso?wcd=14798.

6. Ibid.

7. Campaign Contributions. http://www.opensecrets.org/politicians/contrib.asp?CID=N00026892&cycle=2006.

8. David W. Orr, *Earth in Mind* (Washington DC: Island Press, 1994), 108.

9. Alisa Gravitz, "Commentary: 12-Step Program to Stop Climate Change," *Yes! Magazine,* Winter 2007, http://www.yesmagazine.org/default.asp?ID=194.

10. Janine Benyus, interview, Big Picture TV, http://www.bigpicture.tv/index.php?id=82&cat=&a=216.

Chapter 16. Historical Dividends

1. Staff writer, "New Poll Finds 86 Percent of Americans Don't Want to Have a Country Anymore," *Onion,* March 13, 2006, http://www.theonion.com/content/node/46227.

2. Marianne Williamson, *The Healing of America* (New York: Simon & Schuster, 1997), 38.

3. Jeremy Rifkin, *The European Dream: How Europe's Vision of the Future Is Quietly Eclipsing the American Dream* (New York: Jeremy Tarcher Publishers, 2004), 126.

4. Tijn Touber, "Think Global, Act Natural," interview with Elisabet Sahtouris in *Ode* magazine, no. 35, http://www.odemagazine.com/backIssue.php.

5. Alfie Kohn, *No Contest: The Case Against Competition* (Boston: Houghton Mifflin Co., 1992), 25.

6. Michael Hopkin, *Nature,* June 1, 2005, http://www.oxytocin.org/oxytoc/trust.html.

7. Natalie Angier, "Why We're So Nice: We're Wired to Cooperate," *New York Times,* July 23, 2002, http://www.nytimes.com.

8. Williamson, *The Healing of America,* 38–39.

9. Hawken, in *Imagine,* ed. Williamson, 6, 7.

10. Robert Hinkley, "28 Words to Redefine Corporate Duties: The Proposal for a Code for Corporate Citizenship," in *Democracy's Edge: Choosing to Save Our Country by Bringing Democracy to Life,"* by Frances Moore Lappé (San Francisco: John Wiley & Sons, 2005), 86.

11. Jonathan Rowe, "How to Create a Real Ownership Society," *Ode* magazine, no. 31, http://www.odemagazine.com/article.php?aID=4245&PHPSESSID=d96c4eb7e5f60d71d4a409606eefdd4d.

12. The National Coalition on Health Care, http://www.nchc.org/facts/coverage.shtml.

13. Thomas Berry, *The Great Work: Our Way into the Future* (New York: Bell Tower, 1999).

14. Wangari Maathai, Nobel Prize acceptance speech, City Hall, Oslo, Norway, December 10, 2004, posted on the Green Belt Movement Web site, http://greenbeltmovement.org/a.php?id=34&t=p.

15. Wangari Maathai, "Trees for Democracy," *New York Times*, December 10, 2004, A41.

16. Louise Bernikow, "Night of Terror Leads to Women's Vote in 1917," *Women's News,* October 29, 2004, http://www.womensenews.org/article.cfm/dyn/aid/2048/context/ourstory.

Chapter 17. Cultural Prosperity

1. Williamson, *The Healing of America*.

2. Marilyn Ferguson, *Aquarius Now: Radical Common Sense and Reclaiming Our Personal Sovereignty* (York Beach, ME: Red Wheel/Weiser, 2005).

3. Mariano Grondona, "A Cultural Typology of Economic Development," in *Culture Matters: How Values Shape Human Progress*, ed. Lawrence E. Harrison and Samuel Huntington (New York: Basic Books, 2000), 54.

4. Taichi Sakaiya, *The Knowledge-Value Revolution: or a History of the Future* (Tokyo: Kodansha International, 1991), 311, 312.

5. Jared Diamond, *Collapse: How Societies Choose to Fail or Succeed* (New York: Viking, 2005).

6. Jeremy Rifkin, *The European Dream: How Europe's Vision of the Future Is Quietly Eclipsing the American Dream* (New York: Jerem P. Tarcher/Penguin, 2004).

7. John de Graaf "What's the Economy for, Anyway?" Center for a New American Dream, http://www.newdream.org/newsletter/economy_for.php.

8. Rifkin, 13.

9. Ibid.

10. Ibid., 22.

11. Andrew Kohut and Bruce Stokes, "The Problem of American Exceptionalism," Pew Research Center, May 9, 2006, http://pewresearch.org/pubs/23/the-problem-of-american-exceptionalism.

12. Paul Ray and Sherry Ruth Anderson, *The Cultural Creatives* (New York: Harmony Books, 2000), 340–41.

13. "Discovering the Cultural Creatives," *LOHAS Journal*, March/April 2000, http://www.LOHASJournal.com.

14. Fareed Zakaria, "Does the Future Belong to China?" *Newsweek*, May 9, 2006, http://www.msnbc.msn.com/id/7693580/site/newsweek/.

15. Lester Brown, *Plan B 2.0: Rescuing a Planet Under Stress and a Civilization in Trouble* (New York: W. W. Norton, 2006).

16. Ornish, 16.

17. Paul Hawken, *"Blessed Unrest: How the Largest Movement in the World Came Into Being and Why No One Saw It Coming"* (New York: Viking, 2007), 134.

Suggested Reading List

Ackerman, Diane. *Deep Play*, New York: Random House, 1999.

Bakan, Joel. *The Corporation: The Pathological Pursuit of Profit and Power*. New York: Free Press, 2004.

Barber, Benjamin. *A Place for Us: How to Make Society Civil and Democracy Strong*. New York: Hill and Wang, 1998.

Berry, Thomas M. *The Great Work: Our Way into the Future*. New York: Bell Tower, 1999.

Bingham, June. *Courage to Change: An Introduction to the Life and Thought of Reinhold Niebuhr*. New York: Scribner, 1972.

Brown, Lester R. *Plan B 2.0: Rescuing a Planet Under Stress and a Civilization in Trouble*. New York: W. W. Norton & Company, 2006.

Chiras, Dan, and David Wann. *Superbia! 31 Ways to Create Sustainable Neighborhoods*. Gabriola Island, BC, Canada: New Society Publishers, 2003

Csikszentmihalyi, Mihaly. *Flow: The Psychology of Optimal Experience*. New York: HarperPerennial, 1991.

De Graaf, John. *Take Back Your Time: Fighting Overwork and Time Poverty in America*. San Francisco: Berrett-Koehler, 2003.

Diamond, Jarrett M. *Collapse: How Societies Choose to Fail or Succeed*. New York: Viking, 2005.

Dominguez, Joe and Vicki Robin, *Your Money or Your Life*, New York: Penguin Books, 1999.

Duany, Andres, Elizabeth Plater-Zybrk, and Jeff Speck. *Suburban Nation: The Rise of Sprawl and the Decline of the American Dream*. New York: North Point Press, 2000.

E/the environmental magazine. *Green Living: The E Magazine Handbook for Living Lightly on the Earth*. New York: Plume, 2005.

Ferguson, Marilyn. *Aquarius Now: Radical Common Sense and Reclaiming Our Personal Sovereignty*. York Beach, ME: Red Wheel/Weiser, 2005.

Florida, Richard L. *The Rise of the Creative Class: And How It's Transforming Work, Leisure, Community and Everyday Life*. New York: Basic Books, 2002.

Gladwell, Malcolm. *The Tipping Point: How Little Things Can Make a Big Difference*. Boston: Little, Brown, 2000.

Goleman, Daniel. *Social Intelligence: The New Science of Human Relationships*. New York: Bantam Books, 2006.

Goodall, Jane. *Harvest for Hope: A Guide to Mindful Eating*. New York: Warner Books, 2005.

Henderson, Hazel, and Simran Sethi. *Ethical Markets: Growing the Green Economy*. White River Junction, VT: Chelsea Green Publishing Company, 2007.

Hawken, Paul. *Blessed Unrest*. New York: Viking Press, 2007.

Kasser, Tim. *The High Price of Materialism*. Cambridge, MA: MIT Press, 2002.

Kawachi, Ichiro. *The Health of Nations: Why Inequality Is Harmful to Your Health*. New York: New Press, 2002.

Kunstler, James Howard. *The Long Emergency: Surviving the Converging Catastrophes of the Twenty-first Century*. New York: Atlantic Monthly Press, 2005.

Langholz, Jeff A. *51 Easy Ways You Can Prevent Global Warming (and Save Money!)*. Kansas City, MO: Andrews McMeel, 2003.

Lappé, Frances Moore. *Democracy's Edge: Choosing to Save Our Country by Bringing Democracy to Life*. San Francisco: Jossey-Bass, 2006.

Layard, Richard. *Happiness: Lessons from a New Science*. New York: Penguin Press, 2005.

Loeb, Paul Rogat. *Soul of a Citizen: Living with Conviction in a Cynical Time*. New York: St. Martin's Griffin, 1999.

Louv, Richard. *Last Child in the Woods: Saving Our Children from Nature-Deficit Disorder*. Chapel Hill, NC: Algonquin Books of Chapel Hill, 2005.

McMahon, Darrin M. *Happiness: A History*. New York: Atlantic Monthly Press, 2006.

Meadows, Donnella H., Dennis L. Meadows, and Jørgen Randers. *Beyond the Limits: Confronting Global Collapse, Envisioning a Sustainable Future*. Post Mills, VT: Chelsea Green Publishing Co., 1992.

Merkel, Jim. *Radical Simplicity*. Gabriola Island, BC, Canada: New Society Publishers, 2003.

Meyers, David G. *The Pursuit of Happiness: Who Is Happy—and Why*. New York: Morrow, 1992.

Moyers, Bill D. *Healing and the Mind*. Edited by Betty Sue Flowers. New York: Doubleday, 1993.

Mumford, Lewis. *Technics and Human Development*. New York: Harcourt, Brace, Jovanovich, 1966.

Ornish, Dean. *Love & Survival: The Scientific Basis for the Healing Power of Intimacy*. New York: HarperCollins, 1998.

Pierce, Linda Breen. *Choosing Simplicity: Real People Finding Peace and Fulfillment in a Complex World*. Carmel, CA: Gallagher Press, 2000.

Pink, Daniel H. *A Whole New Mind: Moving from the Information Age to the Conceptual Age*. New York: Riverhead Books, 2005.

Ray, Paul H., and Sherry Ruth Anderson. *The Cultural Creatives: How 50 Million People Are Changing the World*. New York: Harmony Books, 2000.

Rifkin, Jeremy. *The European Dream: How Europe's Vision of the Future Is Quietly Eclipsing the American Dream*. New York: Jeremy P. Tarcher/Penguin, 2004.

Rogers, Carl R. *Carl Rogers—Dialogues: Conversations with Martin Buber, Paul Tillich, B. F. Skinner, Gregory Bateson, Michael Polanyi, Rollo May, and others*. Boston: Houghton Mifflin, 1989.

Roszak, Theodore, Mary E. Gomes, and Allen D. Kanner, eds. *Ecopsychology: Restoring the Earth, Healing the Mind*. San Francisco: Sierra Club Books, 1995.

Ryan, John C., and Alan Thein Durning. *Stuff: The Secret Lives of Everyday Things*. Seattle, WA: Northwest Environment Watch, 1997.

Seligman, Martin E. P. *Authentic Happiness: Using the New Positive Psychology to Realize Your Potential for Lasting Fulfillment*. New York: Free Press, 2002.

Steffen, Alex, ed. *Worldchanging: A User's Guide for the 21st Century*. New York: Abrams, 2006.

Susanka, Sarah, and Kira Obolensky. *The Not So Big House: A Blueprint for the Way We Really Live*. Newtown, CT: Taunton Press.

Terkel, Studs. *Working: People Talk about What They Do All Day and How They Feel about What They Do*. New York: Pantheon Books, 1974.

Whybrow, Peter C. *American Mania: When More Is Not Enough*. New York: W. W. Norton & Co., 2005.

Williamson, Marianne. *The Healing of America*. New York: Simon & Schuster, 1997.

Williamson, Marianne, ed. *Imagine: What America Could Be in the 21st Century: Visions of a Better Future from Leading American Thinkers*. Emmaus, PA: Daybreak (Distributed by St. Martin's Press), 2000.

Index

(Boldfaced page numbers indicate photographs.)